GET THE HELL OUT

To order additional copies, please contact us.
BookSurge, LLC
www.booksurge.com
1-866-308-6235
orders@booksurge.com

FORRESTER CLARK SMITH

GET THE HELL OUT
HOW TO SURVIVE A
DYSFUNCTIONAL FAMILY

2006

GET THE HELL OUT

This book is dedicated to the memory of my beloved wife, Harriet (Patsy) Sturgis Smith, who spent twenty years putting up with my severely dysfunctional behavior while giving me three unique and glorious children—Harriet (Bambi), Forrester, Jr. (Chippy) and Lowell (Welly).

She deserves undying praise for her valor in coping with me as my subconscious ran amuck and hurt her and all those around me. It haunts me to this day that I did not get the "hell" out of my system before so many of my family members and friends were forced to suffer and were ravished so unjustly and unnecessarily. I would never have gotten to where I am now if it had not been for my wife Patsy.

PROLOGUE

Irrational behavior occurs in practically every family on earth. It would be a good bet to say that such a thing, as perfectly normal behavior does not exist. Who is there to set the norm? Perhaps following the teachings of one's religion is the answer but there are rafts of dogmas out there that demand different ways of living. Which is the right one to accept? We must also assume that no person is perfect or that their behavior, teachings or beliefs constitute the only or correct way to live. All people are different and sometimes have strange ideas or quirks.

All children question the directives of their parents, or at some time or other feel that they have been given conflicting messages. This is usual. Unfortunately, offspring of irrational parents see it all too often but don't know if they will be kissed or kicked, hugged or hit, even loved or loathed when their words or actions cross some arbitrary boundary set up in their parents' minds that triggers bizarre adult behavior. A child can't comprehend how to behave in this type of family and, to survive must develop specific skills and even assume adaptive roles to feel safe in the family.

My parents lived with this blight of inherited irrationality, now called dysfunctional behavior, and, as they aged, it intensified as they consumed more alcohol. Thus we children, without ever consciously realizing it, adapted roles in order to survive and feel secure within our family. We never knew what was going to happen to us next so we sought a degree of control, through the well-documented roles of "super hero," "scapegoat," "lost child" and "mascot." However, these guises, though seemingly helpful to the children's peace of mind, promote greater dysfunctional behavior in the child. They preclude living a well rounded childhood but only act as a specific way of survival living. This unfortunate pattern of irrational living lasts a lifetime, unless corrected, and can cause serious family problems and mental afflictions with dire results as one matures.

The role-playing web the children weave to hold their family together is such a strong structure that when a member becomes functional, that person is ostracized by the remaining players. The other siblings believe their world will fall apart and they will not survive if the web is cut apart in any way. They imagine that the very structures of their lives will crumble to dust. To save themselves, when siblings sense the slightest attempt of one of their number to get out of role-playing, they will try in all manners and ways to force the potential deserter back into the accepted model. It helps allay their morbid fears of losing control of their lives. Control is paramount to survival.

Within the last decade the word "dysfunctional" has come into common usage. It aptly expresses the irrational, mostly alcoholic, behavior of the people within its clutch. My mother and father had practically a birthright to behave the way they did and little chance of escape. For generations, though it was for the most part swept under the rug, my extremely privileged family had had suicides, depression, alcoholism, tragic accidents and severe financial swings coursing through it. How could anyone in a family such as this have hoped to have a semblance of normalcy? I certainly did not and neither did the majority of my family. It nearly destroyed me until I forced myself to seek help and find answers to my problems.

I wrote this story to paint a picture of the destructive lifestyle that I was brought up in. By showing my slow descent into a living hell, I hope that people, be they rich or poor, with the same family problems of alcoholism, dysfunctional behavior, depression, feelings of rejection and severe anxiety that I had, will find a way out as I did. By coming to understand these seemingly insufferable agonies and seeing their consequences and causes, it is possible to shed them and find a life of peace and love.

The sporting events, (some quite savage) parties, schools, colleges, vacations, possessions and trappings of wealth described in the book contributed to making my world seem utterly perfect and beautiful yet they insidiously brought about my downfall. My life was what people fantasized about, but underneath it all, there were pains of insecurity lurking within me which were destroying me slowly but surely. This fast way of living screamed for heavy drinking, irrationality, and abusive behavior. Too much money creates too much free time and too much useless time practically begs a person to drink alcohol and seek strange diversions. Alcohol is the most needed and basic ingredient in creating a dysfunctional lifestyle.

I have not meant to paint a picture of any person other than myself or to say that any other person or family is functional or dysfunctional. This applies to my siblings portrayed in the book. I am sure they consider themselves to be far more normal than I. A book of this type could not be written without including all members of my family. Most are not specifically named in order to protect them. I do not intend to point a finger at anyone. My siblings lead completely different lives from mine, and contact does not exist in any way between us. The end of my role-playing was the major factor for our rupture.

I have absolutely no feelings of antagonism towards my mother or father, both of whom were guilty of verbally abusing me throughout their lives. They did not mean to mistreat or hurt me, except for the spankings, for they loved me in their own ways. However, their dysfunctional behavior towards me, a constant and painful spike being driven into my heart, was simply a reflection of their alcoholism and dysfunctional behavior they had assumed in order to survive in their families.

There is a common consensus among mental health experts that there are always four roles that the children play in an alcoholic/dysfunctional family. If one is an only child, then all four roles must be played at different times, and if the children are in large numbers, they share the roles. We Smiths were three siblings so a double up had to happen. Two roles came my way, though I was never aware I was playing them until I got psychiatric help. Children have no choice in picking a role for it is the family dynamics that determine which role devolves on whom. It fell on me to be the mascot and the scapegoat. As I look back, I realize that I played both superbly both as a child and as an adult little knowing that they were causing my near destruction.

Scapegoats are the bad actors in the family. Their behavior is odd and usually quite noticeable for they spend their time trying to draw attention to themselves and away from their alcoholic family. They do not want people to see their parents acting intoxicated so they put on quite a show and say the stupidest things to get the spotlight. When very young, if they feel a parent is acting irrationally, they want no one to see it so they misbehave, say ridiculous things and generally act foolish. As they mature, they do the same things with alcohol now as their crutch.

It really should be no surprise that they usually become alcoholics. They also are like puppets on a string in the hands of the super hero. The hero uses the scapegoat as a foil and as a jester for he wants attention away from the parents as well as himself. The scapegoat gets the blame for everything that goes wrong even if he is not the cause of it. This "court fool" really is the family whipping post and the one that suffers the most. The super hero makes sure of that.

The mascot has an important role to play for he tries to always show the good side of the family and prove to the world that the alcoholic family is actually not alcoholic but, rather, quite wonderful. The mascot, as a child, is sent forth much like an ambassador-always dressed in the best clothes, well mannered, knowledgeable about the family and always amusing. As maturation takes place, the mascot learns the family history, marries the right person, sets up a special style of living and, basically, is the epitome of what the family should be if alcohol wasn't a problem.

The super hero tries desperately from youth till old age to hold the family together and uses any means possible to achieve this. Force, control, misplacing blame, cajoling, bullying, teasing, deviousness and even lying are the means used to weld the dysfunctional family's siblings together. The super hero feels infallible and brooks no criticism, the worst affront possible to him. He feels above the other siblings whether he is bright or stupid. He is merely a figure head for the real father is not being a role model. He tends to be mean or take offense at any questioning of his supposed authority.

The lost child wants to avoid all confrontation and manages to be absent when there is conflict or alcoholic behavior nearby. They want complete control of their lives. It is not difficult to hide in most families and the lost child knows how to do this both physically by being out of sight and mentally by playing dumb. Cleverness is not their forte. These children tend to have few friends for they do not want anyone to see their alcoholic parents. They also tend to be under achievers for then no one takes notice of them. It is a lonely lifestyle from youth to old age.

All of the things in this book happened to the best of my knowledge and as I understood them at the time either as a child or an adult. I did not and do not, quite naturally, see things the way others might see them or might have seen them. I am showing how my life became so completely dysfunctional that I was on the brink of committing one of the most heinous crimes that there is. By showing this dysfunctional behavior, I will hopefully help others have an awakening to what dysfunctional behavior is and what it might be doing to them. If they can gain this insight, it can help them rid their lives of its horrors and perhaps, help others.

ONE

I went and got my beautiful Purdy shotgun out of its leather case. I put one twelve-gauge shell into it and went back into my bedroom. I was going to end this terrifying life. Nothing ever worked, and I had nothing to live for. I lay down on the bed, flipped off the safety, turned the gun around and put the barrel right beneath my chin. I wanted out. I'd had enough. I'd come to the end of my rope. I reached down and squeezed the trigger. I heard the click. Cold terror and fear swept over me as I waited for the deafening blast and the end of my life.

But no blast came! Just waves of numbness sweeping over me as my thoughts began spinning in and out of focus. Was I dead? What had gone wrong? Was I alive? There was nothingness. A feeling of emptiness and total fear engulfed me. I could not move a muscle. I lay absolutely motionless, terrified out of my wits. I was waiting for a delayed action or an explosion, but nothing happened. I suddenly remembered that there were two triggers on that double-barreled shotgun, but, in turning the gun around to put the stock at my feet with the barrel under my chin, I had reversed the triggers. I had pulled the wrong one.

I stared blankly at the ceiling, looked down at the gun on my chest and then started sobbing, shaking and sweating. I had brought my very being as low as I could go. I did not want to try again. I fell into an alcohol-drugged sleep while still clutching my loaded, safety-off, steel blue shotgun. Just the lightest pressure on the right-hand trigger during the night, as I lay there stuporous, could have spelled my death.

The morning arrived all too quickly, as the first crack of light crept into the room, I awoke with a start. A drenching sweat poured all over me. I threw the gun on the floor. It could have exploded but that never occurred to me. I was afraid and feeling sick—but I was alive. As the terrors of the night started to replay themselves, I called out to God for help. My despair was absolute.

What had brought me to this horrible point? Again and again I asked myself how could I, a person with everything given to him on a silver platter, never wanting for money, education, connections or privilege, descend to such a depth? It was obvious to me, even at this moment, that I must find the answers or I would do this again. I was as low as I could get.

Desperately pushing past the pain, I tried to think about the patterns I knew were there. It was clear my life had become riddled with alcoholism, depression, addiction, rejection, obsession and self-destruction, and that I was very nearly a disaster beyond repair.

Again I called out to God, the only person I could trust. I knelt beside my bed and began praying for all I was worth. One thing I knew for certain: I had to "get the hell out" of my system if I was ever to function again as the kind of man I wanted to be.

It is of little consequence if a child is rich or poor, black or white, male or female, if his environment is marked by bizarre or irrational behavior on the part of those responsible for his upbringing. Children are sturdy creatures, but they are also at the mercy of those with whom they are intimately connected: parents, grandparents, other family members, nursemaids, teachers, or anyone else in a position of trust. Inevitably, tragedy will ensue whenever children are mentally abused, either knowingly or unknowingly.

My own parents never meant to cause me harm, but not only were they mismatched, they drank heavily as they indulged in the pleasures common to their class and era. Unfortunately, their repertoire of skills did not include anything useful for dealing with me, a very sensitive boy and forgotten middle child. I was neither the first-born nor the cuddly baby, so I always felt I lived on the fringe of their lives.

Each stage of my development—from infant to toddler, to preschooler, to school age, to puberty, to young manhood—was built with blocks infused with the dysfunctional elements of their lives. The things they said or did rarely made good sense, and because of this I reached adulthood without ever having truly grown up. They basically wouldn't let me.

Perhaps, as I go on to bare my heart and soul in this book—which deals with a completely delightful but totally destructive life—readers may find some echo of their own experience. One has often heard that no man is an island, yet it can take a lifetime to understand that truth. Once

I became a survivor, however, I discovered a world beyond any I had ever dreamed of. What it took was the miracle in the form of a "divine spark" within me to save me. This "spark" had always been with me and, I am convinced guided me to pull the wrong trigger.

TWO

I arrived on this wildly spinning earth on August 29, 1931—an event my family hailed as a catastrophe: I wasn't the longed-for girl and I interfered with my parents' promise to be in Tenants Harbor, Maine, with my brother Philip. What's more, I had the temerity to be born on Philip's second birthday. They never quite let me forget this transgression, for their plan was to have me delivered by Caesarean section on the first of September in Boston. When I crossed them up by starting to fight my way out of the womb a bit too early, our chauffeur rushed them from Tenants Harbor, to Newburyport, Massachusetts, where my mother's uncle, who was her surgeon, was summering in regal splendor on the banks of the Merrimac River. Thanks to his skill, I came into being and gasped my first breath as a pink and beautiful baby boy with no battle scars caused by labor. I certainly was lovable then, even if it was for only an hour or so!

I was always reminded, by my parents, Philip Webster and Cornelia Clark Smith—nicknamed Nip and Nina—that they had wanted a girl. They already had a beloved son, Philip Webster Smith, Jr. He was the apple of everyone's—and I mean everyone's—eyes. He was my parents' first born, the first grandchild on both sides of the family, my father's namesake, and the heir apparent to follow my father and grandfather's paths to Groton and Harvard, where Smiths had been sent for generations. These Philips (my Smith grandfather was also a Philip) had never excelled while being schooled there, but it didn't matter because they adored the old school-tie tradition of it all and made friendships that would last a lifetime.

For his part, my father managed, somehow, to learn little but how to make over consumption of alcohol part and parcel of his life. Unfortunately, this was never clear to him, since he firmly believed he was imbibing in the most perfect "Harvardian" way. Even worse, he completely mastered the art of over imbibing in excess and then never faltered in his lifelong dedication to it. One might say that he made a success of his failure, but it is difficult even now to joke about a habit that was to haunt our family and have such a lasting effect on my own life.

Even though my early appearance on my brother's birthday had been a major strike against me, causing, as it seemed, my mother's and father's peculiar apathy toward me for years to come, I was one heck of a lot more fortunate than ninety-nine percent of the people born on that day, for I had everything on this earth going for me. My genes were those of the generations of this country's truly great patriots and leaders. Coursing through my veins was—and thankfully still is, at my present vintage age—the blood of some of the most privileged and exceptional individuals from America, England, Scotland, France and the Netherlands. Cells of Farrs, Websters, van Courtlands, Dudleys, Bayards, Stuyvesants, Schuylers and even some kings of Scotland contribute to my DNA.

My mother had among her illustrious ancestors not only the Civil War Governor of Massachusetts, John Albion Andrew, but also a drafter of the Declaration of Independence, Robert Livingston as well as a signer of the Declaration, Philip Livingston; a United States Congressman, John Forrester Andrew; a Boston financial genius and major benefactor of Harvard, Nathaniel Thayer, and the last of the great New York Dutch Patroons, who actually ruled the Hudson River Valley for hundreds of years, Stephen van Rensselaer. Her family had married into most of the prominent families of Boston and New York, including the Warrens, the Forbeses, the Wolcotts, the Reveres, the Winthrops, the Ameses, the Bigelows and the Storeys, as well as into many titled families of Europe. And on the literary front, her family figured prominently as a major Boston institution in John P. Marquand's satirical 1930s bestseller, *The Late George Apley*. In short, Nina Smith rightly could consider herself the *crème de la crème*. Every door was open to her, and she loved it.

Such a background even entitled her, she felt, " after a martini or two and with no particular provocation," suddenly to turn to my father and announce how frightfully common he was. She was convinced, as were old school Bostonians, that anyone who lived west of Dedham, a Boston suburb, was a savage. As some of my father's paternal ancestors had lived west of Dedham, she loved to torment him with this fact. It mattered little to her that they ran vast mills in and around Worcester, forty miles west of Boston. His forebears were the Worcesters and the Smiths who had settled the entire area generations earlier and actually owned most of the land and industry there. His great, great grandmother, Clarissa Worcester, was a descendent of the Earl of Worcester.

I know now that such put-downs, in fact, are an old trick used by many dysfunctional and depressed people, who feel raised up if they think someone else is beneath them. Not just my mother but also my entire family made a habit of this "downgrading" practice. It wasn't snobbery but a compulsive reaction usually brought on by drink.

Paradoxically, my mother continually reminded me not to get "puffed up about your ancestors, but make them proud that you're their descendant." Seeming contradictions like this were confusing to a child, and I simply accepted them, for what was the alternative?

Still, even given the enormous potential for success I was born with, I was from the start shadowed by family history. My heritage though extraordinarily distinguished, held within it seeds of darkness that were equally powerful and could spell out failure. Afflicted with dysfunctional behavior, my parents were not the least bit aware of it, as it was all that they knew. They behaved selfishly and irrationally, never having the slightest awareness of the effects their actions might have, especially on a small boy. In my earliest days it didn't matter so much, since I could easily command the small world around me. Nurses and maids scurried to grant my every wish every time I gurgled or cried.

My parents despite being relatively rich in 1931, nonetheless, suffered the effects of the Great Depression. My grandparents did not, for both sets were rich beyond most people's most extravagant dreams. They lived in splendid comfort in well-staffed city mansions of twenty or thirty rooms, as well as in rambling country houses on large landholdings that spread out over many acres. There were outbuildings for their help to live in and massive garages, built originally as carriage houses, which held many cars.

Just one small part of my grandfather, Philip Lees Smith's property holdings consisted of almost an entire Maine village called Elmore. He was a small and rather nasty man, who, from about 1915 on, lorded it over his entire family who came there every summer. It was like a feudal barony, with a bailiwick consisting of hundreds of acres, twenty-five houses, several yachts, two docks, barns for his horses, storage garages for old Pierce Arrows and Packards, tennis courts and sprawling flower and vegetable gardens. Very few people liked my grandfather, and he, in turn, liked few people. Other than his children, mostly sycophants and poor relatives came each summer to breathe the salty, fresh Maine air as they sponged off him. This petty tyrant expected all to do his bidding as well as to jump at his every command. They did just that, and got the use of houses, boats, tennis courts, and docks, not to mention constant trips and free fruits and vegetables, in return for exalting him.

On the surface, therefore, we Smiths, an attractive and socially prominent family, seemed to be on top of the heap. But, underneath this façade of aristocracy, bad habits were starting to erode our sensibilities. Too much alcohol, which was such an integral part of this post-Prohibition era, wreaked havoc with sensible living, created devastatingly destructive behavior, fomented depression and destroyed individuals' personalities. Alcohol was everywhere. Whenever people dropped in to visit, no matter what time of day, they were offered a drink from the grog tray set up in the library. If one went fox hunting, one always took a saddle flask. If a person sailed, drinks were served on board. If a tennis match was being watched, drinks flowed around the court. The evenings revolved around the consumption of exotic cocktails such as pink ladies, old fashioned, martinis and manhattans, with wines accompanying dinner and brandy and stingers after the meal.

When prohibition was over, people were determined to make up for lost time, by quickly abandoning the puritanical lifestyle it had encouraged. No one forsook alcohol's pleasures. During prohibition, our butler had made gin in the bathtub, and my father had smuggled booze in from Canada on my grandfather's yachts. Now, with alcohol legalized again, there were stashes of it in our cellar, enough to sink the Titanic and supply every guest with whatever they wished whenever they wished it.

My mother and father were suited for each other only because both were accustomed to privilege and social standing. In temperament, they resembled a mongoose and a cobra. Each went into the marriage expecting to change the other, but change for either one of them proved impossible. Because of this, they drank to try to ease the pain of their differences. Sometimes they could be sober and quite civil, but moments without a drink in their hands were fleeting, especially since everyone they knew drank. Anyone who did not was considered an oddball.

In 1931, parents like mine did not bother with the care of their children. That's what servants did. Due to their rarefied upbringing, my mother and father had never learned how to nurture and care for children, nor were they expected to. They, themselves, had never experienced such parental attention and thus had no role models. It was always assumed that others would do the dirty work of getting up during the night, changing diapers, burping a child, cleaning up vomit and walking a colicky baby. I never once saw a friend of my mother's cope with anything more demanding in the way of maternal activity than handing out a cookie at teatime.

So, immediately after my birth, my parents turned me over, lock, stock and barrel, to nurses and maids. Their time was so totally taken up with social engagements and sporting pastimes that children registered more often than not as bothersome intrusions into their self-indulgent lifestyle.

As my nurse once explained, I and other children in our circle were really just showpieces, exhibited briefly to guests as evidence of our parents' virility and fertility. We were clearly an extension of them but at the same time, not very interesting. Of course, any bad manners or misbehavior were reflections on them. If our actions were considered wrong or our timing inappropriate, we were punished.

"The passing of wind" meant banishment or a spanking, a high price to pay for gas. Equally, the failure to smile, to speak, or to bow low at the correct moment elicited a reprimand. As infants and toddlers, we were expected to gurgle and smile contentedly every time our parents approached with friends, but, alas, we usually screamed and they would instantly send us in shame to the nursery.

My brother and I each had our own nurse. My beloved Miss Campbell made sure I got some love and attention, which, otherwise, I'm afraid, would never have come my way. In pictures I have seen her sitting comfortably by my carriage while crocheting or knitting something for me or herself. She doted on me, and I was told by aunts and uncles, I far preferred her to my mother. This wasn't so surprising, really, as I rarely if ever saw my parents. They were like strangers when they appeared.

Our family was a part of the horsy set. In Far Hills, New Jersey, riding to hounds was what you did, and my mother, in particular, rode every chance she could. A day-spent fox hunting started at dawn and ended in the late afternoon or early evening. Until children were old enough to ride with their parents, they were not a part of their parents' lives. In my family's group of friends, you hunted three or four times a week and your energies were devoted to the world of horses. In addition to hunts, there were hunt breakfasts, teas after hunts, hunt race meets, hunter trials and hunt balls. It was a universe unto itself, one that we young children were virtually excluded from.

When he was first married, my father was not an accomplished rider. My mother insisted that he become one, so she outfitted him with various hunting habits. Hunting habits are the clothes—jodhpurs, breeches, boots, hard hats, hunting jackets, and the like—which one wears when one rides to the hounds. Then she started to teach him all the necessary points that he would need to put on a good show in the hunting field. The first time he went hunting in his new attire and with his mind full of instructions, he was swept off his horse by a tree branch when his horse jumped a fence too high. A friend found him swinging on the branch and my mother soon noticed his horse-galloping rider less alongside her.

When not out fox hunting, Mother had her breakfast brought to her in bed. As she munched her buttered and marmaladed toast, she would telephone every person she had seen the night before at some party or other social event to find out the latest dirt and learn who had too much to drink after she and my father left. She did not want to miss a bit of gossip, and I'm sure one thing she always hoped was that someone had made a fool of himself by being even tipsier than my father. This took the onus off him. After nibbling and gossiping, she'd bathe in leisurely fashion and finally come down at noon, just in time for a drink or two and luncheon with friends. Some days she lunched out with people. The afternoons were usually arranged for the playing of contract bridge, followed by tea, a nap, dressing for dinner, a cocktail hour or two and then, finally, a late, late formal dinner.

When my father returned each evening from Wall Street and walked in the front door at 6:35 p.m., he was usually already somewhat high. It was easy to tell, as he slurred his words and stumbled a bit. My mother was always angered by this behavior, but it did not change my father's actions at all. I think he did it to help them and others make his conversation with her flow better and to dull the sharpness of some of her remarks. Any number of friends might join them or they might go out to a dinner party. It did not matter what night of the week it was, for people did not wait for the weekends to be entertained. How our servants could stand it, I do not know. Their days began at five-thirty in the morning, when they came downstairs to stoke the enormous Aga coal stove, and ended when they put the last clean wine glass in the corner cabinet of the dining room somewhere around eleven o'clock.

On weekends in Far Hills, the landed gentry spent its energies in foxhunts, cockfights, bird and deer shooting, greyhound coursing and beagling. Tennis and golf, the only other sports considered acceptable by the community, were for those times of the year when the seasons for hunting, etc., were over. All too often as a small child, my father took me to the "blood" sports and we watched the carnage. I can't imagine why he did this. It had a lasting affect on me.

The idea of country life practiced in Far Hills was styled after that of the English aristocracy. This meant taking advantage of great wealth and power to have the best of everything available. To enjoy life in this way meant the wherewithal to keep great houses running filled with servants inside and out. Not only was everything done with perfect ease and taste, but also all the "toys" were the best, from the horses to the hounds to purebred dogs. Cats were out of the question except in barns to kill rats.

When a person hunted, he or she went on horseback to a "meet." A group of riders, called the "field," would be assembled at the meet. The hounds were gathered together at the meet and then taken to a "covert," a wooded area, where foxes were known to live. The pack of hounds, upon drawing out a fox, gave tongue and then chased the quarry for miles and miles until it was caught. Then came the kill. The field had great sport watching the hounds work the scent and following them at full gallop, while jumping fences, banks, streams, chicken coops, stone walls and any other impediments in the way. It went on for hours, yet was exhilarating beyond belief.

The end result, however, tended to be gruesome. If new riders were present, they would be blooded with a fox paw dipped in the fox's blood. Others might be awarded the fox's mask (the head) or the brush (the tail), if they were first at the kill.

Beagling was done on foot with the Master and hunt servants dressed in green jackets and white breeches. The field was dressed in the best tweeds possible, and stout boots were worn to help navigate the rough, frequently wet terrain. One ran after a pack of beagles or bassets, which were chasing hares or, sometimes, rabbits. It was wonderful exercise after a big Sunday lunch, and children often were allowed to come. It was a good introduction to sport for many, although the death of the hare was not at all pleasant.

Coursing, as barbaric a pastime as one could imagine, was outlawed in New Jersey but the fact made little if any difference to my father's circle. The local police or sheriff was generously paid to turn the other way.

People would bring their greyhounds to one of the great cattle-grazing fields of someone's huge estate for an afternoon of speed and speedy death. Two kennel men stood at one end with leashes on the greyhounds' collars. In the middle stood a gamekeeper with a cage full of hares. On the signal of a flag, a hare was released and the leashes unsnapped. The dogs sped like wildfire toward the hare, and each tried to be the first to catch it and kill it. The hare was tossed in the air and then torn apart while emitting an intense, bark-like squeal. The crowd of men, women and children stood along the fences, walls or river banks surrounding the field cheering for their favorite dog. I couldn't watch when I was taken at a very young age, as it was too awful even to think about.

Cock fighting was another favored weekend sport of the wealthy. In a special barn on a large estate every other Sunday during wintertime, the gentry would bring their specially bred and highly trained bantam cocks to fight each other to the death. It was a great chance for these men to gamble, their wives were all home playing bridge. The carnage was awful, but the spectators' ruckus was even worse as men cheered and bellowed for their cock to win. My father raised bantam cocks until one day they all simply vanished. It seemed that a friend of his, Ted Clucas, with his pack of beagles, had come through our place hunting hare but somehow ended up with the beagles taking the heads off all the bantams. My Father's friendship with Clucas went downhill from then on.

There were always animals to shoot in the countryside, but in Far Hills the feeling was that one should never be disappointed. Therefore, hunters arranged to have bird drives of hand-raised birds such as ducks and pheasants, rushed along the ground by beaters or thrown off towers toward the hunters. These events produced hundreds of game birds for their larders. The killed birds were driven in to the Racquet Club in New York to be plucked and then brought home—packaged and aged. One of my friends once went on one of these shoots and shot the gamekeeper's prized dog. There were so many birds coming at him he found himself unable to distinguish the right creature to take aim at. The dog could never be used again as a working animal and my friend was not asked back to shoot again. Eventually, I joined in these blood sports, as was expected of me.

In Maine, during the summers at Tenants Harbor, life was simpler and much tamer. There were activities such as sailing, tennis and picnics, although there was no golf. My parents like so many of their cronies, constantly craved diversions. Being alone or just staying at home was much too boring, for, after all, they had no chores to do.

The ever-present booze relaxed the people of their set and made them happier, and as participants in sporting endeavors they became more fearless. They might say, "We have more fun and play better with a drink," but actually, they were reaching the point when not drinking rendered them unable to function as they wished. They were virtually inoperative without the chemical calming of their egos and bodies. My parents' friendships with stylish and witty people too often necessitated reciprocity of repartee and cleverness. Alcohol helped here, too.

We were always well taken care of before the Second World War, our household consisted of a butler, a footman, a cook, two nurses, a laundress and an upstairs maid. Outside were a gardener, a groom and a chauffeur. This was small potatoes compared to my mother's family, who had employed thirty people—fifteen inside and fifteen outside—to care for them in their two imposing houses. These Clark grandparents' highest paid servant, in the early 1900's, was my mother's nursemaid/governess, who got $15 a month and luxuriated in a tiny bedroom off the nursery. The other servants lived in attic rooms, freezing in winter and stifling in summer. This well-known Boston "torture" was instituted to keep the help downstairs and working and not relaxing in their rooms on the sixth floor. My Smith grandparents had more than ten in help to see that all went smoothly in Maine and New Jersey.

My grandparents' servants stayed with them for years and years, so they must have liked their life or possibly they had nowhere else to go. My parents' help stayed for years as well, and really became a part of our family. Sixty years later, I still remember the days on which their birthdays fall, for they, not our parents, basically acted as our loving family and they had brought us up. They knew it and we knew it, but nobody said it. It was an accepted fact.

From what I have been told by relatives, I apparently could not tolerate anyone except my nurse picking me up. I only trusted my nurse, whom I had started to call "Nee." When the rare threat of being lifted up and exhibited to company by my mother or father occurred, I would howl for Nee at the top of my lungs. Not wanting me to embarrass herself, my mother took the hint and stopped this "show and tell."

From my birth on, my hair was allowed to grow and grow. I had masses of golden curls and everyone called me "Fuzzy." My mother dictated that I be dressed in pastel-colored linen wash suits, never shorts or boy things, as she thought that I was too pretty not to be all dolled up. Many a time I was mistaken for a girl. Nee once told me that she could scarcely remember my mother showing me off to friends without saying, "It's a shame he wasn't a girl." This was a constant reminder to me of the obvious blunder God made when organizing my gender. When I was quite young, I remember that I sometimes wondered what it would be like to be a girl. Would they love me more? However, these thoughts were easily banished from my mind for I looked up to Philip and longed to grow up like him. When I was bigger, I hoped it would be my turn to get the kind of attention he got and be idolized and bathed in love by everyone the way he was. It's sad to say, it never happened.

My first two years were spent between Far Hills and Tenants Harbor. Our season in Maine was long, for Philip and I were sent up with the first battalion of servants early in May and did not return to Far Hills until late September or early October. My parents would arrive in Maine later with the rest of the help, who had been needed as the mainstays of their high living in Far Hills. It was a fabulously comfortable way that they existed.

Polio was rampant through most of the United States when I was young. People knew little about this crippling disease and had no idea what caused it. All one tried to do was to get as far away as possible from its ravages. It was everywhere in large cities. Now we know that it is a virus passed from one infected person to another, but then people thought it might come from the fuzz of peaches or unwashed fruit or swimming pools or warm weather. In Maine, where the population was sparse,—especially in Tenants Harbor,—cases of polio were unheard of, making another reason to whisk us up there early in the season.

During my second year in Maine, I ran a high fever and was desperately ill. My family rushed a doctor up from Boston who said he thought that I had infantile paralysis. My parents were flabbergasted, for they had tried so hard to keep me away from this scourge. However, I recovered with none of the telltale signs of wasted muscles, and everyone assumed I'd escaped the pestilence. Many years later, however, doctors began theorizing that, like measles, practically everyone got polio, but most cases were simply too mild to detect. It's interesting to note that my left ankle has always been very weak. Perhaps I did have a brush with polio, because from my youngest years I could never easily ice skate a circle to the left. My ankle would buckle. It's smaller and weaker than the other one to this day.

Stories abound in our family about my older brother's problems with me as his new sibling. On one occasion, he came into the nursery and squeezed toothpaste into both my eyes, though he was never punished for this. My beloved Nee believed I might go blind, but I survived this and many, many more of his pranks. His constant badgering did not scare me as much as it made me want to dissociate myself from him and turned me into seeking others to play with. Playing with him was impossible for me. He bullied me far too much when we were together. I was a great deal more comfortable with my little friends and other relatives. This certainly was not peculiar behavior, for what older boy doesn't want to get rid of the baby brother siphoning off some of the attention he's used to having all to himself. Thank God Nee could make anything right for me. Life went on happily.

My mother, Nina, was beautiful, glamorous, athletic, charming and truly loved by all her society friends, her family and anyone else, rich or poor, with whom she came in contact. She also had diverse talents. She could entertain the Duke of Windsor or the Secretary of the Treasury one moment, and the next moment she might be showing the groom how to muck out a stall just the way she wanted it done.

When His Royal Highness, The Duke of Windsor, and his Duchess came to Far Hills, they stayed next door to our place at the Cuttings'. Helen Cutting was a great friend of my mother's and so my parents went there for dinner to honor the Windsors. Everyone was gaga over him as, after all, he had recently been the King of England.

To my mother's surprise, Helen Cutting asked her to have the Windsors to tea two days later so they could see what a rambling American farmhouse filled with exceptional American furniture looked like. Without even the bat of an eye, my mother agreed. Our servants, who were all British subjects, were overjoyed and my mother was ecstatic. When that special day rolled around, our house sparkled, as did every brass button on the butler's coat and vest. Our butler told me my mother gave a wonderful tea, which mostly consisted of cocktails. He said he had never shined the tea service better.

Because of the makeup of the wealthy Far Hills community, it is little wonder that people there were frequently named to ambassadorships or the President's cabinet, or became governors. It was not unusual for one of these individuals, such as Douglas Dillon, an Ambassador to France and later Secretary of the Treasury, to come to our house for dinner. Douglas had roomed with one of my uncles, George Clark, at Harvard.

My mother never slowed down until later years, when her too-fast life finally caught up with her. She never really found time to stop and nurture me, but I suspect she loved me in her own way. As she had never felt the warmth of love from her own mother, she never cuddled or hugged me during my infancy. Obviously, this was her loss as well as mine. My father, meanwhile, partied too much to take time to be with his children. From the day he left Groton and sallied forth on the social circuit of debutante parties and then on to Harvard, there were few times, until I was much older, that he was really sober.

Communicating with him was a bit difficult, for he always slurred when drinking and had the odd habit of holding a handkerchief up to his mouth when he had one too many drinks. He could be very sweet about people, and yet one couldn't help but notice all his words were qualified with "but". When crossed or criticized, he would never forgive the accuser. Instead he drank to ease the pain of being rebuked and also to build his ego. Forgiveness meant having to face that person again, and he could never cope with this kind of confrontation or communication.

My father was completely self-centered. His father had severely wounded him though "mentally castrated" would better describe it. I never heard Grandpa praise him. My grandfather never confided in him and said many times that he could not trust my father to do things well or right. Once, when we went up to a launching at my grandfather's shipyard, I heard my Grandfather tell my father that he was ashamed of him and then asked him to go home. I think my father was a bit intoxicated. The remark made a lasting impression on me. Never did my grandfather visit my father in our house when we were in Maine or

Far Hills. When Grandpa went sailing, my father was left behind. They were like oil and water yet were partners, at one point, in a New York brokerage firm.

It's oddly amusing that, as I was growing up I learned so little from my parents and that what I did learn was so banal. "The upper class never wears jockey shorts" and "the long, hanging piece of a roll of toilet paper should always hang next to the wall" were maxims I recall. I wish I could remember more, as they were so stupid.

My mother, bright as she was at this time in her life, had little time for intellectual pursuits and only read the serials in the Saturday Evening Post. My father read only newspapers or self-help books like *How to Improve Your Memory*. The first day he had this particular book, he left it on the train.

Even with these odd bits of parental behavior manifesting themselves around me, my life seemed wonderful though it really wasn't. Children take in far more than one probably realizes, and some of the peculiar antics and unheeding machinations of my family would eventually make themselves loom large in my view of the world. The lack of real love and acceptance that I was feeling soon would overshadow the simple satisfactions of physical comfort.

As I search in my memory for the events and sensations of those early days and learn more about them from my research of family letters, diaries and other documents, I keep coming back to the fact that I was a child with everything my heart could desire but the security of feeling wanted. I never remember being hugged by my parents, but I do remember seeing them and other people always hugging others and especially my older brother. Looking back even more deeply into that early formative era of mine, with the knowledge that education and life experience provide, it is not possible to emphasize too much the key truth at the heart of my message: the building blocks necessary to reach a successful and fruitful adulthood must be wisely developed and cemented at the very beginning of our lives. If we do not receive love as babies and young children, we unfortunately develop bad traits and habits to compensate.

Lack of love in infancy sets the stage for compulsive behavior in adulthood. The void inside us can never be filled by anything but love. As we grow older, we tend to try to make ourselves happy and shake our depression by acquiring masses of material things to make up for our feelings of emptiness. However, no amount of houses, jewels, money, cars, furs or gold can make us joyful for more than a short time. Only love can fill that empty hole. We become compulsive in our attempts to fulfill our craving for love. Rich or poor, black or white, upper or lower class, unconditional love is the cornerstone of an emotionally healthy life. My dysfunctional life was launched at an early age.

Stephen van Rensselaer, painted at age four, is one of my great, great, great grandfathers on my mother's side. He was the very last of the great Dutch patroons and died in 1868. Most of New York had been given in the 1600's to our family. He married Harriet Bayard, a descendant of Peter Stuyvesant.

John Albion Andrew was the Civil War Governor of Massachusetts and a great, great grandfather of mine on my mother's side.

Cornelia van Rensselaer Thayer was a great, great grandmother of mine. She married Nathaniel Thayer.

John Forrester Andrew was the son of the War Governor. He was a Congressman in Washington, D.C. He was Cornelia Thayer Andrew Clark's father and one of my great grandfathers. He died at a very young age.

In 1904, Cornelia Thayer Andrew married John Dudley Clark. Both
are seated in the center. They are my maternal grandparents. This was
but one of Dudley's marriages. His brides all died within a few years
of marrying him. Each wife was richer than the one before. He died
at age 96. It is rumored that all Trinity Church in Boston tittered
loudly when he said "I, Dudley, do to you, Cornelia, all my worldly
goods endow." He was a poor but charming rake who went to Harvard
and had met my grandmother at a dance in Boston. She was as rich as
Croesus.

This charming house in the country was given as a present to my grandfather by my grandmother. She also gave him a brokerage firm in Boston and life memberships in all of Boston's exclusive and best clubs. This house burned down when my great grandmother, Gaga, put her corset on a heater to dry it out.

This was the Boston townhouse where my grandmother was brought up and into which my grandparents moved after their wedding. The balcony was brought over by Sanford White, the architect, from France when the Tuilleries was burnt down. Marie Antoinette is said to have given on it her famous speech about giving the peasants cake, if they had no bread, but my mother once told me differently. She said the Queen had stood on it and said, "Shoot if you must this old gray head but spare my little Dauphin." Of course, this was after Mother had started to drink too much in her later years. Fifteen servants were needed to run this house, since it took up about a third of a Boston block. The top floor was not heated in order to keep the servants downstairs and working.

My grandfather, J. Dudley Clark, was a dashing figure and did all of the right things except misappropriating most of my grandmother's money after she died. He traveled the world and had a well-born mistress in tow. He only cared for his four sons, though some of them he did not like a great deal. He had little if any time for my mother. He never felt that she held a candle to his beautiful wife, Cornelia Thayer Andrew.

This picture of Cornelia A. Clark, my grandmother, was taken the year she died during the influenza epidemic. She was a social leader and generous patron of many charities in Boston. She tended to favor her eldest son to the detriment of the others.

This is my grandmother the night she was presented to Boston society at a ball for one thousand people. Her mother and father had both died by the time she was ten. She was brought up by a maiden aunt in absolute luxury.

My great grandmother, Lula Hensley Clark Englemann, seated at the far left, next to my grandfather, was an imposing, yet small, woman with a commanding aura swirling about her. Her stature was enhanced by the coal black wig perched high on her head. Always on top of this was a cascading floral or feathered hat. She was smart, conniving and clever. She, for the most part, dressed in black when I knew her. She acted as a mother to my mother and her brothers when Grandmother Clark so tragically died. She managed to make life hell for my mother because of her drinking habits. Though my mother hated her, I really quite liked her. Maybe it was because our common enemy was mother.

There's an old European saying that the reason grandparents and grandchildren get on so well is because they share a common foe. Gaga was strict and demanding and she brooked no crossing her. In this picture she is with her second husband, Dr. George Englemann, and two of my older uncles, Dudley and Forrester (Tim) on the right.

My Great-grandmother was born in 1855 in St. Louis, and her family owned slaves. She was ten when the Civil War ended, and she could tell me about it and the horrors of slavery. I was twenty-one when she died and had loved to hear her memories of her long talks with her Great-grandfather, who lived through the Revolutionary War. Her personal experiences covered the entire history of the United States.

The only time I remember her not making good sense was when she asked me if I would ask the man at the end of the living room to stay for dinner. She had asked him twice and he had not answered her. It was General Eisenhower on the television screen.

Philip Lees Smith, my grandfather, was a rich, antagonistic, mean-spirited person. He was short and had what one would call "a Napoleon complex." He spent his life trying to prove himself and fight his way out of his five foot five inch frame. Obviously, his stature and pugnacity did not bother many women as he was always involved in a lot of female entanglements. His father, my great grandfather, had always ignored him, and, when my grandfather's mother suddenly died, he was sent away to Groton School at a very tender age. Grandpa Smith was perfectly frightful to his wife, my grandmother, Belle. He not only flaunted mistresses in front of her but constantly put her down in public. He had never learned how to love or be loved. His father was an alcoholic and committed suicide.

My grandmother, Belle Webster Smith, was a manic depressive and spent a good deal of time in sanitariums trying to cure this affliction of hers. It was well before the days of antidepressants and weaving and crafts were her therapy. When she would get out of the institutions, she would usually find my grandfather emotionally entwined with some lovely young woman. One time my grandmother went to see him off on a ship bound for Europe and found the ship's purser's log had a Mr. and Mrs. Philip Smith booked in a certain cabin. As she wasn't going, she fled from the ship and had the chauffer take her directly to her favorite sanitarium.

This is the large country house, named "Hillcote," that I was raised in in Far Hills, New Jersey. There were gardens, stables, garages for six cars, paddocks, orchards and acres and acres for all kinds of play. We had horses, ponies, chickens, sheep, ducks and dogs everywhere. On an early fall, a hunt came through the place and the hounds snapped the heads off all my father's bantams. In 1952 my father was burning leaves and he set fire to the stables and the garages. This time, not like the time Philly and I set fire to them, they burned to the ground. I lost a beloved car, my grandfather's special-body, twelve-cylinder Packard. It was mine to drive at will.

This is my mother, age three, with one of her younger brothers, George. The expression on her face is one of total arrogance and disdain. If looks could kill, the child in her arms would be dead.

My father, Philip W. Smith, and his sister, Helen, in early childhood.
They remained close throughout their lives but really never
communicated well as the whole family was too dysfunctional.

This is my mother, Cornelia A. Clark, on her wedding day in 1928. She is standing in the front hall of her family's house. The wedding reception for 1,000 guests was held here. Years later I found this wedding dress in my mother's closet and wore it to a costume party on a dare. In the process, I split every seam. As she had no daughters to wear it, it never bothered me in the least.

My mother, Nina, was a true beauty, though she never believed it. As a child, she had been ignored, shunted aside and ridiculed for not being as beautiful as her mother. The servants in her house brought her up after her mother died during the influenza epidemic of 1918. My mother always thought that she killed her mother because she had carried the influenza bug home from school and infected her.

This is the wedding of my mother and father in Trinity Church. The place was packed. There were sixteen bride's maids and sixteen ushers. Bishop Lawrence and the Reverends Endicott Peabody and Henry Know Sherrill assisted.

The design of this church has now changed. There is a free-handing cross over the altar which is about where my mother is standing in the picture. It was given by my great aunt in memory of my Grandmother Clark. At the dedication, Aunt Eliza, who gave it, said to the assembled throngs that "it was the most expensive piece of costume jewelry she had ever bought." I believe she gave a million dollars for the honor of naming it.

The reception following this ceremony was held at my Grandfather Clark's Boston townhouse.

THREE

The inner core of people's personalities is formed from the way they are treated by those individuals around them in their formative years. It is important that they be brought up in their family world with acceptance, love, understanding, freedom and joy. The interaction within this family is a dynamic that gives depth and meaning to a person's rationality, self-esteem and security, which will forever be an integral part of them. During every stage a child lives through, be it infant, toddler, preschooler, or school age, interaction has a major influence on that child's eventual disposition, individuality and ability to cope with adult life. When parents bring up their children irrationally, there is hell to pay.

Before I reached the age when I could finally reason why people were acting the way that they were, the dysfunctional behavior I had experienced had been internalized either as a problem or pain. My ego, the person I was to be, was forming, and I had little control over the abuse it was getting. Only my family had real control over me and they were themselves victims of dysfunctionality and depression. Their depression was caused mostly because of their genes, while the dysfunctionality had been brought on not only by the irrational behavior of their parents and grandparents but also by alcohol abuse. It is important to look at the odd deportment of many of my family members and even some of my ancestors to understand why my immediate family behaved as they did and how this behavior squared (or didn't) with what was expected of them in their social class. It had everything to do with how I was brought up.

My parents really were not so different on the surface from most parents in their social set, but underneath the facade they presented to the world, the imprints caused by their family's behavior made them poor bets to be proper parents. The amount of money they had and the particular eccentricities they derived from their upper-class upbringings and educations made them seem somewhat strange—but then, many households around them were similarly peculiar. I often wished I had some of my friends' parents as mine instead of my own, but it did not take long to see that they shared many characteristics with my mother and father.

The world that I had been born into in the 1930's was changing, everywhere. Everyone felt extreme tension. The dark shadows of the Great Depression and financial ruin spread poverty and destitution throughout the United States. Even wealthy families, including my own, were beginning to hurt a bit. Yet Far Hills was still in high financial gear, as nobody liked to admit that they had lost anything. Men put up brave fronts, even as some of them contemplated suicide.

Clarence Dillon, the great financier who started Dillon, Reed Co. and bought the Dodge Automobile Company, was advising everyone, including my father, to buy, buy, buy all the stock that one could at these depressed prices. He could afford it, but Nip Smith couldn't. My father lost his underpants as well as his shirt, and Mr. Dillon probably tripled his fortune.

Entertaining on a vast scale continued. The ranks of maids, butlers, chauffeur and gardeners actually increased as people were desperate for jobs of any kind and the rich were desperate for help, especially low-wage servants. We took in many of the relatives of our servants who were unable to get jobs anywhere. We paid them a pittance, but, at least, they had shelter and food, while we lived like kings with a footman in attendance. Our houses in both Maine and New Jersey had room for lots of staff, and Mother, a kind person, saw it as noblesse oblige to help our help in this way.

Two or three years later, after we had assumed the responsibility for these extra members of the household, the United States banks began to fail and suddenly closed for a bank holiday. My parents were stunned and decided to close our Far Hills house for the winter. They had to let go of five servants when they moved our household, together with the remaining four servants—a butler, cook and two nurses—into my grandparents' place in Short Hills, New Jersey. This Smith estate sat on a hilltop surrounded by twenty acres of beautiful grounds dotted by barns, garages and formal gardens, along with a lovely shaded pond ringed with thousands of lilies-of-the-valley. My grandparents had been the third major family to build in Short Hills. That was in the early 1900's, and they now had a beautiful, prime piece of land swept by cool breezes and illuminated by the sun in all its brilliance. Nowadays, Short Hills is a suburban community with perhaps four houses per acre, but back then it was rural farmland and a fashionable place to live. It was only a short ride from New York.

My grandparents were the leaders of that local society; though my grandfather, in fact, was as unsocial as a snake and let my grandmother, with her grace and charm, do the entertaining. All he wanted was to have total control over any area where he lived. In Short Hills he was looked up to as the squire on the hill, so this helped bolster his sense of power. Impressed by the splendor surrounding him, many neighbors and acquaintances took advantage of his largesse to visit the Smith compound in Maine during the summers. There his image as a ruler was his delight.

Before long, other families came to Short Hills. Among them were the Thomas Watsons, who moved close by. He, of course, was the founding father of International Business Machines (IBM), and he talked most of my grandparents' friends into investing in his company. They made financial killings as a result. My grandfather did put some of his money in too, but not as much as his friends did. This was because Mr. Watson was known to drink cocktails at night and my grandfather was sure that this would eventually be the ruination of the IBM Company. In time, I would inherit some of my grandfather's stock with a cost basis of fifty cents.

My mother was a true Boston Yankee as well as a fine horsewoman. She decided to save money in her move to Short Hills, so, instead of taking her horse by van the thirty miles between the two places, she rode "Railbird," her favorite hunter, to my grandparents' estate. After that long ride she said her bottom was blistered for two months. But the truth was she was always doing such things to get attention. One time she leapt off one of my grandfather's yachts as it sped out of Tenants Harbor, simply because someone had dared her to do it for $100. It was probably the only time she ever had been swimming in the ocean there. The water was frigid as Antarctica and she was terrified of swimming. Her fear arose from her near drowning as a child while swimming in Farm Pond, a lake near my Grandfather Clark's farm in Sherborn, Massachusetts. She had been horsing around with her brothers and they had held her under water too long.

My father was a senior partner, as was my grandfather, in their own Wall Street brokerage firm. It was called Barbour and Co., and my grandfather had bought it when he came to New York City from Worcester. The gyrations of the financial world at this time kept them both upset and jumping with anguish. One day they might make a fortune and the next day lose it. They were always on edge and worrying what the next move was to be. When my father had graduated from college, he immediately came to work for my grandfather and made a great deal of money rather quickly. However, when the stock market crashed just a few years after he had joined that firm, he lost most of that quick money he'd made. At this time my mother's trust funds started to dry up like the Dust Bowl, and neither my father nor my mother really knew how to cope with these losses. They were totally unprepared to live without lots of money. It had been their crutches through their entire lives.

To compound matters, my father was now living with his father, whom he actively disliked. The feeling was mutual. My grandfather had always belittled and criticized him, declaring that he was worthless. My grandfather could not bear his son's drinking and he also opposed what he considered my father's useless social activities.

My grandmother, on the other hand, loved my father unconditionally and most particularly because he was her beloved first-born. He, in turn, loved her, perhaps, excessively. He told us later of the many times that his mother moved into the Copley Plaza in Boston for months at a time after she had had bad fights with her husband. She wanted to be near my father who was at Harvard. Together they would take stylish European or Caribbean cruises during my father's vacations because they got along so beautifully and enjoyed each other's company. Certainly such delightful escapes were preferable to living with a cranky Grandpa Smith.

Living in Short Hills with his parents was tricky for my father because there was no place for him to drink. My grandfather, himself the son of a heavy drinker, never allowed alcohol, let alone my father's favorite concoction, martinis, in any of his houses. As a result, everyone drank closeted upstairs in a room before every evening meal. My grandmother's boudoir was the popular house speakeasy. She loved her cocktails and had them in her boudoir next to her bedroom. She did not share a bedroom with her husband in Short Hills or in Tenants Harbor.

I knew three of my grandparents very well since only one had died before I was born. I also knew one of my great-grandparents, Lula Hensley Clark Engelmann. This great-grandmother was to live to be more than one hundred years old. As we were forever staying with these relatives, I was able to learn good manners—some of them rather quaintly old-fashioned, like hand kissing—and, most importantly, how to act and interact with all kinds of people no matter what their background. My brothers and I were always brought into the rooms when guests were present. At very young ages we were expected to show off all the nice graces that had been drummed into us by our nurses.

I happily learned much at the knee of my maternal great-grandmother, called Gaga by all. She was an outspoken and amusing character that quite a few of us great-grandchildren adored being with. She would say the most outlandish and racy things, like telling us about the little girl slave that slept at the foot of her bed in St. Louis, or letting slip swear words that we never heard elsewhere.

My grandfather Clark, with whom she lived, had a mistress on the premises as well. Gaga hated her and every time the woman left the house, Gaga would charge into her room and grab all the jewelry, furs and knickknacks my grandfather had given her. The fights between them that ensued, when the mistress returned home, were wild and sometime ridiculous. We children joined in. Gaga's wig would inevitably fall off as she tugged and pulled to keep what she had removed from the mistress's room. She always wore a wig over her graying brown hair, as ladies did not dye their hair and she hated her mousy gray color.

She told us about people she knew who had "diarrhea of the mouth," at which point we children would get hysterical. Once she described in acute detail how Uncle Gigi, her son and the doctor who delivered me, had gelded her carriage horses so she could try driving them if she ever had to if her Irish coachman got too drunk. I remember so well that nothing was funnier than listening to such adult talk, particularly from a little old lady who, on the one hand, seemed the living embodiment of manners. Yet, on the other hand, told her racy stories as she downed glass after glass of sherry. The drinks loosened her up and every laugh made her and us more raucous. How my mother would glower if she walked in on us.

Every time Gaga saw me, she too never failed to tell me "You should have been a girl, as you are too lovely to be a boy." I hated her for saying this, but I still loved her stories. She also frequently added that since I was a boy it could not be stressed too much that I must learn that boys should "never kiss a girl above the elbow until they marry them." Some of these utterances did endear her to me and her sparkle, wit and frankness struck a happy chord with me. Gaga named every maid that worked for her "Mary." The girl would arrive in Gaga's room and announce that she was, Bridget, but Gaga would announce her intention to call her Mary. When she called out that name, ten maids would come rushing.

My mother's parents, I was told, were a great deal more loving and compatible than my father's parents. My maternal grandmother, Cornelia Thayer Andrew Clark, was a ravishing beauty who had a colossal fortune. Her mother, Harriet Bayard Thayer Andrew, and her father, John Forrester Andrew, had both died when she was young. She and her sister, Elizabeth, or Aunt Eliza as we called her, were brought up by their maiden aunt, Edith Andrew, in the immense Andrew house on Commonwealth Avenue in Boston.

The filling-in of Boston's Back Bay had been financed in large part by my great-great grandfather, Nathaniel Thayer, who kept for himself corner lots on each of the eight streets that crossed Commonwealth Avenue. Each of his eight children received a lot and a house on these large sunny-side parcels as a wedding present. My great-grandparents had a mansion designed by McKim, Mead & White. It took two years to complete and was spectacular. It cost $1,500,000 in those days, which is the equivalent of about $25,000,000 today. The mansion featured ceilings painted by Italian artists, leather walls with brass studs designs in the dining room, cavernous, ballroom-sized halls, brocaded walls in the living rooms, a billiard room, an oval library and about twenty tiny servant rooms in the unheated top floor. This house had been left to my grandmother and her sister, but Aunt Eliza did not want it. She preferred the classic Georgian mansion in Hingham where she and my grandmother had always summered.

As my mother was the only female child in the Clark family-she had two older brothers and two younger ones-the background of her mother should be understood as my grandmother's interaction with my mother was very important in forming Mother's style and governed her conservative way of looking at "how things should be done." She spent her life trying to emulate my grandmother's graciousness and did very well with that aspect but with her behavior, she failed quite badly. My Mother was not the favorite or special child of either parent, but my mother adored her mother and was forever telling us stories about her and the incredible life Grandma Clark led. We were brought up hearing Cornelia Thayer Andrew Clark stories from a teary eyed mother. She told us also, all the tales about my grandfather after her mother's death. He horrified my mother and caused her severe mental anguish by ignoring her and cavorting as strangely as he did.

Before telling about my grandmother, a note should be added here about my grandmother's only and unbelievably close sister, Eliza. She was completely unlike my grandmother and rather like a prune. She was that famous old Boston lady who, when asked where she bought her hats, said quietly and simply, "We have our hats." Her hats were undoubtedly the most terrible looking, maid-like, black, squashed straw concoctions that the world had ever seen. For her huge donations of money for the renovation of Trinity Church in Copley Square, the church let her name her gift after a family member. She said, at the dedication of the gigantic, hanging cross over the main altar, "This is the most expensive piece of costume jewelry that I've ever bought." It was given in memory of my great grandparents, John Forrester and Harriet Thayer Andrew, and my grandmother, Cornelia Thayer Andrew Clark. They were her parents and her sister.

The maiden aunt, Edith Andrew, who brought up the Andrew girls, was the only daughter of the Massachusetts Civil War Governor John Albion Andrew. She made sure that Cornelia's and Eliza's lives were elegant and stylish. They went to private schools, met the right people and made debuts. They also became members of the very elite Vincent Club, traveled grandly throughout the world, joined a "sewing circle" of friends who had "come out" with them, married Harvard men who had been members of the right final clubs, and then had beautiful, well-mannered and athletic children to carry on their bloodlines and inherit their money.

Coming out, sometimes called "making a debut," was a rite of passage for every young lady of society in every major city in the United States. In Boston, it was the obligation of the parents to present their daughter to society and, thereby, announce that she was of marriageable age. Marriage to the right person was frightfully important, for it allied fortunes and families.

The prominent families of Boston had for years sent their children to dancing schools. These young ladies and gentlemen then were invited to small dances in the homes of other prominent families. It enabled them to start meeting everyone worth meeting. All the "right" girls and boys were well known in cities across the country, so all of these privileged youth soon got to know one another quite well. When the year of the coming-out party arrived for a young lady about to be introduced to society, a date was arranged with the city's social secretary. One of the best dates in the social calendar was the night of the Harvard-Yale football game. All the most desirable college men would be in town. A carefully culled list was made, with its roster drawn from the socially elite of Boston, New York City, Philadelphia, Baltimore, Washington and Charleston.

Families from these cities had intermarried over the years when sons had been sent to Harvard and attended Boston parties. Society people just automatically knew society people everywhere! Next, one acquired the lists of the prominent final clubs at Harvard, Yale and Princeton, but in Boston special attention was paid to Harvard and particularly the Porcellian, AD, Fly, and Spee Clubs. The Porcellian was on the very top rung, for it was Harvard's oldest and, it was agreed, best one. Its members came from the most important families all over the world. Actually, the Porcellian considered itself to be the only club in the world worthy of being called a club, and so referred to other clubs as "societies." They even called club soda "society soda." The other girls who were asked were all those eligible, socially prominent young women from Boston who had reached the same age as the debutante, usually eighteen years old. Girls from other cities might be asked if the debutante had met them at boarding school or at a fashionable, summering watering hole. Family members of the debutante, quite obviously, showed up in droves.

If one had a private ballroom, one had the party there, but if this was not possible, a suitably grand hotel like the Copley Plaza was rented. These ballrooms were banked to the ceilings with flowers and made sumptuously beautiful for the thousand or so guests. No detail—from the gifts, called favors, given to each lady attending, to the special ushers on hand for coping with wallflowers—was overlooked. This was the debutante's moment, and it was a fleeting one: she was now ready for the right sort of marriage, and the sooner the better.

From every account I have read, my grandmother's coming-out was a glorious evening. Her appearance that night was described as unusually exquisite, and the photograph I have of her is spectacularly chic. She's holding a fan to her chin, undoubtedly to create a look of sophistication, and ostrich feathers flow everywhere. In fact, she did meet a man from the Spee Club at her coming-out and they eventually married, even though not everyone agreed he was her social equal. Those opposed included my Great Aunt Edith, her guardian. She had an AD club member picked out.

This grandmother did only one thing that was not planned. Cornelia Clark died during the massive influenza epidemic of 1918, leaving five small children, a handsome young husband and a massive fortune. According to newspaper reports, she was mourned by more than two thousand people at her service at Trinity Church. My mother was not allowed to attend the funeral, even though she was eleven and really should have been allowed to go. To my mother's dying day, she had tears in her eyes when talking of her mother's death. Once when I repeated the silly joke, "I opened the window and influenza," I was sent to my room for the day. I did not have the foggiest idea why until years later.

As I have intimated, my grandfather, husband of this paragon, was only relatively well-born, but he made up for it by being sporting, rakish, dashing, and able to seem more educated than he actually was. He was also a ladies' man. J. (for John) Dudley Clark had some money, but not much, when he married my grandmother. He soon found that he had access to her huge and generous pocketbook, so at this marriage juncture, life changed rather rapidly for him. She presented him with a senior partnership in the brokerage firm of H.C. Wainwright and Co. as a wedding gift. To assure him proper connections in Boston society, she also arranged and purchased for him life memberships in the Somerset Club, The Country Club in Brookline, the Dedham Hunt and Polo Club and the Santee Shooting Club in South Carolina, to name but a few. They moved into the massive house on Commonwealth Avenue in Boston, which had been her parents', and as well, she endowed him with a magnificent weekend estate in Sherborn and a wonderful summerhouse in Chocorua, New Hampshire.

Lacking any real intellectual curiosity, my grandfather filled his life with polo, fox hunting, shooting and gardening. As a young widower, he soon became a very eligible man about town. He also had something of a reputation as a seducer. Boston debutantes were warned by their mothers at the start of their coming-out year to accept dances with Mr. Clark but "never, never go into the garden with him." It also seems it was his habit to pace around naked without his curtains drawn in his upstairs suite of dressing rooms in his house. He shocked the Cheever family who lived across from him on Hereford Street. They kept calling and asking him to clothe himself, as their daughters were being traumatized. Apparently he paid little attention and even probably got a vicarious thrill out of hearing about his effect on them.

After my grandmother's death and following many affairs—one of them with a first cousin of my grandmother's and another with a lady whom he had originally met when seated beside her at my mother's coming-out party, Grandpa Clark married a duPont from Wilmington, Mary Chichester Dupont. When she died after a happy ten-year marriage, he took as the next Mrs. Clark an heiress from Cleveland, a Mrs. Ayers, whom we grandchildren referred to as Granny Cleveland. He was always kept in the style to which he was accustomed and died at the ripe old age of ninety-seven while carrying a frosty martini to his wife. He was buried in a baby blue coffin, to every one's horror, in Cleveland, a place he probably had never been. He had met this last wife at the Jupiter Island Club in Hobe Sound, Florida, and stayed there till the day he died. He lived life to its fullest.

His self-indulgent lifestyle had caused some problems with our family's finances, for somehow he had managed to misappropriate a sizable amount of my mother's inheritance. It had been left in trust for her and her siblings, but Grandpa Clark had illegally used the monies as venture capital and to finance H.C. Wainwright & Co. during the Great Depression years. Thankfully, my mother had inherited some additional money directly upon the death of her mother, Cornelia, so she never was without her own assets. My father hated Dudley Clark and spent years trying to have him jailed for squandering my mother's trust money.

A trust that should have been worth $15,000,000 in 1960 (when he died) was worth only approximately $3,000,000. The beneficiaries from it over the years were my mother's siblings who had gone into business with my grandfather, as well as my grandfather's mistress, who was receiving huge cash payments on a yearly basis. The original trustees and the First National Bank of Boston had ducked out of the responsibility, leaving Grandpa Clark to run amuck with the funds. Saving H.C. Wainwright from collapse took the biggest chunk of his wife's trust, but on a yearly basis my grandfather and my uncles Forrester, Dudley and George hauled away great profits from H.C. Wainwright. My mother and her youngest brother, Nathaniel were left out in the cold, as they were not in the firm. Originally, though, they had been named equal beneficiaries by my grandmother.

When my father finally threatened to sue the firm, the trustee, who at that point was Uncle Tim (Forrester) Clark, took money from H.C. Wainwright to set up a $4,000,000 trust. This saved Grandpa Clark from jail, but certainly diminished what my immediate family was to eventually inherit.

Grandpa maintained his mistress in grand style, and she lived extravagantly on what should have been my mother's money. It was a rather peculiar arrangement, for my grandfather paid to keep her husband in fine style in New York City while his mistress lived with him in Boston.

My great-grandmother, Louise Hensley Clark Engelmann, moved in to take control of the motherless household after her daughter-in-law, Cornelia, died. Gaga was not up to the task and came close to ruining the lives of all the Clark children. She ruled with an iron hand, but in a haze of sherry. Her charges could not bear her, but she never lost much sleep over that. She was much more interested in her own life and the sherry supply, which she had the S.S. Pierce man deliver once a week. He would put a case in the elevator and send it up to her on the fifth floor, where her maid would store it and she would drink it. She never gave her grandchildren the love they craved, nor could my grandfather, for his status as a rich young widower meant he was busy being entertained far and wide. As he adored women and was always out with them, he gave his mother carte blanche to raise them-a poor choice.

The official story behind the death of Gaga Clark Engelmann's first husband, George Clark, was that he had perished with his faithful Indian guide while shooting over a waterfall on the Missouri River. Unofficially, rumor had it that he had committed suicide because he had syphilis, a fashionable but usually fatal disease that had also killed such other grandees as Winston Churchill's father.

Gaga had been born to slave-owning, very well to do parents in St. Louis, Missouri, in 1851. She always told me, quite imperiously, that she had had her very own slaves to tend to her and thus she found living in Boston in my grandparents' house not as well ordered, as she would have liked. She could not understand white help. She had settled herself in a suite of rooms on the fifth floor, from which she directed the household. There she sat in regal splendor, barking out slurred orders to the maids and male servants. She was never without a hat perched on top of her perpetually askew brunette wig. She owned and often wore the mad Queen of Portugal's emeralds, donning them in the evenings to spruce up her attire. My grandfather later sold them, when he made a bad oil investment. Gaga had inherited them from her father-in-law, George Engelmann, a well-known St. Louis gynecologist and brilliant botanist.

After my great grandfather Clark had died, Gaga was married to the son of George Engelmann, also named George. As her Clark husband had died when he was relatively young, my grandfather Clark and his siblings always considered George Engelmann their father. The Duke of May, a royal German prince, became a good friend of the senior Engelmann and, for his superb botanical work, awarded Engelmann a title, a crest and the aforementioned emeralds. The set consisted of a tiara, a necklace of huge emerald and diamond stones, two emerald rings and a large emerald and diamond bracelet. It had a value of many hundreds of thousands of dollars when sold and, today, would be worth millions. It must have been a big debt Grandpa had to pay off with them.

The favorite place of all the Clark children was a glorious farm in the Sherborn. In the 1920's, to the Clark children's horror, Gaga accidentally set the large rambling house in Sherborn ablaze. It burned to the ground. She had been trying to dry a corset on a grate in front of the fireplace in her room. The undergarment caught on fire and all forty rooms promptly went up in flames. Only a hole in the ground was left that later became my favorite swimming pool, where Grandpa Clark always let all the grandchildren swim naked. This freedom was one that we were usually not allowed by my mother, who was oddly prudish about such things.

Grandpa built a fantastic Italian villa to replace the original colonial house. It was the antithesis of its predecessor, for it had vast rooms with fireplaces large enough to stand up in and walls covered with tapestries and Old Italian paintings. One was a Botticelli. Iron railings and marble floors abounded and little rooms for *tête-à-têtes* were everywhere. There was a colossal wine cellar under the living room, and Italian gardens surrounded the stucco and red-tiled house. It was about as sympathetic to the rolling landscape as a dead hippopotamus in a New England field.

The Richard Saltonstalls' house across the fields was the most gracious and wonderful New England farmhouse imaginable and to put this absurdity in its view was a disgrace. Eventually the Saltonstalls bought the house and tore it down.

In contrast to my great-grandmother and Grandfather Clark, both of whom I liked but my parents did not, my Grandfather Smith was a horrible ogre to young children. Having spent every summer, until his death when I was twelve, with him, I remember him well and learned what true meanness is from him. He was a nightmare. He never said a kind word to me. Luckily, his domain was large enough that I was able to hide or play far away, thus avoiding him.

He would accuse me of doing things that I did not do, and no explanation I gave was ever listened to. He doled out punishments like a petty despot and I spent day after day banished from boats, the tennis court or the dock. Sometimes he would simply ignore me and not speak to me, and at other times he called me by some nasty nickname like "Little What What," because I asked questions.

Once, when candy and cigars were stolen from a cupboard six feet above the floor—a spot totally impossible for me to reach at five years old—I was blamed and kept off the dock for ten days. I was no goody-goody during those long-ago summers but never as horrible a little boy as Grandpa Smith thought I was. There was just the merest hint of a nicer side to him, for he did have an abiding love for architecture, American antiques, wooden boats and natural plantings. In fact, he had a lifelong love for flowers and shared it with my grandmother. There was neither a stonewall nor a border in Tenants Harbor that did not have nasturtiums, sweet peas, delphinium, petunias, daffodils or wild flowers planted in front of it. But this passion for growing things did not extend to growing children.

As I have said, he came from a very rich, mill-owning family in Worcester, Massachusetts. Losing his mother when he was quite young, he was shipped off to Groton School during its first years. He adapted well there and worshipped the Rector, Endicott Peabody. I think Peabody was the only man Grandpa Smith ever feared as well as loved. The Rector was an imposing figure and a fair man, as well. He took the place of a father for my grandfather, for his own had no time for him. From Peabody,

Grandpa Smith learned to face life head on. Like Peabody, he brooked no opposition ever!

He left the strict confines of Groton at eighteen and went on to Harvard for four uneventful years. By his own admission, he had few friends and never made a final club. These clubs were where all the well-to-do gentlemen in college met and wined and dined. The contacts and friends they made in them lasted a lifetime, and club friends were frequently a tremendous help in business later on. One of my grandfather's classmates, who was in the prestigious AD Club, once told my father, who got into the AD Club later on, that there were so many blackballs in the pot when it was passed around to ascertain whether my grandfather was to be a member or not, that no one could see even one white ball. I have to assume he did not give a damn. Strangely enough, his two best friends were members of the top club of all, The Procellian Club.

After graduating, he planned to go back to help run the lucrative family mills but he fell off a trolley car and punctured a kidney on a metal fence. Wounded and furious, he sued the trolley company and got a huge $100,000 settlement. With this booty he headed to New York and bought a partnership in the firm of Barbour and Company on Wall Street. He had a great deal of money before this windfall but this was the impetuous to move from Worcester.

He became very successful in the financial world, although he can only be dubbed a failure at the business of friendship. A particularly unpleasant habit of his was to say nasty things in a stage whisper about his Wall Street peers when they were near him. Once, he made a cutting remark about Richard Whitney, then the head of the Exchange, and Whitney never forgave him. He eventually paid for having such poor manners by being kicked off the New York Stock Exchange for a minor infraction by the very people he had whispered about. They had come to loathe him. Richard Whitney ended up in Sing Sing Prison for stealing. Grandpa Smith had his revenge.

My grandfather retired to Maine and set himself up there by buying The First National Bank of Rockland, numerous rental properties in

Rockland, and Snow's Shipyard. This shipyard was one of the oldest in Maine and had made clipper ships, fishing boats and sailboats, as well as all manner of wooden boats. Under Grandpa Smith, this shipyard produced wooden minesweepers during the Second World War and won many awards, the most significant of which was the United States Navy Award of Excellence. It was presented with many admirals extolling my grandfather's virtues, and he was given a very large banner with an "E" on it to fly over the yard.

In 1901, in New York City, a Harvard friend had introduced Grandpa Smith to a tall, beautiful debutante named Belle Farr Webster. She towered over him physically, and her family was more socially prominent than his. "After all, they were not from Worcester," my mother was fond of saying. Belle was directly descended from the Stuyvesant and Bayard families and her grandfather, Horace Webster, had been the first president of the College of the City of New York. This background did not intimidate my grandfather, and they, Philip and Belle Webster Smith, were married in 1902.

They immediately moved into a house in New York City on the Hudson River. A year later, their first child, my father, Philip Webster Smith, was born. Following his birth, my kind and loving grandmother developed profound and acute postpartum psychosis. She was immediately sent off to the stylish sanitarium, Riggs, in Stockbridge, Massachusetts, to try to regain her mental health. Unfortunately, this serious condition became increasingly intense with the birth of each of her next three children. Episodes of depression began to come at other times as well. She was finally diagnosed as a manic-depressive. Her mania was relatively controlled, but her depression was severe. She simply couldn't cope with having children, though she adored them after her recoveries. My grandfather, meanwhile, who expected utter subservience from his wife and family, could not cope with her depression. As a result, he took up with many other women, a veritable parade of them.

One of Grandpa Smith's idiosyncrasies was that he was a notoriously punctual man. If he asked you out on one of his yachts at noon, he meant noon, and would cast away as the clock was striking eight bells, a ship's signal of twelve o'clock. Many a child who had arrived a minute or two late was left behind on the dock in tears as he sailed off. On the morning that his beloved daughter, Helen, was born in his house in Short Hills, he left his wife's bedroom just as the baby's head appeared at 7:45 a.m. He did not wait to see if the mother and child were well, or even to see what sex the baby was. Nothing could keep him from the 8:03 a.m. train to New York City. He found out about his new child when he returned home that evening at promptly 5:13 p.m. This baby would grow up to become the apple of his eye, but punctuality took precedence over even the miracle of birth.

He collected clocks, and every room in Short Hills had a striking timepiece or two in it. He spent an inordinate amount of time winding them on Sundays after church and also making sure that they were striking or chiming at exactly the same second. When the hour sounded, it was like living on a carousel as each noisily proclaimed the time.

My father, as he grew up, was the image of his father's grandfather. This patriarch, John Smith, had excused himself from dinner one evening, as the rolls were being passed, and gone upstairs to hang himself in the well of the circular staircase. My grandfather blamed this catastrophe entirely on alcohol and, as a result, never touched a drop in his life. I think the resemblance to John Smith did not help his relationship with his son, my father.

One night, when my father was about nineteen years old, Grandpa Smith was sitting by his study window just as my father lowered a bottle of bootleg whiskey out his bedroom window on a rope to the ground below. My father most likely did this so he could get past his father with no liquor bottle visible on his person. He was headed out for an evening of partying. The ruse failed because the bottle passed slowly down past the window my grandfather was looking out at that very moment. From that day on, my grandfather classified my father as a sneak.

In Short Hills, Nee, my devoted nursemaid, was always with me, and I well remember our daily walks around the grounds. We fed carrots to my mother and aunt's horses and we picked flowers. While I walked with Nee or was pushed in my carriage, my brother Philly was off elsewhere with our parents and grandparents. I remember playing alone in a sandbox installed off one of the terraces. When we got to Maine in the summer the picture changed. There, other children played with me, and my father's sister, Betty, cuddled me and helped teach me what love was. Maine was a far cry from Short Hills. This was particularly so if Grandpa Smith was not around.

As the Depression wore on, I was still living in Short Hills with Grandpa and Grandma Smith. My stay lasted just long enough for me to remember it being a lonely life. There was little warmth in that great house. Someone was always at odds with someone else, and, except for meals, everyone lived quite separate lives. My grandfather had nothing to do with me, but both he and my grandmother fawned over my brother, Philly, their glorious first-born grandson. We returned to our place in Far Hills when I was three, but the feeling that I was second rate in my grandparents' eyes never left me.

After having a baby aborted in 1933, for health reasons, my mother produced my younger brother, Bayard Webster Smith, on July 9, 1934. For his first year, everyone thought he might be retarded. He had little if any forehead and was written up in an important medical paper for his lack thereof. Doctors followed his progress and kept close tabs on him, for there was a question whether a fully functioning brain could fit in his terribly small cranium. As it developed, he was not backward at all. However, the belief that he was "special" made him the cynosure of all eyes, and everyone doted on him.

My mother became pregnant again soon after Bayard's birth. We children were excited, but the doctors did not like the idea of doing another Caesarean section so soon. Towards the middle of June that year, Mother left Tenants Harbor for Boston with a baby in her tummy. When she arrived back, about two weeks later, we met her car on the road. As the chauffeur slowed to a stop, we scampered into the big back seat and demanded to see the baby. She handed each of us a stitch that she had saved from the incision made by the doctors from the removal of the child.

At that instant, I suddenly believed that my mother was a monster. I'm convinced I even thought she might one day get rid of me. After all, she had somehow killed this baby that had been in her stomach only a few days before. I really was terrified. To this day, I never pass that spot on the road, the one where the car stopped, that I don't shiver. For a long time a mailbox stood there, and, year after year, when I rode my bike by it, I tried to stay as far from that spot on the road as I could. Somehow I always raked against the sharp edge of the package hook. I repeatedly lacerated my upper arm at that terrifying spot. I, like every child on earth, felt that my parents had the complete power of life and death over me, not to mention the power to banish me if I misbehaved. However, unlike other children, I actually had a visible sign of their omnipotence, for I had my mother's stitch to prove it might happen to me. Is it any wonder that I had feelings of rejection and depression at such a young age? I had nightmares for years about this particular incident and sometime I dreamt I was pushed out of the car and run over.

I am one month old and being held by my nurse, Campbell, or Nee as I called her. I was always told I much preferred her to my mother or father. I wailed if anyone but Campbell picked me up. Here I look content in my nurse's arms.

I am six months old and enjoying the solitude of my carriage. I guess Campbell must have been pushing it as I am smiling.

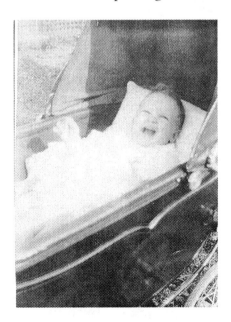

I'm just about a year old in this picture, bundled up in regal splendor. The Smiths never did anything halfway at this stage of their lives. Furs and lap robes were commonplace. I am in our stable yard in Far Hills.

I was dressed in wash suits or dresses, and my hair was always very long and curly. Philly, on the right, was always dressed as a typical boy. I was the sissified one. My family never let me forget they wished I'd been a girl. My nickname at this time was "Fuzzy," and everyone that saw or spoke to me said I was too pretty to be a boy. What was I meant to do about it?

I am with "Taffy", one of my favorite dogs. We always had many of them but my mother would drown puppies to keep numbers down. We saw them put in bags with stones and thrown in the ocean.

Philly, my mother and myself are sitting on one of the porches in Far Hills. Mother is pregnant with Bayard, or perhaps, the baby that died just before him. "Won't they ever cut my hair?" I must be begging.

It is interesting that I never did a single thing with my father. My friends skated, sledded, rode, swam and played with theirs, but mine sat and drank all day or else burned the leaves that a gardener had raked into a pile.

Here I am in the stable yard hugging a beloved dog, Elmer. He was practically big enough to ride and I kept trying to ride him until I was given a pony.

I am brimming with joy and sitting on my absolutely dearest "friend," my pony, Capers. I could ride him for hours and hours around the place or in the paddocks. I was taught to ride at a very young age and adore it to this very day. Capers was killed in front of me.

Living in the country did not allow me to have many playmates until I went to school. Needless to say, my mother never invited children over for me to play with unless they were the children of intimate friends of hers. This meant that they might be GIRLS.

As usual, I am the one on the bottom of the family heap. My mother, Nina, is holding Bayard while Philly is crowd-pleasing. There really are few pictures in which I am smiling.

My hair looks shorter but I still seem sad. This was taken in Far Hills near our barn where I could ride my pony and play with all the other animals. I continually stepped on rusty nails and was forever being whisked to the doctor's for tetanus shots. They hurt like hell!

Doesn't this look like Little Lord Fauntleroy at play in the snow in his furs? It is I and I also had a full length raccoon coat at this age. I was mortified to wear it but was forced to.

(L to R) Forrester, Bayard, "Duchess" and Phillip. This was the favorite of the family dogs for years and years, and it was she that had puppies twice a year. We would save one from each litter and the rest were drowned in pails in Far Hills or thrown in the Maine ocean in a weighted bag.

These are my brothers and I sitting with three playmates. The bonneted girl in the middle grew up to be one of my best friends, Apple Parish Bartlett. D.B. Parish is hidden in the shadows.

I am sitting on the left and probably trying to bite my toe nails. I was an habitual nail biter and scared of my own shadow. My hair was, as usual, curly and long. I loved Maine in the summer and, except for the continual punishments of my Grandfather Smith, would go off with aunts or cousins to play and read.

This is Grandfather Smith steering one of his many yachts with a
sycophant friend aiding him. He was a wild sailor and went aground
just to torment my grandmother if she was aboard. He was small,
abrupt and nasty. He wrote in his diary the day of his daughter Helen's
birth, "…daughter born at 7:46 AM at home. I make the 8:15 AM train
to NYC." Punctuality meant everything to him.

I cannot believe I was allowed to steer this rather large sailboat, but pictures do not lie. I remember greatly relishing such a privilege, for I was mostly relegated to a role as the sissy of the family. My hair did not help my ego.

FOUR

L ife is not always what it seems to be when looked at by others. It appeared that I was living a life that Little Lord Fauntleroy might envy, but, as must be clear by now, I was haunted by the behavior of others, kept off balance and never allowed to develop the confidence that would help me thrive and mature properly.

Mary Raitt, my new governess, for Nee had left, was not only well educated but also utterly capable. She could do anything she wanted to do. She brought sanity to the Smith household and was a loving and sweet woman. For the most part, when she was able to influence our daily lives, I was blessed with a safe, comfortable and secure existence. Our large estate, "Hillcote," was my playpen when Mary was around. She instilled a tremendous amount of love, fun and knowledge in me.

As we lived in beautiful rolling countryside, far from any towns or villages, I did not attend a preschool. There weren't any private kindergartens in Far Hills, and I was not allowed to go to the public one where all the locals sent their children. Our tailor Mr. Lucio's children went there.

"Heaven forbid that you should go there!" my mother once said. She had seen the back of his house, where his children slept five to a bed. Mother was not a snob. She was too sure of herself for that, but some things were just beyond her comprehension.

Children were brought to play with me, and, to my horror, occasionally girls were included. They were daughters of my mother's friends and they were not allowed to get dirty. One of them, Sukie Kuser, would come with her French governess, and sometimes I was sent there. I never understood a word either one of them said because they never spoke English. I do not think my brothers were subjected to playing with girls and I never ever understood why I was. It was the habit of all the local nannies to speak at least once a week, to set up play schedules. Thus, everyone had to play with other nannies' charges. It took only a few boys to be present for the girls to be tormented and their dolls roughed up when no nanny was watching.

There were, however, some things that I liked about Sukie. For instance, there were her incredible birthday parties, staged in her enormous Bernardsville house with forty children running wild as forty nannies chased them! There was always a magician, and a seated dinner with a sensational gift waiting at each child's place. Sometimes there might be more than one. There also would be all our nurses standing behind our chairs to serve us our creamed chicken, rice, peas, ice cream and cake. Though "Happy Birthday" was sung in French, other boys attended and spoke English, so I was delighted to be on hand.

I seemed to be the only child in my family sent to birthday party after birthday party given by strangers. Maybe my brothers insisted that they would not go, but I found myself forced. I think my mother would meet friends out in the hunting field who'd ask her if she had a child or two that might come to a birthday party. It never mattered how many kids attended these events, considering the multitude of servants in most of the Far Hills houses. And it obviously never mattered, either, that the birthday child and guests were unacquainted. My family was starting to use me as a mascot.

The grandest party I ever went to was given for Ann and Diana Gambrill, the granddaughters of the C. Ledyard Blairs. The Blairs were a family who lived in a sixty-room house and owned most of the eastern half of Far Hills. (The Bradys owned the western half.) Mrs. Blair looked like Queen Mary of England, whose pictures I had been shown by my nurse. However, Mrs. Blair was bigger, more bejeweled and dressed more grandly. She sat on a throne in the front hall and greeted all the little guests.

The house was overwhelming to any child. The Blairs' house, "Blairsden," which was constructed between 1898 and 1903, was built on the top of a mountain that had been completely leveled off. A special railroad was constructed to bring all necessary building materials up from the valley below. When completed, the estate required twenty-two household servants and fifty more to maintain the 423 acres of buildings, gardens, stables, kennels and farms. Mr. Blair was an impatient man, so all the trees and huge boxwood bushes were brought in fully-grown by teams of twenty-two horses. The river in the ravine below the house was dammed up and a lake was formed, rightly called Blair's Lake. I skated there all my childhood.

For the party, Mrs. Blair's staff of servants had hidden thousands of chocolate eggs throughout the gigantic house. At the ringing of a bell by the butler, fifty to sixty invitees scampered about, hoping to win a prize for the most eggs found. When the time neared for Mrs. Blair to stop the game and proclaim the winner, I saw a footman rushing about helping Mrs. Blair's granddaughter fill her basket. That fluffed-up little ninny, who had cried most of the hunt because someone had crashed into her, won. She hadn't picked up even one egg on her own, yet I, who had a basket brimming with eggs, had lost this contest to her. Where was justice?

Little unfairness' like this were common in our circle. Once at a party, I saw a parent pull down the kerchief, tied over the eyes of her child while the child was attempting to pin a tail on a paper donkey. He won the game, obviously. The facilitating parent applauded harder than anyone, while the other mothers and fathers gasped in amazement. Again, where was the justice? I could never get an explanation that satisfied me.

Good things did happen, of course. When I was about five, I was given a Shetland pony named Capers. He was a gift from the Rutherford Stuyvesant Pierreponts, who lived a mile down the road. At this point in my young life I did not know the Pierreponts, but a few years later, once we'd become acquainted, I came to love them. They were indeed quite stuffy and old fashioned but also so very sweet to me.

I adored Capers and rode every day that I could. Our groom, George Smith, or sometimes my mother, helped me learn to ride. I became quite relaxed and unafraid. Capers had a mouth of steel and a mind of his own. I could go all over our place, but the instant we turned in the direction of the stable, he seized the bit in his teeth and, at full gallop over the fields, we'd charge towards his stall. Luckily, he slowed to a trot in the stable yard so we never crashed. I learned to hang on for dear life by grabbing the strap at the saddle's cantle that went under his tail. With the other hand I held his mane in a death grip as we pounded home.

I became a rather proficient rider thanks to Caper's acting so capriciously. Our place sat on a hill with sweeping views of valleys and hills, and there was a small brook that ran at the bottom of our hill with a steep bank on the far side. I adored taking him down there for a drink, then slowly walking him up the steep bank. It was so peaceful and lazy, that is, until that potentially lethal turn towards his stall. Truly, my utmost pleasure was just being on Capers and smelling his wonderful pony smell. Riding him gave me a great feeling of control and power, something that I really did not ordinarily have. I always had to wear a hard-hat and promise not to jump any fences. Such strictures made it quite safe to let me go riding on this greatest friend, whom I adored.

Capers was my passport to a different life. As I grew, I was allowed to ride farther and farther afield. I could ride to the Moseleys' and the Bradys' to visit them as long as Philip, on his polo pony, Cecilia, or the groom went along. It was sheer heaven to ride on these trips, if a trifle scary on our return dash. Actually, the speed of Capers was not great, as he was at least twenty years old and rather small. I just thought it was fast. The other horses with me were cantering slowly alongside me. My mother thought it a grand idea for us to ride regularly out in the fields, for she had done this as a child. At this point in her life, she was fox hunting three times a week and anything we did with horses was fine with her. Fox hunting got into my blood later for mascots do what their parents do. It's the way they get praise-usually the only way.

When I was about five, I was asked to be in a pony show given by the Clarence Dillons at their Dunwalke Farm. I put on a magnificent display of walking and trotting, but Apple Parish, the daughter of Sister Parish, the legendary interior designer, looked far cuter sitting on her pony in a wicker basket, so she won the class. Favoritism had reared its ugly head again, and she and her brother, Harry, never let me forget that I had come in second. My red, second-place ribbon, which I kept for fifty years, should have been a blue one.

A monstrous event occurred when I was about four. One morning, my mother came into my room, I was going to the doctor, but she never told me why. When I got there, my pants were removed and the doctor deftly circumcised me. Why I had not had this done at birth, I do not know, but now it was an unthinkable thing for any young boy to be submitted to. Need I say my mother often acted before thinking things through?

For all of my short life, I had been told I should have been a girl. I well remember about this time in my life my mother saying, " We would have loved you if you'd been a girl." Now on my mother's order, my "wee wee" was being cut off. I was beside myself and wept for days and days. I screamed, "You cut it off! You cut it off!" A child couldn't possibly understand any reason for this violation and the terror of it haunted me for years. Had she tried to make me a girl? In many ways it consumed me and not surprisingly brought about severe problems later on. "It will make you a cleaner little boy," is all my mother would ever say, by way of explanation. It turned out my mother had heard from someone at a dinner party that all little boys should be circumcised. Fine, she thought, always eager to act on advice from friends she admired. And so off I went post haste to have this done a few days later.

About this time, my father gave me a dog, a lovely collie named Duchess. Philip coveted Duchess and, somehow, convinced me to trade her for his ridiculous Scottie named Sandy, who spent his life under our large kitchen icebox, scratching his smelly ears and growling. My father had only gotten Sandy to please the help in the house, as they were all Scottish. Sandy had been given to Philip because he was the oldest child. I do not see how Sandy could have ever been lovable. I never liked him and yet he suddenly became mine. My problem was that I could not say "No." Philip could and did force me to do many, many things I knew were wrong. It was my dysfunctional behavior starting.

Neither Philip nor I actually had to care for our dogs, nor were they ever allowed in the front of the house. This never bothered me, for outside the kitchen door we had a large doghouse. I adored crawling in there with Duchess, to hug her and feel the warmth of her soft hair and the sweet smelling hay. That little house was nirvana to me. I felt so secure and I could play there to my heart's content, with a friendly dog that loved me. She usually was pregnant, so I was gentle with her.

However, Duchess, through no fault of her own, caused me severe traumas, usually twice a year, for she would have a litter or two of puppies.

We never could seem to put a stop to this puppy explosion. When she was in heat, we would lock her in a stall in the stable. Only God knows how, but I think stray dogs would struggle up into the hayloft and come down the hay chute to get to her. From each large litter we would try to save at least one puppy, but the destruction of the others was left to the groom or butler on my mother's orders.

Hard as it may be to believe, the drowning of the puppies was always to be done in front of us, even at our young ages, for "Mummy" wanted her sons to be "tough" and not sissies. I can remember the ritual. In the summer, the puppies were put in a bag filled with stones and thrown off the rocks into the ocean in front of our house. In the winter, they were put in a pail in the tack room of the stable and held under water until drowned. Why in God's name we were made to watch, repeatedly, I don't know, but we were. Might my mother soon direct those men to do this to us? It was a terrifying question.

In fairness, my mother was not cruel, but was merely exposing us to the sights she had witnessed as a child on a large working farm with four brothers around her and no mother to calm her. In her girlhood, she had repeatedly been present at the slaughtering of sheep, swine and chickens. It was simply part of living with animals. But my gentle mind could not grasp any rationale whatsoever behind the killing of puppies. It was ghastly and vile, farm background or not.

My parents' friends played a major role in my childhood development. They were ever present, whether as houseguests or appearing on a regular basis for meals, teas, bridge, cocktails or dinner. They seemed to exude love and I relished it.

We children were always brought in by our nurse to be presented to guests. This ritual made us learn our manners quickly, for we might be tongue lashed if we failed to perform according to my mother's high standards. Forbidden to be shy, I soon learned to smile and be polite while decked out in my wash suit and ruffled collar. I also learned at an early age how to make conversation. A dressing down hurt as much as a hard spank, and mother was apt to give the former in front of people if ever I broke one of her rules of comportment.

Among my family's very closest friends were the various members of the James Cox Brady clan. There were masses of them: the Cuttings, the Moseleys, the Brady, Jr.'s, the Scotts, the Cowperthwaites and the Fowlers. They lived well and they owned most of the fox hunting land that the Essex Hunt rode over. All the people in the confines of Far Hills, including my mother, seemed to worship them. The entire Brady family, both young and old, entertained us and we entertained them. We spent time with them in New York, Nassau and Maine. The Brady family and the Smiths were as thick as thieves. Nearly everything the Bradys did was in superb taste and style. The huge dances held in their indoor tennis court, and even the small dances they had in their house, were all wonderfully done. I always felt it was extraordinary how much they would do for their friends in the community and especially for their children. It stood in marked contrast to my own family experience. I was to find out later that all was not as perfect as it seemed to be.

My best friend was James Brady Moseley, the grandson of James Cox Brady. Once he taunted me with the "fact" that he had found out I was adopted. I believed this in my heart for years, because for so long I'd felt so very different from the rest of my family and never really loved by them. I was shattered by this revelation and hid my agony inside myself. I was terrified my parents would send me back to my "real" family, who, in all probability, would turn out to be the Lucios'. Thus I never dared ask my mother if Jimmy's information was true. How could I bear to hear the answer?

In Far Hills, our nearest neighbors were the banking Clarence and Douglas Dillons, the Band-Aid Seward Johnsons, the stock exchange Richard Whitneys, the magazine Henry Luces, the platinum Charles Engelhards, the tobacco Doris Duke and Screven Lorillards, the political Millicent Fenwick, the Brooks Brothers Winstons, the publishing Charles Scribners, the magazine Malcolm Forbeses and the just plain rich Reeve and Ken Schleys, the Richard Gambrills, the Hermann Kinnicutts, the William Kissells and the Percy, Rivington, Grafton and Eben Pynes.

These men and women partied brilliantly, ceaselessly in and out of one another's houses. Being outdoors during the daylight hours was a good way to banish the cobwebs spun at night, drinking and eating and drinking some more. Nearly every member of the group rode to the hounds, much like the English aristocracy did on their vast country estates in England or Ireland. Some non-riders followed the hunt or gave hunt breakfasts and teas. Then there were those who played bridge, usually on their sun porches, in order to feel healthy and to pretend that they had been outside.

Hunting was a glorious sport in such a painterly landscape as Far Hills. The fields were flat and open and there were rolling hills and rivers. The woods provided perfect cover for the foxes that were plentiful in the area.

Foxes were crafty and could run for miles and miles as well as go to ground or climb a tree. The chase was really what most riders came for, as it was one of the most stimulating forms of exercise, galloping across hill and dale while jumping every obstacle in sight. The leader of the field was called the Master of Foxhounds and he or she had a paid huntsman and whippers-in, men or women who kept control of the hounds and made sure they worked together as a pack. Each hound was trained to do a special job. Some would draw the cover to find the fox, while others would form a circle around the cover to start the chase after a fox when it broke cover.

The sight of a hunt passing by was exhilarating. The riders all wore the traditional pink coats—really scarlet, but called pink, as the original London tailor who made them was a Mr. Pink—immaculate black sidesaddle habits, white breeches and polished boots. Above all, the thrill of seeing the hunt came from watching the magnificent steeds. Called hunters, they were sometimes more cherished than the owner's children. Every rider was immensely proud of his or her horse, so they glistened and shone from constant attention. Galloping on a rainy day might smear and spatter mud on the boots and hunting habits, but since there were plenty of people to clean them they were always restored to perfection for the next day out with the field.

The Essex Fox Hounds sponsored these hunts, though participants paid a capping fee. The hounds were kept at the Kennels, as the Club was called by those that hunted, and the fees collected from members fed the hounds, kept fences fixed in the country, paid the professionals and also paid for stabling the professionals' horses. When members' horses got too lame or too old, they were put down and fed to the hounds. I eventually suffered through this practice and was nauseated by it.

Kings, queens, ambassadors, dukes, duchesses, lords, ladies, princes, princesses and even well known actors and writers came for weekends to Far Hills. I can remember being brought to be introduced to many of them as well as bowing, and meeting the Klebergs, the Paul Mellons, Rockefellers, Astors and Vanderbilts, either in our house or at friends' places. I was slowly learning to be an ambassador for my family as I was not shy. People seemed to interest me and they still do.

Even Pope Pius XII came to Far Hills, when he was Cardinal Pacelli, to stay with the C. Suydam Cuttings, our close neighbors. They had a chapel in the house and I thought that was what had drawn the cardinal. However, Helen Cutting's first husband had been James Cox Brady, a Papal Count and Prince of the Church and a big donor to Catholic causes.

A good smattering of uncles, aunts, godparents, and cousins, along with my family's friends from Harvard, Groton and Miss Porter's School, were also frequent guests at our house, especially when large parties were held in the area. They always brought presents for us children. If they forgot to hand them over immediately, we searched their bags for them when they went out to the parties.

I remember, so well, my mother dressing for these dinners and parties. She had a special gold lame dress that she loved. When she put it on, to me she was a shimmering goddess. I would fantasize about who might be coming to our house, or try to imagine where she might be going. When my mother went out for dinner she always came into the nursery to kiss us good night. This was one of the few times I remember seeing her. I think it was done to show off.

My first meal with my family in our main dining room was a memorable one for me, to say the least. I shall never forget it, as I gleaned so much about my family from this one meal. It will always remain as an unforgettable and exceptional meal of my life. I learned, during this

Sunday lunch, that I wanted for nothing material, yet received very little love. I also found out that I was amusing enough to draw attention away from my family when they started acting odd. These antics of mine were the first noticeable start of my playing, in my strange little family circle, the "scapegoat."

This is one of four roles that children of alcoholic and dysfunctional parents take on to assure their survival. The roles for all three of the Smith children, in fact, were already in place, unbeknownst to us, and, as we grew, they took on greater significance. As our parents' dysfunctional behavior was increasing proportionally with their consumption of liquor. We were unknowingly sucked into this role-playing.

This meal—the usual, formal Smith Sunday lunch served by our butler and footman—was unique for me, being the first time I had been allowed to eat with my mother and father in the main dining room of our house. Before this, I had always dined with our nanny elsewhere. On this day, I no longer could act childish, as I must summon up every scrap of my polite social graces and I must be serious. I was in a new Eton gray flannel suit with knee socks and leather shoes. It was a drastic change from my usual frilly wash suits and I thought I was spiffy as all get out. My older brother had already been dining with our parents for a while. My mother and father swished into the living room on the stroke of noon, the sun having risen over the yardarm, to have their cocktails before lunch. Every Sunday they would come in with a friend or two, and have a drink prior to the meal. Today, however, there was no one with them, as they were to have me at the table for the very first time. They probably were just as afraid of being mortified by my actions as I was.

When lunch was announced, we marched single file to the dining room. I rushed behind my mother's chair, first to pull it out and then to try to push it in as she was sitting down. I unfortunately pushed it too soon and she lurched forward and spilled the martini in her hand into her saltcellar. Aghast, I slipped over to my chair, as she made a snide comment about how could I be so rude as to make the butler have to fill the salt cellar again. In this way, the meal began on a decided down note for me. Yet there were more positive moments as it went on.

As the butler's pantry door swung open, in marched our beloved Nelson with a platter of roast beef. My father never carved, as my mother constantly had criticized him for the slipshod product he produced. More help appeared to pass the vegetables, potatoes and gravy. We all helped ourselves, although I got a bit of assistance from Nelson, as my chin was hardly above the table.

When my mother lifted her fork, we started to eat. She turned to me and said I looked handsome in my new clothes, but that she liked the washed linen suits better. I was dumbfounded as she had just bought and had me dressed up in the outfit that I was in. What was I to do to change things? Next she made some snide remark to my father about his drinking at a party the night before. I think she felt she had to pull him down a peg or two in front of us all to build herself up.

At one moment, I dropped my napkin. I went under the table to get it. Seeing my brother's legs, I crawled over and pinched him. Immediately, he dropped down, and we started to laugh, when a snappish voice from above scolded us. We slithered up to our chairs. I was "chewed out," while my brother was reassured that it certainly was not his fault, for my mother said it was my childish behavior that had made him clamber under the table. I basically didn't care as I'd had fun and I was used to being blamed. Yet is emphasized the division of love.

After the plates were cleared, an ice cream mold was brought in on a silver platter. When it was my turn to be served, the ice cream had melted a bit and as I helped myself, I pushed the whole remaining mound onto the table. My father gave one of his usual admonishments, which always included the word "but." This time he said, "You couldn't help it as you're sitting so low at the table, but we never should have had you to this meal and will have to consider whether we have you again."

I started to cry, but nobody paid attention, so I stopped. The ice cream was righted, and Nelson proceeded to pass it around the table, followed by the strawberry sauce. When that heavenly elixir of berries came to me, I put the serving ladle into the silver bowl, dipped it full of strawberries, and brought it to my mouth and ate them. This time near-hysteria ensued. I was the joker and center of attention because I had done a quite stupid thing. Yet I realized I liked being the focus of interest for a change. I somehow understood instinctively that playing for laughs distracted everyone from my mother's cutting comments. Sipping from my finger bowl also brought the house down. I was a hit at that meal!

Months later, I was included in some of the table conversation and felt very grown-up as I talked. We were discussing riding, and, as it happened, I could remember all details of certain hunts because we usually followed in a car. My position was a useful vantage point for knowing who had failed to negotiate a jump and had been left lying under a fence. My parents adored my stories, hearing about their friends' inadequate showings, and by feeding their interest, I was transforming myself into a sort of family "mascot." It was rather a pathetic way of seeking to win their attention, but, like any child who's accustomed to being ignored, I was willing to make use of any resources I could muster. Seeing my success, I was thrilled, and I soon learned to exaggerate when I narrated my tales in order to gain even more attention.

Around ten o'clock one fall morning, Philip and I managed to set our barn and stable ablaze. To build a clubhouse, we had taken a massive cardboard box and propped it against the side of the barn. Inside, for a light, we used a blowtorch and thought we were being clever. Instead, it wasn't long before the heat and flame it gave off ignited our lean-to. As flames began to race up the side of the barn, we fled to the house for help. Nelson instantly called the fire department, and then rushed to the scene. He and George quickly led the horses out of the stables.

The fire department soon arrived, driving over my father's prized lawns. Everyone around was yelling directions or screaming for help as fire leapt to the skies. Finally, I saw my father sleepily shuffle out of the house, gaze speechless at the inferno, and then go inside to fix himself a drink. He, my mother and four house guests had gotten home just before dawn from the annual Hunt Ball and none of them were in any mood for this conflagration. Our governess, Mary Raitt, kept muttering that she wished that we were girls, since they never did this sort of thing. In the end, the fire fighters saved three-quarters of the barns and stables. My parents breathed a sigh of relief, spanked us, and went back to bed.

Mary Raitt was with us for years, and then remained in the family by moving to my Uncle Dudley Clark's family to raise another clutch of children. She was my surrogate mother and was a true godsend to all us children. She was the one who loved us, verbally disciplined us, took us to visit friends and helped us with schoolwork. Every evening, until my father arrived home from work, always a bit worse for wear, she played games with us in the nursery until he came up to kiss us good evening.

Mary was a tiny Scottish woman from Glasgow. She had come to this country to earn a living and help support her family in Scotland. Typically she dressed in starched white dresses with a little white crocheted hat. She was a human knitting machine and was forever making us socks, scarves, mittens and sweaters. Although we truly loved her, we weren't always considerate in the way we acted towards her. It was not from dislike, but from simple high spirits, the kind that turns little boys into demon imps.

We, but usually Philip as he was so big and the leader, smashed her false teeth with hammers, tried to push her downstairs, hit her on the bosom and leapt into her bathroom when she bathed in order to see her naked. She took all of this and more. Yet we did not always get away with this foul behavior. Many a morning after we had been disobedient, she led us into my mother's bedroom, told us to stretch out on her bed and bare our bottoms. Once we were in position, we were spanked with a silver hairbrush that Mary had handed my mother. Mother was usually still groggy and really never knew why she was spanking us. It made little sense to me, as the crime had been the day before.

Mary herself was not allowed to raise her hand against us, even when we painted each other green, flooded the cellar, put mice in beds or rows of nails across the road at the end of our drive. The painful and humiliating swats were left up to my mother. Mary was the guardian angel who nursed us through every childhood illness, read to us every night, played games of Go Fish, Old Maid and Bagatelle with us, and let us listen to special radio programs like The Shadow. My family, busy with other things, left us alone much of the time.

Mary earned about thirty-five dollars a month. Out of this amount she saved enough to help her large family in Scotland, to buy herself a car and to travel home to Scotland every two years. She learned to drive in my mother's car. Her first time alone behind the wheel, she sped down the driveway and ran right into our front hall, removing the front porch in the process. This was not a joy for my father to face when he returned home that evening with his usual martinis under his belt. We all stood in the shambles of the front hall to greet him and see if Mary got a punishment for a change and not us. She didn't.

This was the same front hall into which I had brought my pony, Capers, while my mother was entertaining some stuffy friends. I did get punished after Capers dumped a huge load of manure on the purple rug there. Strangely, one of my mother's friends had started to expire on this very same rug, after a fall from her horse at one of the fences on our place. Her sidesaddle pummel ruptured her bladder and she was lying moaning on the rug in a large puddle when I came down stairs and saw our butler tending to her. Both stains always faintly remained. The woman was taken to a hospital and died there.

Despite our objections, Mary taught us how to knit, sew and cook, even though we were boys. We felt we should not do any of these sissy things, yet she and Mother prevailed. I finally started knitting a scarf for British War Relief. Mary had begun this muffler, but hadn't taught me how to cast off and finish it. When she went on a vacation, I furiously knitted at least a fifteen-foot scarf and was beside myself with grief when she came home and ripped out six or seven feet. I was convinced you could cut it in half and make two scarves. She tried to get me started again, but my fifteen-footer was my last attempt at knitting. Instead, I made a wig out of the skein of yarn she gave me. She had a fit, as she was Scottish and never wasted anything.

One winter, we all went to Bermuda to join Grandpa Clark. I loved to swim each day at the Coral Beach Club where we had a large house. What I remember most about this trip was that I nearly drowned when my grandfather took me quite far out on his shoulders, then lost his balance and fell. I flew off his big shoulders and sank to the bottom. I sucked in water and the sand blinded me, but I managed to break to the surface, went under again and gulped in more water. It was terrifying. After what seemed forever, he found me underwater and rushed me ashore. They held me up by the ankles and slapped me hard on my back so I coughed up the salt water. Injustice again! I was immediately sent up for supper and given prunes that night for desert. This seemed entirely unfair, as I despised prunes and thought, after such a terrifying day, that what I deserved was compassion and attention. I should have known I'd never get it.

During this era of my early childhood, Maine was, more and more, becoming a cherished spot. By the time I was five, I had learned to ride a two-wheeler and could scoot off on my own and visit playmates there. Traffic was no problem, as we owned a whole point of land, and the population all drove at a snail's pace at Grandpa Smith's command. I would pedal alone and always a bit scared, down the road to my cousins the Binghams, the Mallorys, the Russells and the Lloyds, since Philip never joined me and Bayard was too young. We played sardines, tag and hide-and-go-seek, and I gained my independence. On rainy days, we created havoc inside, but on lovely days we were taken out on boats to picnic on our islands either Long or Graffam. If we were on Hart's Neck, we swam in the icy water with our white rubber boots on to protect us from the barnacles, or we learned to play tennis, or we hiked through the woods. It was bliss.

Occasionally, I had to bike down the road for about a mile to a local farm and bring home a closed pail of milk. I loved doing this, as it was responsibility. I hung the pail over the handlebars and only had trouble when I passed the infamous deathtrap mailbox where the "stitch" had been passed to me. We stopped getting this milk, which was not pasteurized, we came down with boils that covered every inch of our bodies. After this, milk was delivered to the house from a different source. Trucks carried in everything from the ice, to the fish, to the bread to the meat. I thought we were very important, as everyone came to us.

Not only were the people who worked on Hart's Neck exceptionally kind to me, but, also, I found a male figure to look up to. His name was Harold Dowling. He was beloved as boatman, master builder, woodchopper, gardener and friend of all the children. He always bent down to talk to us, but stood tall as he carried us onto boats. He built boat models, fixed bikes, taught sailing and picked berries with us. We worshipped him even more when he let us help him with his chores. If Harold was carrying a hunk of ice into a house, he always let me take the other side of the tongs to allow me to believe that I was carrying the ice. He was with our family for sixty-five years and was a true surrogate father and a Superman who could carry a piano single-handed, could sew up a torn sail, could chop fifty cords of wood each winter, and could fix the plumbing in all our houses on Hart's Neck. The boats he built with and for my grandfather were all like H.M.S. Queen Mary to us. Other than Nelson, the butler, Harold was the first man to really pay attention to me.

Visiting Grandpa Clark's houses, both in Sherborn and in Boston, was the "be all and end all" of my young life. There masses of things to do in Boston and I got a glimpse of a city. In his townhouse, there was an elevator I could run, a dumbwaiter I could climb into to hoist myself up and down, and a fabulous six-floor stairwell in which I could pour water down on the maids as they ran to tend to Gaga. There were sidewalks for roller-skating and a pool table in a special men's smoking room, where I could shoot pool as I stood on a stool. I felt grown up in this massive house.

In Sherborn Grandpa Clark had built a thirty-car garage with a colossal turntable in the middle to make it easy to park his many cars. I adored getting the turntable going at full speed and riding on it. What child wouldn't? There also was an elaborate swimming pool in which I swam every morning, noon and night, and always in the buff. My mother was horrified, but this custom was owing to our grandfather's insistence on a relaxed country lifestyle.

As my younger brother Bayard got older, my mother would continually refer to us children as "Philly and the little boys." I hated the phrase, because it meant I had lost my rightful identity as a big boy. Philly was a mere two years older than I, but Bayard was three years younger, "younger" being the operative word. A nurse was still babying him. Suddenly I felt my wings had been clipped and that I was being demoted by three years. Bayard was hardly good company, and I sulked a great deal when I had to play with him. My mother let her oldest child grow up, she forgot her middle one, and she coddled her youngest.

One day my father was in his little garden at our house in Maine. I went over to play beside him and suddenly he snapped at me for lisping, telling me I sounded like a silly little girl. I couldn't help the lisp, because I had lost a tooth, and so I was pulverized by his rebuke. I remember saying to myself, "Now my father has joined all the others in picking on me." My self-esteem plummeted to an all-time low, and, as with that "stitch" spot in the road, I could never again go by this garden without remembering his remark. My father had never "been there" for me, now he no longer was a friend of mine. After years of hearing my mother's repeated criticism of him, it was now easy to look down on him.

The world that surrounded me had the semblance of great security because my parents were rich and we wanted for nothing material, but, in reality, my upbringing made me a poster child for the effects of partial abandonment. Since my family support system was itself so shaky, there was simply no way I was going to be able to grow up and function properly without some crutch or another. Right now, I felt I had a very strange family, but, somehow, I loved them. What else could a small child do?

This picture of me made my mother wild with joy. One of her most
stylish friends, Mrs. C. Sydam Cutting, told her I must be a genius
because the distance from the top of my ear to the top of my head was
so great (room for massive brains). She, therefore, never removed the
picture from our library and never failed to bring others' attention to
her son's innate brilliance. I, of course, adored the picture for it was
about the only praise I ever got. Actually, I was by far and away the
brightest of the siblings but that is not really saying too much. When
I look at the picture, I try to think of all the hurt that was embedded
in the subconscious of that brain. Thank God I finally got the hell out
of there. Notice that finally the hair is like it should be. Miracles never
cease.

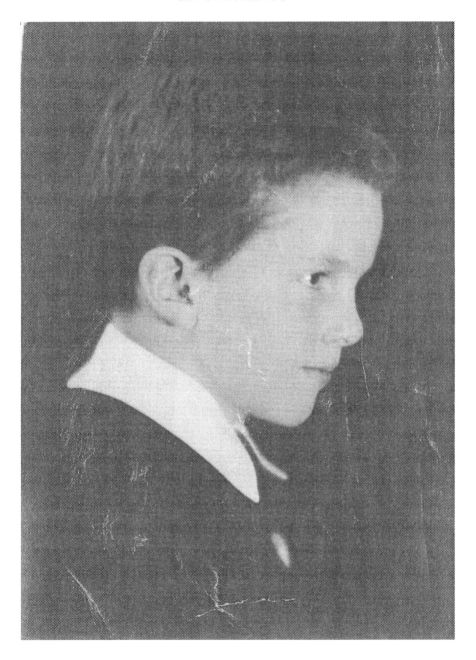

I so well remember going to this birthday party because I wore a tie for the first time. "A boy at last," I thought. Mrs. Blair, a very rich and stylish friend of Mother's, gave the party for her granddaughters and cheated me out of winning the Easter Egg Hunt by telling the ten servants to put all the eggs in her granddaughter's basket. I came in second.

Playing in a boat and relishing the freezing Maine water was my idea of sheer heaven, day in and day out. Alas, the dock in the background is now a bone of contention, with the entire family at each others' jugular veins to decide who may walk on it. Sad but true!

This picture was taken as a Christmas present for my father. We all look a bit normal for a change. My mother is wearing her rubies, all of which she eventually lost by hiding them and never being able to find them again. Two of us got engagement rings from the diamond pin she is wearing. It was a crescent shape, but she always called it her diamond horseshoe, for she liked horses and hated the Turks because she'd heard they were starving millions of Armenians-not that she even knew where Armenia was..

My bike gave me my freedom at last, and I was away from our house at any chance I could get. It was like my pony in Maine. I would run to jump on it, but it was a bit big for me and I nearly always landed on the bar on my testicles. Ouch!

As you can see, I made my home in the bone-chilling water. I never knew any better. I played alone a lot until the Howell clan and others arrived in late June and August. Philly was off with Grandfather Smith or my mother, my father was in New York and Bayard had a cousin just his age to play with. Don't worry about me drowning—a nurse dressed in starched white sat on the beach staring at me. She couldn't swim a stroke and bellowed if I went out up to my neck.

It seemed to be a custom in our family to dress us alike. I hated it, as Philly got all the new clothes and I lived in hand-me-downs. Doesn't Philly look like the cat who swallowed the canary?

(L to R) My Grandmother Smith, Aunt Helen and my mother at the christening of one of my grandfather's ships. As you can see, my grandmother looks sad, and I rarely remember her smiling or having fun if my grandfather was near. My aunts were my saving grace and without their affection I might not have survived.

This was my grandfather's house in New Jersey, where my father
grew up. Out of the window on the right front my father lowered
whiskey bottles to take to parties during Prohibition. My grandfather,
a teetotaler, once saw one coming down, as his study was right below.
He was enraged. We came to live here for a year and a half during the
Depression. I hated it, as everything was a priceless antique and we were
never allowed to play in the rooms.

These are two of my family's summer cottages along the coast of Maine. The one on the left was my grandparents' and ours is the one further down on the right. It was off these rocks that my mother would have our puppies drowned. I adored Maine, though I had nightmares that, perhaps, Mother would get rid of me next. The original house that stood where my grandparents' now is was burnt down by my grandfather, who set a long fuse on fire and then went to sea in his yacht. From far out at sea, he watched it burn. He had his alibi and got the insurance money. He always had his way.

FIVE

My rather cloistered upper-class childhood from the start of my formal schooling to my dramatic whisking away to a boarding school at age thirteen, was not mundane but, on the contrary, was exciting and even explosive. I played with children of the rich and famous and; I learned the facts of life in a dramatic fashion. I saw the world of the upper class change forever as the war exploded over the world. The askew and dramatically tilted building blocks that my family had faultily put together to raise me on were starting to slip more off center and cause signs of real concern. Depression began creeping in and moodiness reared its ugly head. Playing the family roles of scapegoat and mascot became more prevalent and self-esteem came fleetingly and yet vanished on a regular basis. I excelled at many things but my failures were the focus of attention of my family. Superior marks and good behavior at school never took precedence over any infraction of what was considered "normal" Smith behavior. Rejection was more a part of my life than acceptance.

When children go to school for the first time, immense changes occur within them, for they are now interacting with other children and adults in a non-home environment. They must start to learn to deal with the real world, and not just family behaviors and pressures. In my case, school meant salvation, though I was not to realize it until much later. I would surely be a rejected recluse or even dead today if it had not been for my successes at school. My family imprint was already creating havoc within me, and I was subconsciously crying for succor. I got it in school by learning I might be loved for myself.

Through all my subsequent agonies and failures, as an adult, I was always a success with my projects and jobs, and this was because my schooling had given me the confidence in my innate ability to triumph once I applied myself. My parents and grandparents showed me the opposite. They refused to accept me as I was, and by doing so gave me a bitter taste of the futility in relationships and the constant fear of failure.

Horrors nearly beyond comprehension would invade my life later on, but accomplishments at school and the knowledge gained there helped sustain me in my darkest hours.

Truly, my years in school were the most wonderful of my life. Though I was a child of privilege, without splendid teachers and the guidance I got from them, I would have been in grave danger. So many children go to school already marked by the chaos of their home lives. They turn antisocial, aggressive, rude, mean, given to lying and worse. They have no faith at all in themselves. I did not carry these problems to school but I very well might have if I had not had Mary Raitt as a beloved governess. I was a wounded middle child, frightened of my parents, scarred by parental favoritism and fearful of failure. Criticism was an ongoing feature of my life at home. School was to change all that, and I was a happy child, rising above my family's inadequacies. This was to change when the Second World War came with a suddenness that turned my world around.

To this day, I remember deep within me, in these years of my education, a guiding light that felt like a force moving me toward higher and higher goals. I would now call it a "spark of the divine" supporting me, for it seemed to power me to excellence in everything I undertook. My lack of love at home had created a vacuum and this miraculously appearing new feeling of love had come to fill it. Mary was a prayerful person and had imparted a great deal of her faith to me.

I was overjoyed to be sent to the Mt. Kemble School's kindergarten in the fall of 1936. Freed at last from the obligation to play with my younger brother, Bayard. I was equally bored with the various friends continually arranged to be my playmates by my mother. Philip had preceded me there by two years but I was to make a place my own and not try to emulate him. I wanted to be my own person and this drove me though I was so young.

Finally I was outshining Philip in some small way. Throughout those early school days, I took home glowing report cards, and my teachers seemed genuinely fond of me. I was consistently at the top of my class in achievement, deportment and creativity. How lovely this all was, and quite a departure from what I was used to being told.

I even started to get a smattering of praise at home. For some strange reason, my mother was convinced I must take after her scholastically. This was bizarre, for she herself lacked more than a fundamental education at Miss Porter's School in Farmington, Connecticut. Women of her day and age went to school to finish off their manners and to make friends. Upper-class women were never expected to work so their parents reasoned that they did not need an education. But, even given her academic deficiencies, my mother's praise was very welcome to me. My father's remarks were not for if I got a "A" on a paper, he would say, but why wasn't it an "A+."

Curiously, my kindergarten teacher, Mrs. Bessie Coombs, told me just a few years ago, when we met in Maine, that my artistic talent had been far superior to that of any other child she had ever taught. Retiring after more than sixty years, she wound up living right next door to me in Tenants Harbor, and it was amazing, surely, that she remembered my childish work after so many decades! I still paint!

After Mt. Kemble School, I spent the next five years at the Somerset Hills Country Day School in Far Hills. It was an Episcopal elementary school with eight grades and about 140 boys. I was consistently number one in my grade, as well as being either president or vice president of my class. I even did relatively well in every athletic endeavor I undertook, except boxing.

Dr. Fair, the Headmaster, was an Episcopal minister and presided over the daily chapel services. We sang stirring hymns, and everyone became well acquainted with the Episcopal *Book of Common Prayer*. The teachers there had been recruited from the entire Eastern Seaboard, as the school's reputation was so high that its faculty positions were widely coveted. The quality of the students was equally high. In private schools, the teachers could teach to the top of the class, whereas at public schools the teachers had to teach to the middle or below. If you could not keep up with the top students at institutions like Somerset Hills, you did not come back the next year. It gave the students a tremendous advantage, too, when applying to other schools after the eighth grade, the final grade taught at this school. They were usually ahead of their public school counterparts. Money certainly helped the rich kids stay ahead of the poor ones while climbing the education ladder.

I loathed boxing. Every rainy day we engaged in that foul sport in the dank sports area in the cellar. Even now, I tend to get headaches when it rains. Probably it's because I am reminded of being punched in the face by some wildly swinging classmate. By third grade my marks were so good I jumped to the fourth grade. However, I missed my friends too much, so I went back to my old grade and took advanced-study classes. My mother continued to take credit for my academic performance and would always boast about it when I was brought in to bow and say something to her bridge friends. What a change!

Each morning the chauffeur drove my father to the Far Hills railroad station to catch the train to Wall Street. We three boys joined him in the car on our way to school. The school was only about five hundred yards and a tiny street crossing away from the station, so Philip and I were allowed to walk there. Bayard, meanwhile, was still being driven there. We had to pass the local drugstore on the way, and I was soon taught by Philip how to wait for Louie Goes, the owner, to answer the constantly ringing phone in the back of the store and then slide open the glass door of the candy case in order to steal Baby Ruth's and other goodies. When Mr. Goes sent my family a bill for the stolen candy, the jig was up. We were forbidden to walk to school, nor could we have any allowance or candy for two months. I was glad we were caught for I never wanted to participate in this thievery but was pushed into it. Younger children are so malleable.

Each week in chapel we were assigned hymns to learn. I couldn't carry a tune, but I had a fantastic memory and eventually would know by heart every word of nearly a hundred hymns. Knowing them got me a vocal lead in the Christmas pageant, despite the fact that my voice sounded like a sick donkey's. It was great fun being the center of attention in these plays and performing for the crowds of parents. Once, appearing as an angel floating through the air hanging from a wire, I sang "It Came Upon A Midnight Clear." The wire broke and I landed in the crèche. Nothing happened, as I was only about two feet off the ground. I had thought I was about fifty feet in the air! My family, as usual, was not in attendance. Mary was.

Since we also had to study the Bible daily, I took many questions about religion home to Mary, a devout Anglican who had converted from being a Scots Presbyterian. She instilled in me a sound faith in God and taught me the power and beauty of prayer. Although it was many, many years before religion became the true center of my life, I remember as a child that prayer really did help in my life when I was feeling down and needed a sense of comfort and support. This was dashed a bit when mother had a prayer entitled "Make Me A Nice Clean Boy" taped in my Bible. That seemed to indicate she believed I was bad and dirty, and maybe God did too. We young Smiths said prayers every night before bed, but that was just about the extent of my parents' efforts to make us good Christians. I had been hastily christened in our house one weekend only because my parents wanted my brother, Bayard, christened as he was quite sick at the time and they thought him on the verge of death. I got a Mickey Mouse watch as a christening present and it meant far more to me than joining the Christian community.

Occasionally, Philip would deign to make me his accomplice but sadly, it usually would create havoc. For want of anything better to do, we'd stand nails, sharp end up, on the road at the end of our drive in order to catch passing cars. We once got all four tires of one vehicle, but two people riding by on horses saw us hiding in the bushes and told our parents. There was hell to pay, and I learned one of the most important lessons of my life. I had to tell the truth and confess a "crime" to the person it was committed against. Going to the man whose tires had been ruined was an agony beyond belief, and I recognized that I had to think twice before doing something criminal. The consequences of these vandalous acts were building in me a consciousness of what was good and bad. I learned that it was important to understand the difference if I wanted peace of mind. I was so overly anxious when misbehaving.

For a game of hide-and-seek, Phil painted himself, Bayard and me dark green from head to toe so we could hide amid the lilac bushes and not be seen. Mary spent three hours cleaning us with turpentine baths, and it was necessary to cut off our hair. It got a lot of my curls out of my way and I was thrilled, though the stinging from the solvents was painful. Because of such antics, Mary persisted in believing that little boys could be devils incarnate at this time.

School friends were forever coming to our house or I visited theirs. One friend, Billy Woodhull, had a father who was an inventor, so playing with him was especially thrilling. Often we'd go to a gravel pit and shoot machine guns that his father was developing for the U.S. Army. This was one of the most exciting and exhilarating things I had ever done. Philip was gun-crazy and thus jealous of my visits with the Woodhulls. His envy made me feel superior, which was sweet revenge. Anything that gave me positive feelings about myself was great and especially when the "golden boy" was involved in the comparison.

For kicks one day, or for whatever reason, my gun-crazed brother aimed our father's pistol at me and pulled the trigger. It was loaded and the bullet shot past my ear and through a nearby picture, where the hole remains to this day. My father kept this loaded gun in his dressing room closet, as he, like all the Far Hills gentry, was deathly afraid of kidnapping, particularly since the Lindbergh kidnapping happened, five towns away. My family was aghast when they learned of the shooting but gave no punishment out nor did they console me. I felt as if they did not give a damn if I had been killed.

People all around us hired night watchmen or bodyguards. They, and we had special locks installed and armed our houses. They already had shotguns, but now they got pistols. Because of our wealth, people like us thought that their children might be snatched at any moment. Burglary was another worry, and in all the cellars of the great houses there were walk-in safes for silver, jewelry and other valuables. Some people actually stored their liquor in them not as it was valuable but so the help would not steal it.

Freddy Clucas was a friend who lived near me on a vast farm. Here we gathered eggs, poured milk into pasteurizers and shoveled corn into cribs for ten cents an hour. There was a little clubhouse where we went to smoke stolen cigarettes, discuss what we thought was sex and eat dreadful sandwiches supplied by his cook. Freddy loved trains and had a layout that took up nearly the whole attic floor of his family's house. We spent many a winter day there with his marvelous Lionel trains. We had trains at home but only Philip's was a good set up. Bayard's and mine were cheap and only ran on oval, very small tracks. In fact, there were few houses I went to in those days that did not have large train sets. It was the major rainy-day distraction for boys. Freddy considered me his greatest friend, and I learned more about life on his farm than I ever did at home. The farm girls there let Freddy and me take them to our little club to see what they looked like undressed. I had no sisters so I played up my innocence. All we did was peek at them, but afterward we felt ourselves to be men of the world. We were convinced now that we knew everything about everything, and we even learned from these girls how to "talk dirty." But Freddy's clubhouse was the only place we could safely try out this new vocabulary. I still was having my mouth washed out with soap if a bad word slipped out.

Skipper Dorsey, son of the celebrated bandleader, Tommy Dorsey, was another very good friend. He lived on a fantastic place in Bernardsville, the town next to Far Hills. One could only be admitted by ringing up the house on a phone from the front gate so that the gate could be buzzed open. This seemed like cloak and dagger stuff to us children, especially since the whole fifty acres or so was securely fenced like a prison. Tommy Dorsey was the leader of one of the most famous orchestras in the country. Every singer was dying to perform with him, playing, as he did, to packed houses from New York to Los Angeles. Frank Sinatra was one of his vocalists. We could sneak in to listen to his father rehearse for his radio shows. We also liked to swim in the pool, which was one hundred and fifty feet long and had been fashioned after Mr. Dorsey's friend Bing Crosby's pool. It had three diving boards of varying heights and a water slide. I loved the tallest board, which must have been twenty-five feet high. It seemed like a mile in the sky to me and I felt like the greatest daredevil in the world when I jumped off it. It was either an ego maker or a ball breaker, depending on how I landed. Tommy Dorsey and Frank Sinatra were very, very kind to me.

Skipper often came to my less-exciting house to play, until the day that Phil put him in a scissors lock by wrapping his legs around Skipper's midriff. Philip was a large boy and Skipper was small, so the result was painful and terrifying. Skipper partially blacked out and was sick enough to be whisked home. He never wanted to come back to my house, but he still always asked me to his. I never wanted Philip to play with my friends again.

From Skipper I also learned about divorce. His parents split up when we were about nine years old. This was something that was unheard of in my parents' circle. You married for life and put up with everything. I was taken aback by the Dorseys' rather public and nasty divorce, which I first heard about on the radio news as we drove to school one morning. It made me question, in my mind, the marriage of my parents, for they always fought. Might they divorce? Who would take me to live with them? What would happen to the family?

Jimmy Moseley and I were inseparable, and the best of friends for years and years. He might tell me the most untrue and horrible things about his family and others and I loved hearing about fellow sufferers. It made me feel a bit better. We always had the time of our lives together and did things that made our nurses' white hair stand on end and turn whiter. We would go skinny dipping in the river that meandered by his place well before spring had sprung. We would get people we did not like to come to one of our houses and literally torture them by hosing them down in the snow or tying them up and leaving them in a pitch black cellar or in a locked closet. We would spend hours on the phone calling people and saying the stupidest and rudest things, and we tormented our younger siblings, Bayard and his sister, Ailsa. We were hellions. Until the sixth grade, when he was sent to Fay School in Southborough, Massachusetts, we spoke every single day in school and on the phone when we got home. We talked to each other for hours at a time. I am convinced that our nasty and uncalled for behavior was caused by growing anger in us. It was also a way to rebel against our families. He had many problems with his family as well.

Jimmy told me the facts of life over the phone with, unfortunately, my mother and his father listening, quite by accident, on other extensions. My family, as did most families in our set, did not discuss sex in any way with children. Kids had to find out from others, and what we found out usually was like a dose of reality and often somewhat crude. My brother Philip had filled Jimmy in on the facts of life. The people who worked on our places were much more apt to talk about sex, as they were always around animals that they bred and therefore it was a big part of their work. There were children whose parents did discuss sex with them and were eager to share what they knew. What Jimmy imparted to me over the phone came as less of a surprise to me as playing in the clubhouse with Freddy and the farm girls had provided some of the basics of sexual anatomy.

"Everything you were told by Jimmy," my mother said, "was a lie." But I knew it was not, and I felt betrayed by her own falsehood. How foolish, I thought, for I knew why boys and girls were different and I also knew my mother had had babies. How could all of what I'd heard be a lie when it wasn't even entirely news to me? As it turned out, even as I was reaching maturity, I never found out a single thing about sex from my parents, another sad note in our communications. Mother always referred to sex as "married life," and was as old fashioned as her grandmother.

A question that carried with it an aura of terrible mystery with sinister implications and remained unanswered for years was "what happened to the babies Jimmy's mother, Aunt Jane, was occasionally having, yet were never seen?" I was well aware that some years she was very fat and pregnant, yet there never was a baby as the result. I was positive that my mother must be talking her into doing away with these newborns just as she had done with her own babies. As it turned out later, Jane Moseley had suffered miscarriages. I tried to discuss it once with my mother, in a tentative manner, but I was immediately informed that mothers and their children never ever discuss such things. I remained terrified, thanks to my mother. My parents were not only dreadful role models, but communication was absolutely zero. Was I to be a child forever and never allowed to grow up and know about life?

Jimmy and his family were an especially important part of my boyhood. I learned more from them about family life and love than from my own family. Uncle Fred, Jimmy's father, took his boys skating and riding, and he played tennis with them. My own father did none of this. There was less fighting in the Moseley household, too. I always wished they could have been my family. However, I was later to learn from my Mother that things were not as rosy as they seemed. Mother ripped even her best friends down to build herself up.

Life for everyone is chaotic as we hurtle hundreds of thousands of miles through the universe each minute. Each day we awake to a disordered world, which we try to put together piece by piece all day. We go to sleep at night with our worlds pulled together somewhat, only to wake up the next day to face the same chaos. For the wellborn and rich, it is less of an unsure world. They have the money to try to control their world. Thus, in Far Hills, our lives were organized and orderly, at least on the surface, for money could pay the wages of people whose duties were to keep it so. A housekeeper trained the help to carry out the orders and wishes of the house owners. The staff was expected to be prompt with breakfast, lunch, tea, cocktails and dinner. They served meals beautifully and they silently cleaned up behind every move their employers made. Beds were turned down and bedclothes were laid out each evening in all the bedrooms. Fires were lit in the sitting rooms, and the curtains were drawn right before the owners came down for their cocktail hour dressed for dinner. Every morning there was a muffled knock at the door and the chambermaid came in with a cup of tea or coffee and opened the curtains. You were asked what you'd like for breakfast. It was a blissful way to live.

The women servants dressed in white in the morning, gray for lunch, purple for teatime and black for dinner. Men servants wore regular black or white short coats for breakfast and lunch and changed to tail coats for dinnertime. Butlers polished silver in pantries with green baize aprons on and cooks wore toques.

There was no inside or outside work for my family or their friends to do except to enjoy the luxury. Many of the ladies had their own maids who took care of all their personal needs, from cleaning, sponging and pressing clothes worn the night before to drawing baths and laying out dinner clothes and brushing the mistress's hair. One did not have to drive, nor worry about the animals. There were people to feed them, care for the cars and bring the horses to the meets for hunting. Everyone gardened, but that meant going into the garden wearing a huge straw hat and telling the Italian gardeners what to do. Everyone learned to accept this traditional life and they carried it forward to the next generation if they could afford it. It made marrying for money a necessity for many. The Smith family did not live quite so opulently, but quite close to it.

When we arrived each new summer in Maine, there always seemed to be increasing numbers of children and even adults for me to play with. These included friends of my mother and father, my just-married aunts and uncles, their spouses and new cousins who kept being born. They all lived in one or another of my grandfather's houses. One summer we had a tutor, Benbo Merriman, who came to teach us sailing, tennis, camping and swimming. Essentially, he was somewhat odd in his social behavior but he tried to do a good job, and, in the process, caused us, for once, to be thoroughly organized and not just running wild all summer. Benbo set up a track meet for us and, to my great joy, I won the high jump. In typical fashion, my mother ruined the moment for me by coming up and never saying a word of congratulations. Instead, she took the Milky Way candy bar I had just won and bit off half of it. Then she announced that Phil could have jumped higher. What could I do but throw a tantrum and run home, even in my moment of victory? I locked myself in my bedroom and cried and cried. Mother had in essence, totally diminished and dismissed me.

My older brother and I were continually getting in trouble with my grandfather. Most of the pranks we were jointly responsible for. We would, for example, go to the stables and pee down the hay chute on the horses, pour car-starting ether on the animals to see if it would make them sleep, start raging fires on the rocks with gallons of kerosene, or nail shut the seat tops in the outhouses scattered behind some of the houses and used at their request, by staff. In the matter of all these I was guilty, I admit, but for stealing paint from a locked closet, taking cigars from a cupboard and letting a rowboat go adrift, I was innocent. Yet, no matter my indignant protests, I was not believed and I was punished, because Philly said I had done the act. It seemed I was just his minion and whipping post, when, in reality, he had done it.

My Smith grandparents were continually at odds with each other, and too often we children were caught in the crossfire. Grandpa seemed to enjoy making mean cracks about Gran being too dumb, too sad or too forgetful. They hardly spoke, except to argue, and they slept at opposite ends of the second floor in their huge summerhouse, "Munasca." They finally stopped wintering together, which seemed strange to me. We always had Christmas with Gran but not Grandpa. They never played tennis, picnicked or even rode in a car with one another. They truly went their separate ways. Gran's way was not so merry, for she was depressed a great deal of the time, and Grandpa's shenanigans with his many girlfriends did not help. Gran was usually aware of what he was up to, as he had the audacity to house his girlfriends nearby.

Grandpa's demeanor was aloof. He always seemed to have a mistress in tow and he was embarrassed if we caught glimpses of them even just talking together. One of the most charming of them, Carol Woodin, was set up by him in a little chauffeur's cottage on Harts Neck about half a mile down the road from "Munasca." She lived comfortably there with her maid, Bellaeda, a black woman afflicted with huge bunions. Carol had a bedroom on the first floor of the house with windows looking directly out on the path I used as a shortcut through the flower and vegetable gardens to the boathouse.

One day, as I traipsed happily by the cottage on my way to the dock, I looked in the window and saw Carol and Grandpa wrestling in bed, naked. Unfortunately, they saw me. I said, "Hi," and from that moment on I was never again on good terms with Grandpa. But then there was always a lot of "not speaking" and "avoiding" going on in our family, so this was not something new to me.

When I was about nine, I kissed my first girlfriend, my cousin, Farr Bingham. In those days, she was the love of my life. We were exactly the same age and always shared summer birthday parties. It was not at all unusual for one of us to find a little gold ring in a party snapper and have our nurses or parents decide we should wed in a mock ceremony. I think I married her five times. A few weeks after our initial kiss, Farr announced that she thought that she was going to have a baby because her father had told her that when you kiss, you have babies. I was beside myself with fear. My terror abated when I noticed that she did not get fat. I spoke to my mother about my fears, but she corroborated Farr's father's evaluation and emphasized that kissing was a very bad thing to do. From that conversation I judged that's why my mother kissed me so rarely.

Just as I was finishing the fifth grade at Somerset Hills, Mary Raitt got into a fight with our wonderful Scottish butler, Nelson. They were given to quarreling, for Mary was quite moody. After these spats, she'd flounce about the house or else empty her bureau drawers and start to pack her bags. Then her trunks were lowered from the attic and filled with all her possessions. I assumed that this contretemps was business as usual, but this time, to my horror, everything of hers was loaded into her car and she drove off.

When Mary reappeared three days later, begging for her job back, my mother said, "No." I was inconsolable and very scared. Without Mary, I felt abandoned. She had always been my anchor to windward and now I was adrift. My parents would have to call the shots but they hadn't a clue about our schedules or our likes and dislikes. They were rudderless and so were we until our butler immediately stepped in. All children need a framework to live in and my parents had not built one.

So it was to our joy that Nelson and his wife, Sadie, the cook, rose to the occasion and filled the breach. They gave us the security and organization we needed by reading to us, playing games with us, driving us and helping take care of our clothes and our bedrooms with the help of another maid, Elizabeth. Nelson was one of the most capable men who ever lived, and he would have excelled at any job he might have undertaken. It was only the Depression that had made him seek employment in domestic service. He could have been a businessman in any firm, yet when he came from Scotland, no jobs were available. He eventually became the executive director of the Essex Fox Hounds Hunt Club, the social hub of the area. His wife, Sadie, died while working for us, and my mother always teased that she had died in the pea soup she was cooking. I never ate pea soup again, though it was her appendix that burst while she was cooking. She died in a hospital.

We gave a huge party for Nelson at our house after Sadie's funeral and had all of his butler friends. There were more than fifty butlers present, for they had a close-knit group. Whenever there was to be a big party in Far Hills, the butlers worked together at them. There were no catering services in those days and all the people who employed servants shared them with their friends. The help was paid extra for these occasions. Later, when Nelson went to the Hunt Club, he did set up a catering service.

The most tragic ordeal of my young life was the demise of my pony, Capers. One day my mother decided that Capers was too old. He was thirty-two, but I thought that he still had a lot of life in him. To demonstrate, once again, that death was part of the growing-up experience on a farm, and also as a way to toughen me up and assure herself that I would not turn out to be a sissy, my mother had me taken up to the stables in order to be there when the veterinarian shot Capers.

It was a nightmarish experience. I threw up all over Caper's body. As he convulsed and trembled in his death throes, his body was encircled with a chain that was attached to a truck. He was dragged through his outside stall door onto the gravel stable yard and then towed over the roads to the Hunt Club to become food for the hounds. I threw up again, fled to my room and hid for hours under my bed with a splitting headache. One of my very best friends had been killed on the orders of my mother. I was heartsick. From that day on I would get severe migraine headaches whenever I was stressed and I would be petrified of loud noises for many, many years. Panic attacks would come over me whenever they reached my ears. *Would my mother shoot me?* I asked myself.

Out of the blue in 1939, my mother decided that she was going to take all of us to Florida for our Easter vacation. We were wild with excitement and couldn't wait to get away from winter and be warm. Usually my mother and father would go with their friends to the Brady family's palatial establishment, "Old Fort," in Nassau. At last, we were getting the nod. On the morning of the fifteenth of April, the day we were to leave, I awoke with a severe pain in my stomach and began vomiting every minute or so. I was rushed to the hospital and had my appendix removed just moments before it seemed about to burst. It had been terribly inflamed. If I heard it once, I heard it a thousand times, "Forrester ruined the family vacation and made everyone stay home." Pity for my emergency operation was not forthcoming, and I was made to feel like a complete loser for daring to get sick. As a consequence, I learned to go to school even when I did not feel well. To stay in bed when I was ill became anathema to me. Sitting in school with a pounding headache was better than being criticized for having the temerity to suffer any ailment.

December 7, 1941, is a day that I still remember vividly. I learned that this country had been bombed in Pearl Harbor by the Japanese, it was frightening and bewildering to me, for no further explanation was forthcoming. I could not help but worry we would be bombed in the night. Though I did not yet know it, my world was to change dramatically from that moment on, just as the war changed the face of the world.

The First World War and then, with a more powerful stroke, the Second World War, forever altered the life of the upper classes. It was not an instant change, but one that came gradually, blurring and softening the lines of class. Many servants had to leave the great houses. There was little fuel to heat estates, houses were closed and wings shut off, while owners moved into much smaller quarters in the main house or into a cottage on the property. Large apartments in New York City, where so many of our neighbors stayed during the week, were closed, as cities were potentially targets of enemy bombs. Estate farms which were in the Far Hills, were mostly gentleman farms, were let go to seed, for gas was a scarce commodity and farm laborers were needed in the factories. Many younger servants went into war work and found that in the plants they could earn far higher wages than they had ever been used to. They never returned to service again. Only the old retainers stayed, as they were too old to change.

The fifty-four-stall stable at Hamilton Farms, the Brady/Cutting place next door, was turned into a hospital for wounded soldiers and sailors. The men often, while recuperating, took walks by our place and my imagination ran wild, wondering how they had gotten wounded. I dared not ask them. The stable was so beautiful that two of the Brady girls, Victoria and Genevieve, had had their wedding receptions there before the war. It is now the headquarters of the United States Olympic Equestrian Team.

Fathers of my friends went off to war, some would not return. Our big winter house was shut down to save fuel and our own animals were destroyed or given away for lack of help to care for them. The severe rationing of food and gasoline quickly began to govern what we ate, where we went and whom we saw. Such changes all too simply became our reality, yet we were still together and thus better off than those whose families had been split because of military service or war work.

War really seemed right at our front door step, for convoy after convoy of army trucks moved troops, ammunition, tanks and supplies through Far Hills. But as my mother had no idea how to manage a house without servants and as my father had begun to drink more due to his frustration at not getting into any of the military services because of his poor eyesight, we all were like boats adrift in an unknown sea. My father became depressed because of his feelings of inadequacy. About three years into the war, this despondency did lift a bit and the cloud of doom that he had thrown over us children vanished, as he had finally wormed his way into the Coast Guard Reserve. This new status splashed a daily smile across his face. Unfortunately, the only "action" he saw was when he got punched by a fellow Coast Guard reservist who did not want him to keep playing "Begin The Beguine" on a jukebox at the station. That black eye he referred to as his war wound.

It was amazing what my mother accomplished during the war and how she excelled in her new lifestyle. During this period I saw a different person emerge. She planted a victory garden of giant proportions and actually tended it herself. She even learned how to cook, though the meals she made were dreadful, for there was little variety. She ran the New Jersey Motor Corps and ferried wounded military personnel around in our wooden Ford beach wagon. It had been converted to an ambulance by adding a flat plywood floor for the stretchers and attaching canvas sheeting from the back roofline to the end of the lowered tailboard. We loved riding back and forth to school in the stretchers whenever we had the chance. Mother also spotted planes from an outpost on a hill and rolled bandages for the wounded. She was a nurse's aide at the local hospital and an officer of British War Relief. In fact, she was incredible, but wore herself to a shred with far too many activities. We children suffered with her constant outbursts of anger brought on by fatigue but also too much booze.

There were many times when we, to ease her schedule, would take over her plane-spotting job. It made me feel like a man to swing my binoculars through the skies and spot planes, identify their type and call spotting headquarters to report what was passing overhead and from what direction it was coming. We were really doing no more than all our friends in the environs of Far Hills were doing. Every single person had a job of some kind to aid the war effort, from sewing to packaging bandages to patrolling streets of the villages at night to see if enemy agents were on the prowl. I was dying to catch a Nazi but had no such luck.

Without household help or gas coupons, it was necessary to close our house and take an apartment in the village of Far Hills. Our cook and butler went to work elsewhere as there was no longer room for them with us. We were near the train station, for my father needed to commute to New York City. Bayard and I were enrolled in the new Far Hills Country Day School and Philip was sent to Groton, the third Philip Smith to go there. Far Hills seemed like a ghost town. Most of my friends had either been shipped off to boarding schools or were following their fathers and families as they took up various military duties and posts around the country. We couldn't drive anywhere because we lacked the gas, and I knew no kids at all in the village to play with.

I never in my life had felt such loneliness and abandonment. The life I had always known suddenly stopped dead and a new one was beginning. But I was unable to understand how to cope with it, for nothing was ever discussed with me. I felt depressed all the time and had terrible trouble getting on with my family in these cramped quarters. I was forced to keep myself amused, and this was hard in the village. Sometimes I would bike out to our place, seven miles away, and spend the day alone, happy to be once again, in the big but dank, closed house. There I discovered something that offered a window into my family's world. It was my mother's beautifully kept scrapbooks, and they enthralled me. They contained everything from friends' suicides, to a bizarre car accident of mother's, to the jailing of certain chums, to suicides, to marriages, to assorted nasty divorces, to husbands decamping with young call girls, and much more. All of this information I loved to take in and I used to full advantage later in my life, as I became the mascot in my family's dysfunctional role-playing. I knew gossip that could be used to make me the life of the party.

My Clark family was well known in Boston so nearly every move my mother made seemed to have been recorded in the press. She made the front-page headlines with her car accident. The same was true when it came to my parents' friends and acquaintances. I was fascinated by it all—the photos, the exciting headlines, the familiar names—and to this day I remember most of what I read.

The auto accident to which I refer had occurred the year my mother came out. She had run over, but not killed, a working woman carrying a bag of grapefruit home to her dying mother. The headlines read, "Rich Society Girl Crashes Into Poor Grapefruit-Ladened Girl." Mother was brought to trial but got off after Grandfather Clark bribed the judge, or so she claimed. Mother had a police siren on her car, which was wailing when the crash occurred. It is little wonder the young woman got excited and was hit. I never could understand why there was such a big play on some lousy grapefruits. The story also discussed at length the cost of my mother's immense coming out party and her prowess on the polo field with her three brothers as a team.

During World War One my grandmother Clark moved her entire household, minus six servants of the usual fifteen inside help, to a very large apartment in Boston. This was done to save heating the huge house on Commonwealth Avenue. The money she saved she gave to the Sherborn Red Cross, and for the two years she lived in the apartment it exceeded its fundraising goal by 300%. My mother gave away no money like this, but our move, I am sure, was in emulation of her mother's move.

Somerset Hills Country Day School for boys and Mt. Kemble School for girls had combined their teachers, supplies and equipment at the start of the Second World War, occupying for the duration a large house on the top of a steep hill in Far Hills. It became Far Hills Country Day School, which I attended for sixth and seventh grade. Girls were now everywhere and, in fact, far outnumbered us boys. I was starting to get interested in them, but I was also scared of them. I think our class numbered three boys and nine girls. I had no idea how girls really acted other than at birthday parties.

Schoolwork remained easy for me, and I was still a leader of the class and popular. However, I was allowed to get away with too much and soon my study skills started to slide. I was getting no supervision at home and was smart enough to learn how to skirt homework. Good reports were all that were necessary, and I got those sometimes by a little bit of chicanery. The teachers here were far from strict. The best instructors had gone off to war.

I biked up hill to school each morning and blissfully coasted home each afternoon. Gone were the days of being driven to school, unless Freddy Clucas's car came by me and picked me and my bike up. Because his family's cars were considered farm vehicles, they could get practically unlimited gas to drive anywhere. Their farm's produce went towards the war effort.

Tenants Harbor was frightfully lonely during the war, as only a very few young first cousins, some aunts and uncles, and grandparents were there. We stayed in Far Hills later into the summer so Mother could tend her victory garden at our house, which we moved back into during the warm months because then it needed no heat. She always served us the fruits of her labor in jellied vegetable rings. She had never cooked before, so once she learned a recipe we had it constantly. To make this frightful dish, one cut up vegetables, put them in a tin mold and then poured consommé over it before putting it in the icebox. It was a tasteless concoction.

Mother indulged in other peculiarities so that we would always have food on the table. Rationing had put crimps into people's daily meats. From Bloomingdales in New York City, she sent hundreds upon hundreds of cans of vegetables, fish, meat, soup and jellies to Maine. She hoarded to such an extent that other hoarders couldn't hoard. It also helped to save gas by lessening the frequency of shopping trips to Rockland. Yet although this canned goods supply was meant to last for the duration of the war, the tin cans stored in our barn soon rusted from the effects of the salt air fog swirling about them. They had to be thrown out after just a month or so. Mother was enraged at this besting by the elements but chose to blame it on Hitler. According to her, all the good tin was being used to beat the Germans and the bad tin was being used by Bloomingdale's. She never again bought groceries there. Happily, we could still get fresh food in Maine from Grandpa's own extensive victory gardens, so we did not starve.

All of the windows of our house in Maine were covered with blackout shades so that enemy vessels would see no lights on the shore. Otherwise, they might find it easier to land. In addition, car lights had half-moon shields to help prevent Nazi planes from spotting them from above and bombing us. All this was exciting for us kids. We were always thinking we saw subs and German planes. At one point we lived in daily dread because we'd been told that some German submariners had washed up on our family's island, Graffam. It is a place where the currents swirl and fetch up when the tide changes, so it wasn't impossible for such a thing to happen. Yet, if it actually had happened, it was hushed up by the Coast Guard and we heard nothing more about it.

The newspapers were always reporting supposed landings by German spies along the Maine coast, but only three or four ever did. They landed in the Bar Harbor area. Since more than three thousand rugged miles were involved, patrolling the shores was a task best done locally in each town. Tenants Harbor had a special patrol, consisting of those who did not go to war. They watched over the coastline and reported any strange activity.

A few years before the war started, Grandpa Smith had bought Snow's Shipyard in Rockland, Maine. It was a nearly century-old yard with about fifty men working in it when he took it over. It was famous for building very large schooners and fishing boats. In 1940 the government asked the Snow Yard to begin building small wooden minesweepers for the U.S. Navy. The contracts increased, and during the war 800 men were employed. The yard built twenty wooden vessels, ten minesweepers, two sub chasers, two salvage boats and six net tenders, which strung nets across harbors to keep subs out. The sweepers were effective little ships that could speed into harbors in pairs and sweep the place clean of mines. When the mines rose to the surface, the ships would blow them up with machine guns they had on deck. As they were made of wood, they did not attract mines, which were usually magnetic.

My mother, grandmother, aunts, cousins and family friends were among the ladies who christened the Snow Yard boats. We were allowed on them as they slid down the ways. The minute the bottle broke and the horns tooted we would race to the stern and watch the huge plume of water shoot up as the boat hit the water. The tugs would then come and tow us to the docking area for a celebration. The yard was an incredible playground for us children, and, as the grandsons of the owner, we were allowed to roam free there.

As my grandfather's shipyard won the "Army and Navy E" for its exceptional war production, both the Army and Navy honored the Snow Yard with a great deal of fanfare. Brigadier General Thomas E. Troland dramatically proclaimed that we would win the war by sending "Hitler the sound of ringing steel, the thud of swinging mallets, and the clank-clank of the spikes," while Rear Admiral W.C. Watts extolled "the fine spirit of enthusiasm throughout the yard." Everyone was very proud of Grandpa, I never was.

As Grandpa owned a bank, some boarding houses and other businesses in the Rockland area, we were often taken to Rockland but never allowed to explore the town on our own. At this time it was wild and woolly, with sailors and fishermen weaving a bit unsteadily along the streets. It had not weathered the Depression very well and was considered to be nearly bankrupt, with unemployment rampant. My grandfather's yard proved highly valuable in helping to restore the Rockland economy.

In the middle 1930's I remember occasionally seeing in Rockland a tiny old lady dressed in black from head to foot. She had a huge head with a big, black hat plopped on it, and she was always carrying a dark-colored basket. When she came into Grandpa's bank, she scared me, for she reminded me of the witch in Hansel and Gretel. This was Lucy Farnsworth, one of Rockland's greatest benefactors. When she died she left a million dollars, quite a sum for those days, to establish a library there in honor of her brother. As Rockland already had a library given by Andrew Carnegie, her will was adjusted somehow and thus the Farnsworth Art Museum was founded, later to become one of the great regional museums in the United States and a splendid legacy.

Andrew Carnegie, a family friend, endowed libraries throughout the United States, for the reason that he did not want to leave his colossal estate to his children. He believed money to be the root of evil, and that it should be used only for good works. He had actually played a very important part in my family history, for my parents met for the first time at his mansion hideaway on Jekyll Island, off the coast of Georgia. My mother had been staying with the Carnegies and my father nearby with the John S. Phippses. Phipps was the steel magnate who, along with Carnegie, put together the vast steel mills that J.P. Morgan bought and turned into U. S. Steel.

During the war years, both my Smith grandparents died. I was forbidden to attend their funerals and felt very left out. When Gran Smith died, my parents did not discuss her death with me, and since she was the first person I had known really well who had died, I was not just sad but had many questions. However, I was not at all distressed when Grandpa Smith died. Rather, I felt some relief he had gone. I had been a second-class citizen to him. Tenants Harbor was, in a flash, a different place for me without him. I no longer had to be constantly in dread of meeting him.

For one summer during the war, I was sent to Chocorua, New Hampshire, to a Clark family farm and ski house. Bayard and I were both there to avoid the anticipated hand-to-hand combat with the Germans, who, it was feared, might land in front of our Maine house that summer. I was angry, because I wanted to see Germans. The summer turned out to be a bit boring, for Mary Raitt was there to take care of us along with two tedious, little cousins. She had gone to work for my Uncle Dudley Clark after she had left us. In Chocorua I learned to play the card game "Hearts," which became a saving grace that summer. Bayard and I played every night with an aged couple, Mr. and Mrs. Whittemore, down the road. It made us feel quite grown up and took us out from under Mary's surveillance. The Whittemores had no gas so they couldn't go anywhere, and they were glad to have even two small boys as company. I was proud as punch when I won many times.

We also closed down our big Maine house, "Seawoods," and moved to a smaller house, "Haystack." In such close quarters, I really got to know my family's habits, both good and bad. It was an eye-opener and had a profound effect on me. Unfortunately, at this time, my parents' drinking was beginning to get the better of them, and I couldn't help but be aware what was going on. I was right on top of them and could hear everything. The strain of this closeness made us all act more erratically than usual.

We had always, each of us, played certain roles, but we were unaware of them. Now they became more pronounced. My older brother, Philip, tried to control the siblings by the sheer force of his very being. Bayard, my younger brother, mostly just played with a cousin, George Carey, his closest and, indeed, pretty much only, friend. I experienced continual mood swings that often culminated in hysteria. But I also remembered how to use my cleverness to capture everyone's attention. I was at my craziest at cocktail hour for, if there were guests present, I would try to hog the stage by saying ridiculous things or telling outrageous and exaggerated stories so all eyes focused on me and not my drunken parents. Every one thought me an "ass" and I was.

I was also playing the mascot role as I had a sharp and witty mind and my mother's scrapbooks had enhanced and added to my repository of stories. To get even more attention for the stories, I embellished. Such exaggeration became a habit that took years to break and still has not been banished completely. To this day I favor hyperbole and have a hard time foregoing it when I describe something.

As I reached puberty and adolescence in 1943, a carrot was held out to me, namely, "boarding school." I was never shown nor given a choice of schools. My family worshipped at the altar of Endicott Peabody, so Groton would have been the logical choice. Peabody's portrait gazed down on us from our library wall, my father practically never took off his Groton tie, and Philip had been sent there two years before. As he had dropped back a grade, we were now only one grade apart. With our totally different temperaments, abilities and personalities, and the fact that we fought constantly, we should not, it was felt, go to the same school. Brooks School in North Andover, Massachusetts, was picked for me without my ever being told anything about it.

The Groton connections that decided my going there was the fact that Endicott Peabody had founded Brooks to take Groton's overflow. My father's 1921 Groton classmate, Frank Ashburn, was installed as headmaster. Mr. Ashburn was a marvelous head, but the school, at the time I was to go there, was not top notch. It was too new and without a reputation or a steady supply of graduates' children filling its forms and giving the school money. (There are six forms in most boarding schools. First form is equivalent to the seventh grade and the sixth is the twelfth grade). Brooks at that time took anyone who applied, no matter what their grades or abilities. They did prefer the rich kids more for endowment was needed.

My father actually could not bear the sight of Frank Ashburn, whom he always referred to as Peabody's Pet Pig, so I had a hard time figuring out why my family had chosen this supposedly second-rate school, run by a hated man, for their brightest child. But, in the fall of 1943, as the war raged in Europe and the Pacific, I set out for Brooks, smarting from the awareness that my parents thought it an inferior school for obviously, their inferior son.

As I left for a life away from my family, I was a smart boy but lacking in any common sense. I was childish. I had a father that had been the pits as a role model and it rubbed off on me. Completely lacking in self-esteem, despite my prior successes at school, I left home convinced I was a jerk. My family had systematically stripped my ego of any semblance of maturity.

Finally one day my father took me out to ride, but as you can tell from the picture, he got inebriated beforehand and forgot to put on the proper clothes. This is the day he nicknamed me "Pusscat." I thought it was wonderful to be a special person to him. God only knows where the name came from.

Mother was a wonderful rider who would ride for hours and hours
and hours. She loved the hard exercise, and, like me later, she liked
the socializing that went along with fox hunting. She had ridden from
youth and, as any Bostonian knew, "Riders were trusted a lot more than
ordinary people."

My father was a success on Wall Street for a time, but I am sure his lack of drive, his father's manipulations of his company and those six martini lunches finally reduced the level of his drive to that of a sloth.

Mother's war work was top notch. She ran motor corps, worked as a nurse's aid (though bedpans were not her forte), rolled bandages, spotted planes, grew victory gardens, worked for British War Relief and basically gave up all her other interests. After the war, she never really regained them and took up cocktailing, instead, with a vengeance.

This was taken so we children would all have a family picture for our bureaus at our boarding schools. It was taken in our library in Far Hills. Mother, here, is starting to show a bit of hardness that wasn't there before. She has been taking care of us as a family and a big house alone. The help has not returned yet. World War II was just over and Far Hills was starting to swing again.

This family grouping is in front of our smaller house in Maine. We moved here during the war and lived like sardines until we moved again. We went from thirteen huge rooms and plenty of bathrooms to five tiny cramped rooms and two baths. Everyone was at each other's throats. It was not a place for privacy or to enter puberty from. We might as well all have been in bed together.

This is Mother when she ran the entire East Coast motor corps during the war. She could dismantle a car's engine in forty-eight minutes, she said. We loved having our "beach wagon" turned into an ambulance, and we would come home from school each day stretched out on stretchers. All this work took a toll on her and she was a grouchy person when she got home and swung into her drinks. Despite this, she was a true hero to the war effort.

SIX

To be thirteen years old, hundreds of miles from home and no longer living with one's family, is a shock to anyone's system. To do it during the difficult days of wartime was an even greater trauma. Even if one is mature for one's age, it can be hard. And if one has been systematically wiped clean of self- esteem, the change is earthshaking. That's how I experienced it. Distracted by the demands of war work to the extent that she rarely slowed down to notice how I was feeling, my mother had little time for me at home and little idea how to bring me up after the servants who took care of us left. She and my father loved me, but it was a conditional love, with frequent jabs of rejection.

This set the stage I played on, as I got ready to go to a preparatory school. Some years of my life there were to be a disaster and others quite the opposite. School was school, so it all depended on my being able to draw on the wonderful grounding I had gotten at the elementary level. I also had to cope with the hurts dealt me by my family. On my own, I had to find the right balance, probably as all adolescent children do. The trouble was I felt so immature.

Civilian travel in the United States during the Second World War was incredibly difficult. It was a major undertaking of about nine or ten hours to go from Far Hills, New Jersey, to Brooks School in North Andover, Massachusetts. One had to take a train to Hoboken, the tube under the Hudson River to 33rd Street, a subway to Grand Central Station, a train to South Station, Boston, a taxi across Boston to the North Station, a train to North Andover and a taxi or bus to Brooks School. It was out of the question to have anyone drive all the way there as no extra gas was available for such a journey.

We had an "A" gasoline sticker that allowed the Smith family only a pitifully small amount of fuel per month. This would get us occasionally to the village from our country place. We coasted down every hill with the engine shut off for greater gas efficiency. To make travel just that much more annoying, the trains were continually late, always packed with heavy smoking and drinking Army and Navy personnel and no free seats anywhere. One was considered lucky to be able to squeeze into the clanking, breezy coupling areas between railroad cars. Here the baggage was heaped for lack of room in overhead racks in the train carriages. Travel in the winter was the worst.

It had been announced to me one day in June 1944 that I was to go to Brooks School. I was startled, but relatively happy with the news. At least there was the possibility of finding some new friends. On the appointed day in September, after Mother had packed my bags with the prerequisite tissue paper, I was whisked to the station in Far Hills and put on a local train to Hoboken. All the while I was holding back tears and squeezing a note in my wet palm that contained on it directions I needed to follow in order to arrive in one piece at Brooks School, 500 miles away. When the train pulled out of the station, my very first thought was one of joy to be getting away and my second was one of disappointment for why wasn't I on my way to Groton, in keeping with family tradition. What did it say about me? Didn't it reflect on my worth? I was also a bit overwhelmed with my baggage, which I could not manage to lift into the overhead rack. As we clicked ever faster over the rails, I stared out the window in relief for, quickly, I began to realize that at last I was getting out on my own and away from my family, whose effects on me were, clearly, so often deleterious. When I reached Hoboken, I felt strangely more self-sufficient and confident as I dragged my pair of unwieldy bags through the corridors. Against the odds, I was partially growing up and realizing I could cope alone.

In Grand Central Station I met three boys who were also going to Brooks. One of the boys had been at Somerset Hills Country Day School with me three years before, so I felt less lost as we boarded the jam-packed train to Boston. It took but a few minutes before I started to get to know and like the other two boys while we stood swaying in the aisles with our bags pressed between our legs and our lips wrapped around cigarettes. My smokes were Chesterfields that I had stolen from home just before I left. I was trying to prove to the world that I was grown up, but, heaven knows, I wasn't.

What I was, and this I must emphasize, was an adolescent who was just starting puberty, with nary a clue as to what life was all about or even what to make of all the new hair sprouting under my arms and between my legs. That was too unseemly a subject for my family ever to discuss. I was getting to be physically like my father, yet I was treated like a little kid. It didn't help that my mother treated my father as a kid also.

To break the ice with the boys on the train, I reverted to my family-learned "mascot" role, using gossip as a kind of conversational crutch. It was what I'd learned that always worked. After being on the train barely fifteen minutes, I was asked by one of my new schoolmates, "Where do you buy your clothes? I get mine at Brooks Brothers." As the clothes I wore had always been hand-me-downs from Phil, I knew less than nothing about shops and had never thought to look at a label. I felt immediately that it was an odd question, but sensed it was in order to determine whether I would be accepted, this being a factor by which I could be judged. I knew Brooks Brothers was the most expensive place to get clothes, and, certainly mine did not all come from there. I said mine came from my brother and probably some of his came from Brooks Brothers. This was a bit of an exaggeration but it got the boy off the subject.

At dinner, on the first evening of my arrival at Brooks, I was bombarded with more questions. All had to do with placing me. "Where's your girlfriend at school?" "Does your family have maids?" "What does your father do?" "Where were you at school before Brooks?" It was a grilling I never forgot. This inquisition by upperclassmen as well as my own peers conveyed the message that I could not be liked for myself but rather only for the possessions, family, friends or money that surrounded me and gave me identity. I had been one of the most popular and smartest boys at my former schools, yet now I was back to square one. My interrogators made jokes at my expense, finding my truthful answers outside of their comfort zone and not in keeping with their idea of status. When I said we lived in a tiny apartment with no servants, I did not go on to explain that we actually owned large houses elsewhere but because of the war could not use them.

I was being judged by factors that were beyond my control, and truthfulness, obviously, was not a system I could count on. As a way of "packaging" myself, it was inadequate in a situation where presentation was everything. I soon found I needed to "pad" my replies for better results. Yet, in the end, I knew how lies always return to haunt the liar.

Students at boarding schools tend to be a bit snobbish and boastful. It is a mechanism used to get attention and praise, which are just other names for "love." Kids judge each other by family backgrounds, clothes, athletic abilities, girlfriends and appearances, and try to best anyone they are judging. If a guy was handsome, Christian, well bred, rich, athletic and dressed his muscular frame in Brooks Brothers clothes but never—never!—wore jockey shorts, then he was an exalted creature. If he had a picture of a beautiful Miss Porter's or Foxcroft girlfriend on his bureau, he was even a step higher and could be considered one of the school gods. Such fellows could do no wrong. They were idolized, adored and made prefects, captains of teams and presidents of school organizations. Niceness, kindness, politeness and brains were not necessarily regarded by students as desirable credentials for they had little to do with arriving at the top of the pecking order. Showier, shallower attributes were what counted, along with an excess of bravado.

My first year at school, I had a prefect—one of the fifth-form boys who controlled my dormitory—who, every morning, strode naked, his muscles rippling, from his room at the far end of our cubical dormitory to the showers. He had a towel around his neck and a large smile on his face. He was athletic, rich, handsome, nice, popular and well dressed (when he wasn't on his way to shower). This was George Frick, the second formers' god that year. You could tell he knew it just by the way he walked. We all wanted to be like him, including being as well endowed. All that year I tried to look at him as a role model. He never noticed me.

School also consisted of two distinct groups of boys other than the almighty "gods." There were the younger, lesser gods, who would attain that exalted rank in a few years. Then there were the nerds, comprising those boys who perhaps played soccer instead of football, had more brains than athletic ability, dressed in Bloomingdale's, Filene's or Macy's clothes, were considered effeminate, looked funny, were non-Christian, publicly schooled, needed a scholarship or had unpronounceable names. Their lives at schools were usually ones of constant ridicule, harassment, torment and put down. It was true that occasionally a few of these students changed their stripes and slipped silently into the ranks of the "gods," but they had to work hard at it. They recognized that everything about themselves—including their clothes, complexion, athletic ability and dating prowess—must change. Few could make this changeover, and many were simply too hurt, insecure and poorly equipped to cope with life at school. They tended to turn out all right, in the long run, but were miserable for four years or so. College usually was their saving grace.

It would be an unfair judgment, or even a poor assumption, to think that this behavior was only going on at Brooks School or that it was worse there. All boarding schools were like this, male and female, as I learned when I went home for my first vacation and talked at dances to boys and girls from other single-sex boarding schools.

The subscription dances our families sent us to were how we met the "right" people in our age group. At them we were expected to meet and interact with other people just like ourselves. All the best boys' boarding schools were represented by St. Mark's, St. Paul's, Groton, Pomfret, St. George's, Kent, Choate, Andover, Exeter, Westminster, Avon, Milton, Middlesex, Hochkiss, Taft and even Brooks. Brooks was a struggling newcomer but was top drawer socially. The girls who came were from Farmington (Miss Porter's), Westover, Foxcroft, Miss Walker's, Rosemary Hall, Madeira, Garrison Forest, St. Timothy's and Dobbs. These were considered the top boarding schools for girls. Many young ladies did not go away to school and instead stayed in New York City, and went to schools such as Chapin, Hewitt's, Spence, Nightingale/Bamford and Brearley. They were superior schools as well. All of us got together over Christmas. I delighted in these dances, called the Metropolitans, Getogethers, Holidays, Colony's and Cosmopolitans.

I think, at Brooks, my schoolmates regarded me as somewhat of a jackass, nonconformist and outsider. My quick-wittiness worked in my favor, though, and even if other people's remarks might wound me, I was almost always able to snap out a retort. If someone called me a "jerk," I would come back with a cutting remark about his attire, sports record or intellectual ability. (It helped that I was able to glean and remember so much about everyone and their background.) If someone said "Fairy Forrie," even though I would wither inside, I would instantly return some really nasty name for them that I could make up on the spot. There was a Jewish boy in our class who called me a fairy one day. Hearing that, I shot back with "Jewy John." He was never rude to me again. Comments belittling me caused severe pain within me for rejection was a fearful hurt for me but I needed to defend myself even if it hurt others. Then their comments might cease.

I heard once from a teacher that boys could be as vicious as wolves and I believed it. Girls, too, I knew could be just as savage, for one or two went after me or friends of mine when we broke off romances. There was a lift I seemed to get from bringing a person down who had hurt me for I felt more powerful when I saw them suffer. I knew such behavior was innately wrong and used it only as my defense. I was, sadly, still a frightened kid who chewed his nails and banged his head on his crossed arms in order to go to sleep every night.

To me, it seemed as if my whole appearance prevented me from reaching any godlike status. My ostrich-like physique, my "unslickable" hair, my pimples and my lack of toughness made me stand out like a crack in a windowpane. I was jagged, fragile and gangly at this age. I also did not have a girlfriend to use as a crutch. Many years later, at my fiftieth reunion in 1999, one classmate dryly informed me that he thought I had arrived at school acting as if I was brain dead. I had only been trying to find my bearings in this new environment, and, ultimately, to adapt. I think I can understand what he meant.

The traits I learned to rely on eventually became ones that were no longer purely defensive and, as such, could be put to wonderful advantage. Occasionally, when I felt a bit at ease with myself, I could approach anyone and immediately put them at ease, or I could break the ice between groups that took lots of work by me on my psyche but being able to converse with grace and humor, without any edge of aggression, became a glorious gift. It was my diplomatic mascot role rearing its head.

During my five years at Brooks I worked at becoming a god, but I never quite reached that level but came close. Though I grew somewhat better looking, had a better complexion, longer hair, bought nicer clothes with my pittance of a clothing allowance, fell in love with a Farmington girl, excelled at rowing, and became a minor prefect, I could never completely shake my insecurity and childlike way of looking at people and the world. I still became depressed and insecure at the slightest hint of rejection.

I did seek out friends at Brooks because I was so desperate to fit into this world. Jimmy Moseley came to Brooks, but he had fallen back a class so he was no help to me. There were, though, a few guys I felt empathy with and we became good friends. Three of these, stayed friends for years. Peter Winslow, and Charlie Minot and Charlie Pingree, were ushers in my wedding, and Peter and Charlie are godparents to my children. Another great friend was Warren Crunden who died a few years ago trying to save his brother from drowning. I miss him terribly. I am in touch with another one, Cory Kilvert, who had an even sharper tongue than mine. These boys were quick witted, funny and just plain nice to me so we bonded despite some initial standoffishness. As boarding schools create the atmosphere of a large family, great friendships inevitably resulted students from all across the map come together. A social network is woven, and this web of relationships can evolve into a tremendous aid to men and women as they begin their business lives or settle away from their families and hometowns.

To impress my friends, though they accepted me as I was, I soon learned to be better dressed, to rip out non-Brooks Brothers labels and to pull on shirts over my head even if they were not from Brooks Brothers (their shirts were made with the bottom part sewed together as one unit). I reported for football, cursed soccer players, slicked my hair and covered my acne with aftershave powder. I strutted and flexed my body in the showers while showing off my ever-growing endowment. I boasted at meals about family, VIP connections and money, even if it was not all true. I frantically wrote every girl I had ever known in the hopes that at mail call I would get a letter from Farmington or Foxcroft.

Boys' boarding schools are not dens of homosexuality, as people often imagine. However, there always will be tension when several hundred young men live together without the opposite gender. But by doing what every adolescent youth in the world does, we survived our monks' lifestyle. We learned the facts of life from our fellow students and spent time fantasizing. We were all growing up, and sex was a definite force in our daily existence. Sadly, boys who were considered "fairies" tended to bear the brunt of the cruelty handed out. To be poorly built, to talk or walk effeminately, to have erections while showering with others or not to like football, all unfairly categorized a poor soul as a "homo." As such, he was doomed to ostracism.

Problem children were not taken willingly into private boarding schools, as the communities were too close to cope well with them. However, many children, once they were in school, grew into problem children and had a very difficult time. For the most part, they were thrown out for no infractions of the rules were allowed, even if the student was the child of a very rich person or an alumnus. If you smoked, went off campus, drank, swore profusely, insulted a master or had sex, you were out in a flash. Parents did send what they considered their problem children to some schools, and, in many cases, the schools shaped these students up. Often, the children's only problems were with their parents.

A lot of good things actually were part of my experience at Brooks. It had a superb headmaster and headmistress, wonderful teachers, fabulous teachers' wives, a glorious campus, fine sports facilities and nice long vacations. I also loved some of the sports that were offered, crew being my favorite and squash right behind.

Ironically, the man my father abhorred and once referred to as "Peabody's Pet Pig" turned out to be for me the finest gentleman and teacher I have ever known. Frank Ashburn, the headmaster at Brooks, played a major role in smoothing out the bumpiness of my adolescence years, and he managed to mold me over my time with him into a caring, Christian young man. His own Christianity pervaded all that he did, and he gave me positive guidelines that I attempted to follow. He was fair, learned, just, even-tempered, kind and understanding. Looking back upon my time at Brooks, it is not easy to see that I was subconsciously fashioning my life upon his image, but, in fact, I did. His kindness when he dealt with me concerning my family problems and his concern when my depression became all too obvious exemplified his ability to connect with his charges. His influence prevails today in how I treat and deal with my contemporaries; in how I connect with God and in how I interact with the fairer sex. He was my shining star. My run-ins with him were few, for I was well behaved, did a more than passable job with my schoolwork, and was my very best self with both him and Mrs. Ashburn at the supper table. I always raced in to sit next to one of them if it was my month to be seated at their head table. I must add that it took many years for his influence to come to full fruition within me. My dysfunctional behavior kept getting in the way.

One day, in my second form year, Westy Phillips, Charlie Minot and Bob Royce tied me, stark naked, to a post in the auditorium's attic and whipped me with a cat o' nine tails. It was done on Brooks School's hazing day, Bloody Sunday, when all "jerks" were meant to be taught a lesson. After what was really a beating, I caught a terrible cold and was a whimpering mess in the infirmary when Mr. Ashburn came to visit me. He wanted to know what had happened, but I was afraid to tell him for fear of retribution. However, I finally did. The dressing down those boys got was delivered with such grace that, somehow, they managed to be nice to me when I emerged from the infirmary. Charlie Minot became one of my best friends. Mr. "A." was a supreme diplomat and disciplinarian, and I only wish he had dug deeper into my personality to see the repressed psychological problems I had and would continue to have.

The truth is, boarding schools in my day were not prepared for, nor did they understand or take notice of, a student's psychological problems, particularly if they were as well repressed and covered over as mine were. Schools then did not have resident doctors, let alone psychiatrists or psychologists.

During my first year at school, I was picked to play the female lead in the annual school production, Gogol's The Inspector General. (There were no girls at Brooks, so boys were dolled up accordingly.) I did an outstanding job, and many others thought so as well, yet my mother, when she came to see it, was shocked. She told me afterwards that I had been too convincing a girl and that I should be careful lest I get too effeminate. She was never happy with what I did, and this was no exception. I did not sleep a wink that night, as I was so upset. Wasn't it my mother who had told me she and my father had wished I was a girl? It was impossible to win. Each of her put-downs increased my feelings of worthlessness and anger. I tried to scour my mind of her reaction, but never tried acting again.

Brooks had a fine faculty. Some of the teachers had been at Groton in my father's day and had come out of retirement, because of the war, to teach at Brooks. All of these men left their indelible prints on me. Bob Spock, who taught mathematics and coached crew, and Doc Scudder, who was my first dormitory master and taught me Latin and English, were the most important to me. They were both kind, caring men, and both were "oddballs" who played favorites, taught classes in uncommon ways and verbalized in ways no other human did. They had words and phrases to connote the strangest things. A favorite of Scudder's was, "Tet me louch your nose." Whereupon, he'd touch our noses for some unknown reason. We all went along with this, even if we never understood what his words meant.

To be a teacher in a boys' boarding school took a special kind of person and I got along with both kinds. If married, they usually were fairly normal, but if they were older and single, they were likely to turn into characters. It was a monk's life they led; yet they weren't in religious orders. They did not have romantic attachment and the school was their sole interest, also some had just come from college or the military and were single for a while but had obviously picked teaching as a career and soon would settle in as married men once they were established. They seemed like contemporaries as I got older and they were great fun to be with. They treated us as adults.

Teacher's wives became my surrogate mothers and they worked to try to build my self-esteem. For this I am eternally grateful. Alicia Waterson, the art teacher, and Janie Jackson, my football coach's wife, were sensational with me, and I relished their kindness. Janie's husband was my housemaster. For my last two years, there was very little I did not discuss with her. Every boy at Brooks was in love with her, but I felt that I had the inside track. Her brother-in-law, Jimmy Jackson, later to be her husband after her husband died, had been a beau of my mother's and this, I felt, sealed our closeness.

I was moderately athletic, because I was well coordinated, but most major sports like football, basketball, hockey and baseball were never my strong suit. I tried some of them, as I was forced to under school requirements that we had to play some sport each semester, but I was only medium-good at them. I went out for football my first year and made end on the most junior of the junior club teams, the Medes. The Persians were the other club and we Medes hated them. I loathed every minute of the fall term's sports activities and relished the end of the football season. The body contact, even though we had pads, and the smashing of heads in helmets, always reminded me of my despised boxing days at Somerset Hills. I continued to play football until my sixth-form year, for I was afraid to go out for soccer and be called a fairy. At this time in my life it was impossible for me to do what I really wanted to do, being part of the pack was too important.

My last year at Brooks, I found a distraction that I truly relished. It was squiring Nancy Ashburn, the headmaster's daughter. She was home from Farmington on sick leave and I was, by some fluke in the rules, being allowed to take no fall sport. They wanted me to study as hard as was possible for my College Board examinations in the spring. I roamed free, and it was a delightful autumn that Nancy and I had for ourselves. We were forever driving off campus in her Chevrolet convertible, and I smoked up a storm, and we necked. It was a term to remember for, suddenly, I had all the advantages of coed education in a boy's school. No other classmate had the perks I had. It was heaven. "To hell with Groton, " I said to myself. I had a girl at Brooks and she liked to go out with me. Groton certainly could never be like this. Most importantly, I felt really loved for myself and boys envied me at last.

When not studying, I played squash relatively well during the winter terms, and, for two years, I tried hockey. My bad ankle, probably a legacy from my bout with polio as an infant, made that game a disaster for me, as I could not turn to the left without my ankle giving way. Each spring I went out for rowing, enjoying it immensely. I worked my way up to the varsity's number-one boat and rowed oar number two for my last two years. Finally, I had found a sport in which I could excel and one which made some of the younger boys respect. One of my greatest triumphs was winning my crew athletic "letter" in my fifth-form year. I looked muscular in my bulky letter sweater and tried to never take it off.

In 1949, with my mother and father both watching, my crew beat Groton's varsity. My mother wept at her beloved Groton's defeat, and my father said the race had been well rowed BUT my form was poor and he had really wanted Groton to win. I, literally, could barely speak to them for the rest of the weekend that they were with me. They had squashed every bit of pride I felt in my victory. If they were using forceps and a scalpel and operating on me, they could not have done a better job of taking away such a huge chunk of self-esteem.

Not only did we have to wear starched, stiff collars and blue suits every evening for dinner and on Sundays, but we had to attend chapel after the evening meals and twice on Sundays. I never complained and was delighted that we had to go, for I found tremendous peace and strength in prayer. It was in the Brooks chapel and from Mr. Ashburn's Headmaster's course on Bible study, that I found a powerful faith. In my last year, I became the head chapel usher and I always felt a sense of tranquility while I did my job. Mr. Ashburn's sermons were geared to growing young men and the obstacles faced by them. There were few of his homilies that did not impress me, and most hit all my "nails" on their heads. My first year at Brooks, I requested that I be confirmed and never missed Holy Communion at school from the day Bishop Sherrill laid his hands on me until the day I left. I had found a firm rock to stand on, and I forever repositioned myself on this boulder when things seemed to be going poorly. It never failed to protect my life and give me peace even at my darkest moments.

When VE Day was proclaimed in April of 1945, the school became hysterical, very nearly insane. The incessant ringing of the chapel bells loudly proclaimed the Allied victory. We all had been advised at our daily assembly that this day was soon coming, so we congregated, wildly screaming, in front of the Ashburn's' house and filed into the chapel. I found myself walking in with Billy Roosevelt, President's Roosevelt's grandson, and making a totally unnecessary and nasty remark to him about his grandfather. Though I liked Billy very much, it had been ingrained in me to hate Democrats and especially his grandfather, the traitor to his class. At that point I did not really know what this meant, but I did know that there were few people I knew in Far Hills, New York City, Boston or at Brooks who were not Republicans. My Grandfather Smith, to indicate his total disdain, had a portrait of his Groton and Harvard schoolmate, Franklin Delano Roosevelt, hanging in his little office in Maine, framed by a toilet seat.

Eleanor Roosevelt had come to Brooks in 1944 to visit Billy, and she had taken me out to lunch with him and a group of our friends. When I shook her hand to thank her, it felt like a damp dishrag and I never failed to remind Billy of this supposed affront to me. My mother had taught me that a gentleman or a lady always looked a person in the eye and shook hands with a strong grip. She had not done this, and I was sure it was because she was a Democrat and not a lady.

On my summer vacations in Maine, I tried to avoid our house as much as possible. Being with my parents, whose evening amusement was cocktails was not a happy time for me. Their civility with one another would wax and wane, and it was difficult to know which side to take. Many an hour was spent sulking in my room or playing tennis with my younger brother. There was no gas, so no motorboats were in the water and there was no place to go without cars. It was impossible for us to do all the wonderful things Maine is known for. We were not permitted to spend time along the shore, nor could we sail to our islands or camp out. None of our sailboats had been launched and no equipment was available in stores so that one could stay outside. We could visit nowhere. I had one of the most sublime vacation places in the world as a playground and yet it was hardly possible to play at all.

After the war was over, life, obviously, improved. During my last years at Brooks, I had at least four girlfriends, with whom my correspondence was voluminous. Two were at Farmington—Sheila Scott and Lisa Brady, another—Phyllis Dillon -—was at Foxcroft. The fourth—Farr Bingham, my third cousin—had had the temerity to go to the Master's School in Dobbs Ferry, New York. (Farmington and Foxcroft girls enhanced my status, but Dobbs was a misstep up the ladder of success.) I was forever having my picture taken so I could send it to these girls, but I never dared to ask them for one of theirs. I brought Farr up to my school dance one year and plotted for six weeks beforehand how I was going to kiss her. When she finally got there, I think we only got close enough to dance cheek to cheek. At the last moment, I was too scared. I thought she might reject me and fear of rejection ruled my life.

In 1946 I was fifteen and eligible in Maine to get a driver's license. Suddenly, after I acquired it, vacations in New Jersey and Maine became marvelously entertaining. We kept a unique car in Far Hills, though it was registered in Maine. It was my late Grandfather Smith's special body, twelve-cylinder, standard-shift Packard. It was black, stylish, huge and wonderful and it was a sensation among my group. None of my friends in Far Hills were able to drive legally so I was the hit of the century with the girls. I had spent a few years illegally driving two-cylinder Crosleys around the dirt back roads. These forerunners to the Volkswagen Beetles got eighty miles to the gallon and had to be pushed up steep hills if two were in the car. They were pitiful to what I had now. I loved thundering down the dusty roads in the Packard to the Moseleys', Dillons', Whites', Scotts' or Bradys', and taking girls on the running boards was heaven for me, particularly as they had to lean in the window on my side for supposed safety's sake.

My family had rented an apartment at 245 East 72nd Street in New York City in 1947 so my father would not have to commute every day to the country. They hardly used it at all but, on the flip side, I stayed there on a regular basis. I was going to all the subscription dinner dances in New York City. As we were getting older, all our mothers were arranging new dances so we could keep meeting the right people from New York, New Jersey and Connecticut. There were now the Senior Holidays, Senior Get Togethers, Groton-St.Marks and the New York Junior Assemblies. The girls' families all paid for us young men to come as their guests. Each girl brought along two or three escorts. We presented them before hand with smelly gardenias but never orchids. The girls could never wear so many flowers so I pushed for mine to be the special one, worn over the shoulder. I was an elegant dancer, having been taught by my mother in our front hall. Also, I had the good fortune to be coordinated. I loved girls and I never missed a dance if I could help it. Girls were starting to like me, too.

In New York, away from my family, I could live life as I wished it. I could drink, smoke and continually go to movies, F.A.O. Schwartz, Hamburger Heaven, Brooks Brothers, hockey games and the Central Park Zoo. I was allowed to go to one nightclub, Larue's, with my dates, because I had been told that this was "one place where they were so nice to prominent children." Cokes cost six dollars, but I could not have cared less, as I had learned how to wheedle money out of my parents by playing one against the other. My visits to Larue's, however, were stopped abruptly the minute the papers announced that the headwaiter had raped a society girl. The drinking age in New York was then eighteen, but they never asked for identification in those halcyon days.

When in Far Hills, I never, if I could help it, stayed around my family or in our house for any length of time. As a young guy with a driver's license, there were a multitude of friends for me to hang out with, many of whom remain my friends today. Each night I would head out for evenings of bridge or supper or night tennis or swimming or just talking. I had far more pals in Far Hills than I ever had at school, and I loved every one of them. Most of my friends did not drink, as their families were around, and I never even dreamed of having any liquor, unless at a dance. My bridge was quite good, so it made sponging meals easy.

As I still loved riding and as all my friends in Far Hills rode to the hounds, I took it up. We would wake at the crack of dawn and hack to the meets. This way of keeping myself busy was healthy, and it was exciting, too. Our family had gotten rid of all of our horses and ponies when the war had started, but I was not too shy to ask the Bradys or the Dillons to mount me. If that was not possible, I could rent a hunter for the day and charge it to my parents.

At this juncture in my life, the island of Dark Harbor, Maine, became my focus each summer. There I could enjoy the company of vacationing Far Hills girls. I would drive to Lincolnville and take the ferry across for splendid summer parties and dances and fun-filled weekends. My favorite destination was the Douglas Dillons' house, where their two daughters, Phyllis and Joan, were ensconced. I adored them and their parents as well. They all made me feel like a special prince every time I saw them.

Many of my friends from school now summered in various spots on the Maine coast and I could easily fit in different trips to see them. There was little for me, I felt, back in Tenants Harbor, with my parents, brothers, aunts, uncles and cousins boringly in residence and annoying me.

However, if I had to be on home turf, necking with baby-sitters was a preferred pastime. The girls were rather unimpressive and slaughtered the King's English but were definitely sexy. One evening, my mother caught me with one of them down at our tennis court in a reclining position. The sitter and I had few, if any, clothes on and I was decidedly caressing her when my mother, who was quite tipsy, yanked the door open. When she asked what I was doing, I calmly replied, "I'm just saying good night." She then told me in no uncertain terms that that was not the way she had ever said it in Boston. She slammed the door and walked home. The subject never came up again.

Tif Bingham, who often accompanied me on these sexual escapades, and I were the scourge of Hart's Neck. No girl, we thought, was safe from our clutches. Nice girls still scared the life out of me, and this meant I only held hands with the socially acceptable ones but petted the less social ones. What a snob I was, but I was terrified a nice girl would reject me, just as my parents always did.

By my sixth-form year at Brooks, it seemed that I was on every debutante list in the USA. I was asked to dances nearly every night over Christmas vacation, as well as every evening during the months of June and September. Tappan & Tew ran a social secretary service in New York, which kept the debutante list. If you were prominent, you stayed on the list for four or five years, and you got invitations whether you knew the girl or not if it was a big party. The schedule for the parties was carefully organized so there would be no overlaps, mistakes or dances on the same evening. As I actually knew most of the young women who were coming out and since my family was well known socially, I was busy nearly every single night.

These parties were truly out of this world, but they are, unfortunately, a thing of the past. The great houses in which they were held are museums or torn down. Huge coming-out dances in the country are also gone. A terrible accident in Darien, Connecticut occurred when two drunken minors' cars collided and both were killed. They were going home from a debut party at which liquor was served them. The debutante's parents were sued and a huge settlement was granted to the parents of the minors. Nobody could afford this price to pay, so the dances ended. Many young women now want to avoid the pressure of coming out and prefer to be debutantes in name only. They can be listed in their cities as debutantes and come out at a group party, with the subscription profits usually turned over to charities.

The majority of the parties that I went to had lavish dinners preceding the dances. These in themselves could be considered debutante parties, for one arrived at seven o'clock and never left until midnight to go on to the actual coming-out dance, another long lasting delight, usually going till seven in the morning. At the dinners, hundreds of guests would be served such fare as exquisitely poached salmon with hollandaise sauce, rare filet mignon, buttered asparagus, puffed potatoes, endive salads and chocolate soufflés. Magnificent wines were the accompaniment. There might be lovely dry white Cabernet Sauvignon Bordeaux wines for the first course, followed by Bordeaux reds from Chateau Haut Brion, Chateau Lafite or Mouton Rothschild for the main course, while for dessert there were champagnes such as Bollinger, Moet et Chandon or Piper-Heidsieck. No host ever skimped on the wines and liquors, as everyone assumed terrible hangovers would follow only from the consumption of cheap booze.

Each party seemed more spectacular than the one before it. I reveled in each one and never got over their beauty. I invariably followed the same routine, heading directly to the bar where I would immediately drink five glasses of champagne usually in five gulps. This unfortunate habit began to help make it easier for me to face and talk to all those brilliantly shining people. Liquor loosened my tongue and transformed me into Fred Astaire. Being convinced that some young lady or other might put me down or refuse to dance with me, I used champagne as a magic weapon. With it in me I came to enjoy these evenings, much more as I was whirling the night away with well into the next morning. There usually were fifteen or twenty glasses of champagne under my belt when I left the party. Only God knows why I made it anywhere to sleep.

Mountains of flowers helped bathe the debutantes in a soft glow as, under the pink and white tents, they vied with each other to be considered the most beautiful girl there. Ailsa Mellon Bruce gave on Long Island one of the most exquisite dances I have ever been to. It was in the country where the lawn was like velvet as it swept down to a shimmering lake where swans were swimming and lights were floating. The little tables had flowers and candles on them, and the whole place magically shone with sparkling lights and lanterns. It was like something out of a fairy tale as the guests, perhaps 750 people, floated around the dance floor to the strains of Lester Lanin's full orchestra. There were two of his bands so the music never stopped when musicians took a break. When breakfast was served at five o'clock in the morning, we were still caught in the spell, ready to dance on.

I am ashamed to say that I had only one summer job during my whole time at Brooks, and it lasted for only one day. I went to work on the Dillons' farm at six o'clock in the morning and returned home at eight o'clock that night, exhausted and with bloody fingers from handling wire on hay bales. That ended my attempt to be useful and mature during my adolescent summers. Parties were far more fun, and sleep more soothing. Without being aware of it, I was heading down the road to alcoholism. Despite my young age I was, owing to heritage, at a high risk to become a victim of this horrible disease.

My last year at Brooks was uneventful except that, for three or four months—the equivalent of two marking periods—I actually ranked second in my class. There was a reason for that progress. I was trying to go to Harvard and, therefore, putting a great deal more time into my studies. Phil had gotten in the year before, albeit with tremendous help from my father and my father's great friend there, the dean of admissions, Frankie Kinnicutt. I wanted to go there like hell on wheels. My family feigned interest but really was paying the usual scant attention and never once mentioned to Frankie that their second son was now applying. I had an acceptance there one day, and then saw it rescinded three days later due to an inordinate number of servicemen returning to Harvard after the war. Veterans got the first shots at empty slots, and well they should have. But I was stunned to find myself the first in my family in generations not to go to Harvard.

A quick call by my father to a cousin of my mother's at Trinity College in Hartford got me in there, instantly. This, as it turned out, was probably one of the best things that ever happened to me. I went there with eight Brooks School classmates and, except for one whom I loathed at both Brooks and Trinity, we all became good friends. Peter Winslow, the Brooks School senior prefect and crew captain, was to be my freshman roommate. We ended up rooming together all four years.

On the day of graduation I left Brooks overjoyed. One reason was the splashy yellow Jeepster that was my graduation present. It became my key to wild freedom. With college looming, I planned to celebrate all summer long, partying in Long Island, Boston, Philadelphia, Far Hills and Maine. A job was out of the question. Champagne was not. I was proceeding to my young adult stage of living still immature and a person who needed liquor to be prop himself up socially. This did not portend well for my future.

This photo was taken during my first year at Brooks School. I was constantly beaten up and jumped on, but so were all the other young kids.

I actually made friends during my time at Brooks, and two of the boys in this picture, Billy Cox and Cory Kilvert, I still see very occasionally. The other boy has died. Hikes in the woods were organized to take our minds off girls, though, at this point, kissing was the height of my sexual interest. I was scared to death of all girls. It took every bit of my will power just to manage to hold a hand.

This faded snapshot is yours truly in costume for the Brooks School play. I had the lead female role and was quite good. However, my mother came to see the play and I'm sure she thought, subconsciously, that that meant I wanted to be one. Christine Jorgenson wasn't around yet, so sex change was not fashionable. Mother, for the life of her, could not compliment me on my acting. The sight of me in a dress terrified her too much.

I had such an inferiority complex that I was convinced at this age that I was ugly as sin. Yet, when a friend took this snapshot so I could send a picture to various girls I knew, I thought I looked pretty good. It helped my ego, especially when young ladies begged for one. What bravado I put on to mask my terror of life itself.

This picture was also taken for some girls I had a crush on. I really cannot remember which ones, since I was in correspondence with about fours girls at this time. One can tell how shy and unsure I was. I remember (with dread) this gray pin stripe suit, which would have looked more at home in Harlem, where zoot suits were the rage.

Perhaps the achievement that I am most proud of at Brooks School was not squiring around the headmaster's daughter, but making the varsity crew. We had for two years a quite honorable record, winning more than we lost. On the Brooks crew I made lifelong friends. Peter Winslow is on the far right and he was my roommate for four years at college and godparent to one of my children.

I loved to dance, and here I am in my first dinner clothes. If this was today, people would say I looked like a band member or a waiter, but I thought I looked great.

My first true love, Farr Bingham, is on the left. Her brother, Tiffy, one of my best friends, is in the middle and her sister, Heidi, on the right. Their entire family played a major role in helping me through life. I really was wildly infatuated with Farr and devastated when Phil stole her away from me. "Our song" was the Missouri Waltz and my heart beat rapidly whenever I heard it played. She gave me a copper ring, which nearly rotted my finger off, and it was, until she went to Groton-St. Marks Dance with Phil, my most prized possession. Heidi became a girl friend of mine much later on.

This was life in the Big City for me. The picture was taken in the Stork Club and shows Phil with a girl friend, and my mother. Mother was wearing a veil and how she sipped drinks through it I do not know. She was a lovely lady, but one can see the first signs of "booze" taking its toll.

During my adolescence these absolutely ravishing Dillon girls (Phyllis on left and Joan on right) started to mean a great deal to me. I had known them for all my life, for they lived at the place next to my family's and their parents were friends of my parents. I spent so much time in their house that I felt like a member of the family and I often wished that I was.

SEVEN

When I arrived on campus in 1949 in Hartford, Connecticut, I was still rudderless and adrift, and also a terrible snob. I was using my disdain for others to cover my lack of self-esteem. Though I felt that I had started to grow up, both physically and mentally, when I left Brooks, in fact, I was not maturing well at all. I had spent the past summer drinking far too much and taking nothing in life seriously, I was barely connecting with the people around me, especially if I felt the slightest bit ill at ease with them. This was a poor way to start college.

Being reasonably intelligent, unfortunately, had its down side. As I never had to study very hard to get passing marks, my time was generally spent cocktailing, taking out a plethora of insurance company secretaries who lodged at the local YWCA, or going to the movies. We were not allowed to have cars our freshman year, but I brought mine up from New Jersey as soon as I could find a way to break the rule. I got around it with the help of a good friend, Dick Stewart, who was from West Hartford. I let him use my Jeepster to commute from his place to college, but he had to release it to me on weekends, when I always planned to be off and running on my round of social escapades.

At college I was making some friends, not just being forced together with them as I had been in boarding school. I was also focusing on what actually interested me. Making my Trinity life easier and pleasanter was my roommate, a great and delightful friend from Brooks, Peter Winslow. Peter was great with everybody but I remained a snob, as deep down I felt inferior and leery of people. We drank alot in our room and all too soon I learned that too many of these drinks could make me surly and nasty with anybody that disagreed with me. It was a bad sign for I was taking "disagreement" as "rejection."

The required freshman courses were not very taxing. My private school education had put me at least a year ahead of the majority of my public schooled classmates, so I managed to sail through with relatively high marks. I played on the freshman squash team as the number four men. There were six of us, and I was thrilled to win most of my matches, becoming the first member of my family to get a college "letter." My father, whom I immediately told of this accomplishment, assured me he was a far better player than I, for hadn't he once beaten me at Brooks when I was fifteen? He was a master "balloon burster." Nevertheless, doing well in my studies, getting on the dean's list, and competing in sports were real tastes of success for me. This appears odd with all the alcohol I was pouring down my gullet.

Classmates from Brooks, whom I had not known well while I was there, became great friends of mine at Trinity. I had lived with them so long at Brooks, I never had to be a snob in their company. It was a new experience for me and I carried this ice-breaking image further by making new friends with about twenty other men, some who roomed with the Brooks guys, as well as others who lived in my entryway and nearby. Unfortunately, I was still far too shy and insecure to go out and participate fully in my classmates' activities. I had all the social graces but not self-confidence to be a man among men. I just couldn't turn this participation on at will. I feared rejection intensely. Something in the back of my mind told me that if I did not open myself to intimacy, I could not be hurt. If I acted superior, others could not get to me. Consequently, I kept my distance and seemed aloof to most of my schoolmates when it actually was due to sheer fright. Being snobby was my defense.

We could not join fraternities our freshman year so there was little to do over the weekends at college. On Fridays—for I had made damned sure I had no Saturday classes—I would vamoose by three o'clock Friday afternoons. My roommate, Peter Winslow, lived in Boston, so I would stay with him there and go to sea breeze parties, followed by football games at Harvard. Alternately, I went home to New York and Far Hills even if my family might be in residence, for lavish debutante parties and fox hunting were my passion. I adored these pursuits and returned to college on Sunday nights hung over and very tired. Playing hard never affected my schoolwork so I inevitably played as exhaustingly as I could each weekend. I avoided my hatred of being alone with myself by keeping a full schedule. I just might have to face too many fears without one. That was far too painful a possibility to allow to happen. Depression deepens when alone.

Coming-out parties in New York and Boston were arranged in the fall to coincide with the football schedules of the Ivy League colleges. The most celebrated of these matches was the Harvard-Yale game, and the number-one debutante or the richest family had the splashiest party on this night. One year it would be in New York and the next year in Boston, depending on whether "The Game" was in New Haven or Cambridge. It was usually the be-all-end-all of the season. Each weekend in October and November there was a coming-out party in Boston, usually held at a debutante's house, a country club, the Ritz or the Copley Plaza hotels. In New York, the ballrooms at the Plaza, the old Ritz or the Pierre were the choicest, although the Waldorf or the St. Regis Roof might be used. Sometimes a grand house, if it was near the city, was picked. Whichever was chosen, they were all opulently decorated, and the events lavishly planned and stylishly presented, each party seemed to be trying to outdo the one just before it. I dressed in my black tie outfit, put on my pumps and went to them all.

As I did not stay at college for the weekend social life, except for some wild football and partying weekends, I haunted the debutante circuit. I soon knew nearly every girl on the East Coast who "came out." All of these fascinating young women certainly did not know me very well—mostly because I wouldn't let them close to me—but they paid attention to me as I was attractive, well-bred and an excellent dancer. I always made a beeline to the dazzlers like Kitty Douglas, Lisa Brady, Winnie Trimble, Phyllis Dillon, Joan Dillon and Lily McKim. They danced beautifully and were so popular that nobody was ever stuck with them. Sooner or later I would have to move on to the agonizing chore of duty dances with the children of my mother's friends. This was obligatory, and I often got stuck with them-sometimes for an hour.

I became altogether too dependent on champagne for a good time at these soirees, and I drank it down as if there was to be no tomorrow. It made the evenings float on air and helped me break the ice with those young ladies with whom otherwise I might feel too shy. But, interestingly, one of the byproducts of these parties was the communication I began to have with my mother and father. As the family "mascot," I was now, their social butterfly, representing them in the outside world. This was because they tended to stay more and more at home in the 1950's, and it was I who spent time in the company of their friends. We, therefore, endlessly discussed these people and their foibles. They knew everyone who gave the parties and wanted to hear all about what happened and who did what. Though they barely knew where I was going to college or what subjects I took there, they cared intensely about my social activities. They were always inquiring about who behaved the worst and drank the most and with whom I had or had not danced. As far as who had acted the worst, it surely was I, but I wasn't going to tell them that. Other than these parties, however, my parents and I still shared few interests or conversations. They were up on all Philip's activities and they would tell me about him constantly. My life was unimportant to them. I hadn't gone to Groton or Harvard.

One weekend while visiting my grandfather Clark's country house, I found the key to his huge wine cellar hidden in a wall sconce. He had amassed a vast cache of booze during Prohibition. I soon began returning to college, after stopping there on many weekends, with case upon case of scotch, bourbon, gin and sherry. Grandpa Clark had moved to Wilmington, Delaware, right after marrying Mary Chichester DuPont, but he had always kept this house with a small staff running it in order to make a home for my great- grandmother, his mother. She had moved to the country from her top floor dig's in Boston. She was the excuse I used for the drop-in visits to the house, though, in truth, I would only talk to her for five minutes or so. She made more sense than I did as I was always in a big rush-especially to grab the liquor.

Not a person in the household nor any relative ever seemed to notice how the cellar's supply was dwindling, so I was free and clear to keep "borrowing." During my years at Trinity, I, in essence, maintained a small speakeasy with the fanciest of liquors in my chambers. Winslow's and my room became a popular gathering place during the few football weekends we stayed in Hartford and for most special evenings as well.

Those bottles of liquor, with their old-fashioned white porcelain tops, were incredibly delicious, for each was the grandest of its type and as smooth and mellow as possible. There were no tax stamps on the bottles, as bootleggers had supplied them to my grandfather. It should be noted that no booze was allowed in rooms at Trinity. Breaking rules, or bending them, as I preferred to call it, had been part of my childhood, so I continued in that tradition. My parents had set the example that the upper class could do things that might be a bit dishonest if it didn't hurt anyone.

Good horsemanship and sportsmanship while fox hunting soon earned me the honor of being awarded hunt buttons and a hunt collar by Mrs. Charles (Vera) Scribner, the Master of the Essex Hounds. Now, gleefully and proudly, I could wear a pink coat for the hunt. An uncle had given me a pink coat and also an old and exquisite scarlet tailcoat, the evening dress equivalent of the pink coat. It was faced with glorious apricot silk and worn with a white tie. It was never off my back when I went off gallivanting to dinners and dances in the country. I wore it at the slightest excuse, for I felt I was fantastically dashing in it. I was puffed up with myself at all the parties, but failed to understand what was really going on. The clothing afforded me a false sense of security and belonging. This was something new for me.

As I was on a minimal clothing allowance, I scrounged my riding habit—meaning fox hunting clothes, which consisted of white breeches, black boots, vests and stocks—from my father's and mother's closets, from relatives and also from friends of my mother's. My parents regarded my fox hunting passion only as a passing fancy and did not want to help outfit me. They didn't understand that there was no way that I would ever drop trying to be a dashing gentleman in the hunting field. It staked out for me a unique place with my horse-oriented friends. It wasn't long before my mother took exception to this assumption. She informed me, quite emphatically, that she had been an incredible rider, fox hunter, polo player and steeplechaser and, though she had not been allowed to wear pink, she said she had been awarded buttons and collars from two hunts, The Norfolk and The Essex. She had to belittle me.

At college I never had a special girl in tow. I was afraid of nice girls and, without a drink, I could never relax with them. I did have platonic relationships with some terrific women and weekends with them could be wild but far from sexual. The sex began only after serious drinking, and my partners were local Hartford secretaries or Hartford Hospital nurses. I felt and acted superior to this type of woman, so I never had a fear of rejection. They always had marriage in mind, but I had only sex on mine. Once I drunkenly tangled with one of them when she pushed me, and, lo and behold, she called the police. They came and I was put in jail, much to my mother's horror, when I had to call her for bail money and the lawyer's fee. She never let me forget this indiscretion and was continually telling me that Phil would never do this type of thing. That was a predictable fact, though far from what I needed to hear. I once told my mother of my wild exploits at Miss Porter's when she asked if I ever went there from Trinity. I told her stories that curled her hair. She never quizzed me again.

One evening we Trinity men sent an undertaker to Miss Porter's School to collect a supposed "dead girl" whose death we had fabricated out of whole cloth. We told the funeral home that a student had tragically passed away while singing in the Gundy. As we watched from the bushes and roared with laughter, the hearse arrived. Another time, we climbed in the second floor window of one of Miss Porter's seniors. Though it was at her behest, she suddenly got frightened, as we squirmed in, and she called the housemother. This old woman, whom I had seen on other occasions as she padded around Farmington, then called the police. It was legal to call on these girls for tea on Sundays, but such an approach was too demeaning for such masterful Lotharios as we felt ourselves to be. We preferred to live dangerously and continued to besiege these girls until we got too old for them and moved on to the college girls at Briarcliff, Bennett, Bennington, Smith and Vassar for our kicks.

While at Trinity, I introduced my roommate, Peter Winslow, to my cousin, Farr Bingham. He was very taken with her and this put pressure on me to find a girl of my own so we could be a foursome. He was her boyfriend for three years. I was still too damned scared of permanency and would only ask a young woman to college if a specific occasion called for a date. This solitary life made me not only an outsider—for most of my friends had girlfriends—but it made me continue to be unsure of myself and to remain given to heavy drinking to liven parties up. I could never rid myself of the feeling that nice girls would inevitably repudiate me if I tried to get too close to them. This had happened to me a few times when I had been serious about a girl. Philip had stolen one of my girls and Jimmy Mosely another one. If I made a pass, I was afraid that the damsel might jump up and leave, or laugh or call me immature. My mother had done all these types of things to me since I was a baby, so in my mind why shouldn't these young women do what she did. My subconscious dominated my actions and would not let me grow up.

In my sophomore year, to my great pleasure and excitement, I was invited to become a member of Psi Upsilon Fraternity. Four of my classmates from Brooks were also asked, as were five friends I had made during my freshman year. I really think I would have quit college if I had not made a fraternity. I would have felt completely rejected, abandoned and left out. For their part, my mother and father knew nothing about fraternities, only Harvard final clubs, and had heard of only one fraternity, St. Anthony's Hall, which an uncle of mine, who had gone to Trinity, had joined a quarter of a century before. When I informed them that I had joined Psi U, they never said congratulations but only that it was sad I had not joined St. Anthony's Hall. Why, they asked, was I so foolish as to join Psi Upsilon? In fact, I had been asked to join the Hall, but had refused. My parents never could understand, but I did not regret my choice for a single moment. I was gaining a bit of confidence and some friends, and that was all that mattered. Would my parents ever be congratulatory?

Unfortunately, my fraternity life would lead me to develop some very bad habits. We ate and spent most of our time in the fraternity house. Against the rules of both the college and fraternity, I sneaked local girls in for drinks and other delights. No holds were barred, and some passionate times were had by all. When my mother drove me up to Trinity for the start of my freshman year, she had told me emphatically that "naughty" women hang around college towns and I should be careful and stay away from them. At this point in life, Mother's warning seemed to compel me to spend my entire life at college looking for the "naughtiest" and trying to seduce them. Living in a fraternity house my final year made such a goal a snap for me to accomplish.

My major in history proved so fascinating to me that I happily immersed myself in all the courses associated with it. What's more, the history and religion professors became good friends, and they gave me more credit for research and hard work than I probably deserved. I managed to make the Dean's List a few times and became eligible to take honors courses involving reading and research with no class attendance required. This meant I could be off campus for weeks and still not be cutting classes, which was pretty much an invitation to the kind of self-indulgence I was majoring in. I never once thought I was in college to actually study and learn. I figured that college was there for my fun and my family and their money would always take care of me in later life.

I did have to show up for history classes and these I went to eagerly. The head of the history department had seen my name in a New York newspaper's society column as an attendee at the Autumn Ball at Tuxedo Park. I immediately became his favorite, even though I did not know why it was so important to him. It was while attending a dinner at his house to meet his charming daughter that I was introduced to his most cherished collection of books, forty years' worth of Social Registers. From the moment he discovered mention of me in the paper, my marks were better than I often thought I had earned. He would continually ask questions about my background, and the instant he found out that I had van Rensselaer, Livingston, Bayard and Stuyvesant's blood in me, I could do no wrong. Strangely, my roommate, Peter Winslow, fared less well at the hands of this professor, for he was in no Social Registers at all, despite the fact that the Winslows had been on the Mayflower and were a prominent Boston family. How amusing to be graded in such a snobbish way by the head of the Trinity history department! But what is genealogy but history, after all.

During this time there was a limited war being angrily fought in Korea. I expected to be drafted at any minute. To avoid this fate, I joined the United States Naval Reserve as a lowly seaman. Once a week I was required to go to an evening drill session, and for two weeks in the summer I had to attend a boot camp in Newport, Rhode Island.

After a bit more than a year, this nighttime naval activity was interfering with my social life, so, against Navy regulations, I stopped attending drill meetings. Understandably, the Navy did not take too well to this and sent orders calling me to active duty. Now it became apparent that I would have to leave college and go off to war as an enlisted man, a seaman third class. I immediately called my father, who, pulling all the strings he could, got me an interview with a high ranking Admiral in New York's Naval Headquarters. It did the trick, for I was immediately accepted into the Reserve Officer Candidate Program. This program let me stay in college, but it required that I attend, without fail, the weekly drills in Hartford and that I go to California to study for eight weeks during the summers over two years. These were to be the first summers of my life that I had ever had to work.

In 1952, after my junior year, I spent a hard summer working at the Reserve Officer Candidate School in Long Beach, California. I used every brain cell I ever had. When all the drilling, hard studying and Naval history indoctrination, stopped each weekend, I set about having a glorious typical Forrester Smith summer. I got on the phone and called two great young ladies. These two women who had been debutantes and had had lavish coming-out parties in New York. I had been invited to their dances and gotten to know them. One was Barbara Warner, who father was Jack Warner of Warner Brothers fame, and the other was Jean Stein, whose father was Jules Stein, the legendary head of MCA, the Music Corporation of America. They were the crème de la crème of Hollywood society, and I went up from the base at Long Beach each weekend to stay at their houses. What an eye-opener this was for a shy kid from the East who still bit his fingernails. The first dinner party I went to was a dream come true. I was seated next to Elizabeth Taylor. She was swathed in a long, loose, white Grecian-goddess toga, and her cleavage took my breath away as no bra was visible. Also at my table of eight were Jennifer Jones, Debbie Reynolds and Judy Garland. The men were Van Johnson, Monty Woolley and Tyrone Powers. With the aid of six or seven glasses of champagne, I became quite talkative and, as they loved to meet representatives of what they considered the "Eastern Establishment," the evening went swimmingly for me. I was a hit with them all. I danced with each of the women several times that evening. I got to know them well enough so that I was asked to join them often during that summer. I could not believe my luck.

On another amazing evening, while dining with a similar group, I went looking for a bathroom. I was directed by a maid towards the library of the house. In this beautifully paneled room Judy Garland was dancing rather naked with Cole Porter playing his own music on the piano. Porter informed me that Garland tended to do this if there was a full moon, and, as I looked out the window, I became aware that, indeed, the moon was full. I sat down on a sofa, squeezed my legs hard together so that I did not have to go to the bathroom. I was overwhelmed. I've always loved full moons since that night.

It seemed to me that Jennifer Jones always had bodyguards hovering around her. It was something I could not comprehend but I wanted to test it out so I asked her to dance. These fellows were not pleased when she accepted my invitation and moved about the room to be near her as we tripped the light fantastic. I think her husband wanted to make sure what she was up to was on the up and up.

It was a let down when the summer of 1952 was over but back to Trinity I went to continue my rather odd life of work and play.

On Sunday afternoons on the rare weekends at Trinity, that my friends and I would stay in Hartford, we might have milk punch parties. By the time the booze in the milk punch caught up with our systems, we were bombed beyond belief. It was nothing for us to consume ten mugs or so of the stuff at a sitting. After all, it was just creamy milk with some liquor flavoring it. Sometimes we would have mock funerals for friends who had passed out. Many a time I was laid out on the top of the downstairs piano while a fraternity brother banged out funeral hymns. My binges were bad and well documented by many due to a very noticeable horticultural disaster. I killed all the lovely ivy growing up the wall outside my room by throwing up out my window when suffering from intense hangovers. Alcohol was increasingly ruling my life then and I had no choice but to put up with vomiting.

On one Boston weekend, I staged a horror show that has embarrassed me ever since. The setting was a debutante dinner dance in honor of Jane Weld, held at Brookline's fashionable Country Club. At the cocktail party, which must have lasted for an hour before dinner, I consumed martini after martini after martini. By the time I got to the dinner table, I was virtually toxic with the stuff. The room seemed to be spinning in circles. We sat down and started the first course. Suddenly, to my horror,

I felt that I was going to throw up. No way could I make it to the men's room. I dove under the table, pretending to look for my napkin, and let fly from the depths of my guts. I then crawled out, thinking I had gotten away with this subterfuge, but, alas, I had filled the shoes and sprayed the feet of my dinner partner, Lee Bouvier, the sister of Jacqueline Bouvier Kennedy. A friend dragged me to his home, and, for the next week, I wrote letters of apology to at least ten people. It mortified me for years, and still does.

I was required by the college to attend chapel on a regular basis. It was one of the best things that could have happened to me, for I did believe in the power of prayer and knew deep down that the way I was living life was not as it should be. My connection to religion and prayer held my life together at that time and was the single thread of sanity that gave me hope and strength. I could talk to God in prayer, feel forgiven, and have a friend I could trust with my darkest secrets. I knew He existed and that He listened to me. He was the spark of the Divine within me. Yet sadly, at this time in my life I was living in fear and trepidation of God, for I thought of Him as a vengeful God ready to strike me down dead when I sinned. I was always asking for forgiveness, yet it didn't dawn on my sodden mind to stop drinking and change my life to get to know God better and to think of Him in terms of "love."

I had miraculously survived drunken car rides, wild sex bashes, heavy drinking, as well as studying rather lackadaisically, when, finally, the time came for me to graduate.

My mother and father had come to Hartford for my graduation, not as sober as one would have wished, but why should I have expected otherwise? At the lunch before the final graduation exercises, I myself got as drunk as possible, playing the scapegoat as wildly as I could. This was done to draw attention away from them.

My classmates at the lunch seemed sober, as far as I could ascertain, but I was far from it. In the gymnasium, where we went after lunch for the graduating exercises, I tripped on the stage as I received my degree and nearly went headfirst into the audience. As I turned and looked at my mother and father, I saw that they were politely applauding from the audience and not even looking at me. They were talking to old friends sitting next to them and were totally uninterested in me on my important day. I was their second son but the first to graduate from college, as my older brother had not gotten his diploma from Harvard. My siblings did not come to my graduation. I really never expected them to come.

In 1953, I was on the West Coast again to study navigation, gunnery, naval history and military drilling. I had an even wilder social summer than the year before with members of the Hollywood set I had met but I also had a lot more Naval responsibility. I had to cut down on my social life-but just a bit.

The Navy course of study was more difficult and intense in its second year. There was an immense amount of assigned reading to do every night and only about two hours available to do it in. Some evenings we were expected to read three gunnery manuals and memorize all the types of armament on a battleship. Needless to say, this was impossible to do, but the Navy was testing us to see how we stood up under the pressure. Some of the men became too stressed out and left the program quickly and quietly. I held my own and even thrived, for my memory was sharp. I was my company's student commander. I had never been a leader before and the experience was a revelation. I found that I could lead and be an officer.

On the day of my commissioning, the Secretary of the Navy, Thomas Gates, came to award us our commissioning papers. After the ceremony, the loudspeakers boomed that Forrester Clark Smith should report immediately to the Secretary on the podium. I started to tremble all over; for I was sure I was to be decommissioned and told that they had found out I had been in jail while at Trinity for messing with that slut in Hartford. To my astonishment, Secretary Gates said he wanted to have dinner with me, for he knew my family and had recognized my name when it was read off. Every admiral and officer on the base was instantly jealous of me, and they fawned over me in the Officers' Club all evening long. With the help of five or six rum-and-cokes, I played my aristocratic self to the hilt. The next day I was a full-blown hero to my instructors and classmates as well as very hung over.

A day later, when my head had cleared, I set forth for my first assignment, a destroyer berthed in Charleston, South Carolina. The Korean War was now over, and I was to be stationed on a high-speed destroyer minelayer, the USS Shannon, DM 25, in the Atlantic. This ship was preparing to partake in NATO exercises by shadowing the Soviet fleet in the Arctic Ocean. I felt like a pretty important guy at last, though I was starting at the bottom of the chain of command, as all junior officers do.

What the Navy did was help me grow up somewhat and reshape my opinions, values and lifestyle. I was completely on my own and strings could not be pulled so easily. I had to succeed on my merit, and that took some real willpower for me. There were fellow officers on board who had trained at the Naval Academy, and others who had been in the ROTC while working their way through college. They had lived far different lives from mine, but I soon realized that we could all work well together if I gave of myself. I found that I admired them for what they could do. They changed my outlook on people forever. One of the officers who shared my cabin had not had running water in his house in the Midwest and another had never seen the sea before the ROTC sent him on a summer training cruise. I had taken bathrooms for granted and had sailed every summer on my grandfather's yachts.

From time to time I was sent to technical schools to learn antisubmarine warfare, combat information center operations, officer-of-the-deck duties, and cryptography. I came out of all this schooling as the Shannon's general quarters officer of the deck, the ship's antisubmarine warfare officer, the top-secret cryptographer and, strangely, the officer in charge of administering liquor as a medicine. I had to account for the booze, so I never touched it even if we were at sea for two months. If I did not have liquor, I did not miss it. It was always that first sip that made me want more.

I got along famously with my fellow officers and the men in my division. I was an usher in four of my fellow officers' weddings and took part in three enlisted men's weddings, one that had "The Muskrat Ramble" played as the bride came down the aisle. I had a difficult time with the technicalities of naval gunnery and ship's machines, but I was a whiz at navigation and submarine warfare. I felt I was a great success as an officer in the U. S. Navy and was truly proud of myself for the first time.

I "saw the world" with the Navy. As an unmarried officer, I traded "standing duty watches" in foreign ports with the married officers. This ensured that I always got both the girls and the drinks in foreign ports. When I was stationed in Key West at antisubmarine warfare school, I flew round trip to Cuba most evenings, for about fifteen dollars, to enjoy glorious times with a Miss Rosemary de Havana. She was my favorite "friend" on the island. This was all in the pre-Castro days when Cuba was wide open and hedonistically swinging along with me. How could I have not like the benefits the Navy was giving me?

My Navy service brought me to Charleston for the first time, and it was love at first sight. Inevitably, as I had in most of the fashionable cities I ever visited, there, too, I had entrée—a key to the top social set. My mother's brother had married into a prominent Charleston family, the Rutledge's, and this opened every door to me. My fellow officers, on the other hand, hated the place, for it was far less welcoming if one had no connections there. I got to know six or seven ravishing beauties that I could ask out, and I liked Charleston so much that I spent the holidays of Thanksgiving, Christmas and Easter there. When not actually standing watch on the quarterdeck, I was entertained like a prince during these times. I went to debutante parties, weddings, beach picnics, plantations for shooting and the most fashionable church for services.

Charleston was and still is one of the most beautiful and aristocratic cities in the world. It had not yet become a tourist attraction and money was scarce. Everyone claimed the Yankees had seen to that. I might go to a dinner and have some of the plaster ceiling fall in my soup or my chair splinter, but it was all so gracious and Southern that these incidents mattered little. Once I fell downstairs at a dance when the banister gave way. Two butlers who were serving the guests picked me up gently. The parties usually had servants in threadbare uniforms and white gloves, with fingers of the gloves missing, but they knew how to serve beautifully. Nothing was forgotten, even when the hosts probably could ill afford to pay for the party. Style, beauty, elegance and charm were the bywords of Charleston society, and all of these things, I realized, were possible without money, or, at least, without the kind of money I'd been used to.

I grew up considerably, both mentally and physically, in Charleston. Being away from my family demanded of me that I act as a mature individual and not just as a role player in a dysfunctional family's survival structure. It was sad for me to return to my family after my stint in Charleston was over. To ease the pain of seeing my family again, I took two charming Charleston ladies, Libby Maybank—her father was one of South Carolina's United States Senators—and Alicia Walker, along with me for a vacation in Maine. It was glorious fun.

Still, after the Navy, I was not as mature as I would have liked to have been when I went to Boston to find work. I was still drinking far too much and was without assured financial means. I had cut my financial ties with my family when I entered the Navy, being the one son who chose not to be on an allowance, though I certainly could have used the money. My family had never provided any distribution of their capital to set up trust funds for us, nor had my grandparents left us a cent. All of us boys were given a clothing allowance when we reached fifteen. My mother considered these small stipends as her umbilical cord to control us. I hated that control so I cut the cord. Now I suffered as I looked for a job.

The Navy had done wonders for me, but being back in the environs of my family made me slip back slowly into dysfunctional behavior. I suffered from any number of anxiety attacks as I started my business career. Serious conversations with my parents about the future and what I intended to do had never taken place, and what I actually was suited for was a big question mark to me. My psyche had been so trodden upon that I had little if any drive to get ahead. If it had not been for my Navy experience, I would have been hopelessly mired in despondency. No foundation to support me was in place. With no drive to succeed instilled in me by my family, I had good reason to feel that the chances of my flourishing in the business world were dim. Training had helped with my naval career, but I had no training for business. For the time being, I could not seem to build on my successes as an officer, and the steps I now took were backward.

I had this picture taken in Hartford while I was at Trinity. I look as if I'm fifteen. I went to have it done at Bachrach, and it cost a bloody fortune. The idea was to give it to my family for Christmas. My mother and father paid little photographic attention to me or my brothers. Pictures were never thought of by my family. That rubbed against my grain, for all my rich friends constantly were having their pictures taken or painted and there was nary a one of me at home. I just had to be like others and feel wanted. When we were little, pictures were actually taken of us, but that was before the days of heavy drinking. I was twenty years old in this picture. Mother's remark upon getting a copy for Christmas was, predictably, "you're so pretty you should have been a girl."

This is my mother gazing fondly at her firstborn grandchild. Sheer love, I am certain, is passing between them. As you can see, she really kept the usual ravages of alcohol-induced unattractiveness away. With her hair dyed and an every night spreading of cold cream on her face, she held onto her looks. She was such a wonderful person when sober, and in this photo it shows.

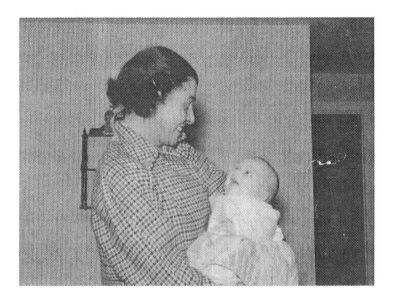

I am sitting on the front porch of my family's place in Bermuda. I probably have already had a few rum drinks even if it is only ten in the morning. I was not staying with them, but had come down on my own for College Week. Boy, did we raise hell! I think I looked pretty nifty in tropical garb. Notice the dangling cigarette. I was told it would stunt my growth but was already 6'2". On this trip I had such bad hangovers, mostly from drinking Pernod, that I soon learned every cure there was.

Sometimes it made the hangover worse when I gulped down Italian bitters. Our college group still won the College Week volleyball trophy, though none of us could see the ball.

This is the Psi Upsilon fraternity house at Trinity College. It's where I learned to drink in a really insane way. To hide my shyness, I would be bombed at the drop of a hat. I could tell some amazing horror stories about what went on in Pete's and my room (second floor bow window on the left). I adored college and the wild life in Psi U.

I couldn't find any pictures of my life at Trinity so here's one of my
fraternity brothers sitting on Psi Upsilon's front steps at our twenty-fifth
reunion. I seem to have grown a moustache and started to part my hair
oddly. I am in the middle of the front row. These guys and gals were
wonderful. Within two months of this picture, one of the wives arrived
in Boston at my front door for a little hugging and stroking.

I spent nearly three years on the *USS Shannon*. It was a destroyer used at times for high speed minelaying. Its home base was Charleston. Here it is tied up to a pier in St. Thomas where we operated in the winter by supposedly guarding the Caribbean and the Panama Canal from Russian subs. We were ashore a great deal. Married men stood the duty in foreign ports while the bachelors ran wild with liquor and women.

How the Captain, shown leaving the *Shannon* for the last time, ever put up with me I will never know. I was like a man from another planet. I gave him a party at my family's place when we docked in NY. He, the Executive Officer, my mother and my father, drank themselves under the table. The Captain fell across the hood of the taxi which came to take all the officers back to the ship and was badly bruised. Mother was unable to say goodbye and my father sat in a corner with a handkerchief stuffed in his mouth. Many of the officers, fifty percent at least who were Southern Baptists, were not quite as familiar with cocktail parties as I was—some literally lived in houses without running water and had worked their way through college. Thus, you can imagine how absolutely horrified I was with my family's behavior. It is I saluting on the far left.

While stationed at anti-submarine warfare school in Key West, a friend and I would fly over three nights a week to Cuba for wine, women and song. Pre-Castro Havana was an unbelievably wild city. We picked up some fabulous women there. I'm sure I had this picture taken only to fan an ego fire. I wanted to prove to the world that I was a real man who could sleep with attractive gals. A picture would tell it better than a boast. I wonder if I have any Cuban kids. When in foreign ports, I always made a point of spending the night with the women because, when I returned to the ship for duty in the morning everyone would realize where I had been.

Of all the things I ever did as a young man, getting commissioned in the United States Navy as an officer (and gentleman) was my greatest triumph. It did more for my self esteem than anything I had ever done. I did it on my own, did it well and was near the top of my class and a cadet officer to boot. The day I received my commission from the Secretary of the Navy, Thomas Gates, was a triumph.

I really loved being in the Navy. I was not a particularly good officer, but tried hard and was given quite good assignments aboard my destroyer. The Navy offered me a broader idea of what people were like and for the first time I realized that socially elite did not define humanity. Far from it. I was fascinated by all my new experiences. Even crashing into sixty foot waves over the Arctic Circle in the winter was interesting to me, though shore leave and liberty were my favorite times.

EIGHT

There are major steps in a young adult's life that are so complex they require a tremendous amount of rational thinking and planning. Entering into marriage, having children, finding a job, getting living quarters, developing a spiritual life and making friends all are tasks that are absorbing, demanding and fully challenging. Facing such issues as an insecure person and as someone with already-developed bad habits is a poor formula for success. Factor in an immense tragedy, one that is completely unforeseeable, and one's life can fall utterly apart.

When I returned to the Northeast, I missed the Navy and, particularly, Charleston. I was still much too insecure to stand on my own. I needed relatives and close friends around me to keep me propped up. That's what role-playing's web does to a dysfunctional person. I had been forced by world events, namely the Korean War, to go into the Navy, but since that was the most controlling of all environments, I had had little trouble surviving it without family. I had been told what to do during every second of my Navy life.

Setting out on my own to pursue a career in business was an obvious next step. In September of 1955, I moved to Boston to do just that. I knew my family connections in the area could support me, at least non-financially, and that I could lean, also, on my many friends from college who were settling in and around the city. Their presence made my move there an easy choice. Boston had Charleston's quaintness and intimacy so I soon fell under its spell.

I found an extraordinary, whole-floor apartment that looked out over the Public Gardens, Boston's equivalent to New York's Central Park. It was at 75 Beacon Street, a fancy location. With the pay I had received for mustering out of the Navy, I fixed it up in a rather elegant manner. I found roommates—my brother Bayard and an old friend, Charlie Pingree—and off we roared to address ourselves to the business of business, partying and sports. During the weekdays, we all labored at our jobs. I had gotten one in advertising, and both my brother and Charlie worked for car companies. We played hard on the weekends, and some weekday nights as well. We slowly but surely met lots of other people our age who were living in town and who, like us, now were beginning adult lives on their own.

Whenever there was snow, we drove to Franconia, New Hampshire, to ski, and whenever I could, I went fox hunting or riding either on the North Shore or in the Dover area with my uncles, Nat and Tim Clark. I was healthy enough and good enough to play the number-one position for the second squad of the Racquet Club Squash Team in the Evening Squash League. I appeared to be living a relatively normal life, though scads of fears continued to fester in turmoil underneath the façade I had constructed. I was vaguely aware of their debilitating effect, but alcohol was a fine mask behind which to hide. I did not miss any chance to drink.

My job was with a large Boston advertising agency for thirty-five dollars a week. The days of my high living on Navy pay were gone, but roommates sharing expenses made living manageable. One of the main reasons I was hired by the Dowd Agency, Boston's second biggest advertising firm, was because my name was so similar to my Uncle Tim (Forrester) Clark's. He was the owner of major businesses throughout Boston, and Dowd was obviously anticipating making use of my supposed connections through him. Just the way I carried myself and spoke spelled "class" to them. Dowd was a very Irish firm, and Dowd wanted a bit of polish in the form of a Boston Brahmin working for him. My upbringing seemed never to fail me and give me an advantage over others. It was totally unfair, but there was no reason to fight it, and, in fact, I liked it. There was no way my friends or employee could spot what demons— what hell—lurked inside me.

My assignment, at the start, was to inspect major grocery stores' displays throughout the Boston area. I was to observe the way they marketed specific products, the accounts, which my agency wanted. I did not mind doing this roaming around the city at first, for it meant I could set my own hours. But it wasn't terribly creative so, eventually, boredom set in. At this point I pushed my boss to let me get involved in actual advertising work; success soon followed as I worked my way up the agency ladder. Eventually I was writing copy for some of the food lines we represented. If I came up with a slogan, I was supposed to test it on the public. I accomplished this by stationing myself on the corner of Boylston and Arlington Streets, in front of Shreve, Crump & Low, where I would stare at the jewels, and stop people to ask them to choose the best slogan from my list. Naturally, I made sure that my ideas won the most votes from the men and women on the street when it came to tallying the results. I did not consider this cheating but, rather, a smart way to get ahead in business.

I was responsible—and got credit—for some well-recognized lines on products. "Sooner or Later You'll Buy Educator" was one of mine. Educator Baking Company was a mammoth New England baking firm, and I became a star in the Dowd firmament when my slogan was plastered on hundreds of thousands of boxes of their baked goods. The agency also used me as a model in ads for cars, cigars and drinking straws. I was their suavest employee, the thinking went, and, as such, was very useful. My upbringing set me apart from my coworkers, and it was easy to impress clients by trotting me out. The way I was treated at Dowd suited me because I loved showing off. I also found that showing the portfolio of my ads to guests at parties was a fantastic way to attract new girlfriends. I was a good model.

The birth control pill had not yet been developed, which meant that sexual intercourse with nice girls was too risky. Who needed a shotgun marriage or parents counting the months before the delivery of a child after a wedding? Most of the young women I hung out with were virgins on the day of their marriages. Some had been affectionately and thoroughly mauled in their bedrooms before their weddings, but their virginity had not been compromised and they were left intact. They might have gone as far as they could without doing "the deed" so they could still be considered pure. All this is not to say that "all nice girls" did not sleep with men. Some did, but they remained in the minority before reliable contraception came on the scene. As I was always taking out nice girls, I had no fear of rejection for they would only go so far. "No" was understood to mean " no farther."

The uninhibited parties in my apartment attracted more young women than I was able to handle. Needless to say, they were all well bred and eligible. At one of these bashes, I made the acquaintance of one, Jean Sturgis, who would turn out to be my sister-in-law. She saw me dance in my nightshirt on my mantelpiece, and, as I found out much later, she told her parents about the wild evening she'd had with Forrester Smith. This was long before I had met my future in-laws, but when we finally did come face to face, I'm sure that they considered me debauched and uncivilized and not the polite young man I was trying to be to impress them. My face like that portrait of Oscar Wilde's Dorian Grey, had not quite begun to crack. I had been nicknamed Dorian in college by my history professor, and his prophecy was about to be realized.

Such wild parties meant I was drinking a lot, and alcohol consumption led to severe hangovers and depression. Alcohol lifts one up when first consumed, and then drops a person down as it wears off. My depression was starting to become more pronounced as I drank more and more. Occasionally, if I found myself alone in Boston, I would spend weekends in bed to help me deal with my loneliness. I would only occasionally get up for a drink. It started to dawn on me that I basically needed alcohol to make my life worthwhile. On top of the frequent binges, there were few, if any, evenings that went by sober. Yet, no matter how much I consumed, I was convinced I was not an alcoholic, for I never drank in the morning to feel better, as many of my friends did, nor did I drink at lunch for I did not want to ruin my day. I knew if I took one drink while lunching, I probably would have more and would not be able to accomplish anything in the way of work for the rest of the day. A martini at noon was the kiss of death for me. This illusion of control over my drinking falsely assured me that I was certainly not an alcoholic like my parents or some of my friends. On more than one occasion, I found I could stop for a week or so, but I did not do this often. The only way I managed this was to promise God I would not drink for a certain period. I was terrified of God and thought I'd be struck dead if I broke the promise.

Around my family, I still acted as a mascot or a scapegoat. I could be pouty, sullen, wisecracking, foolish or even rude. I was an exceptionally good scapegoat, trying so hard to take the focus off my family. I was a marvelous mascot, as well, for in an instant I could become a sweet and social character, whenever my family was on its best behavior. With my friends I tried to be Mr. Congeniality, but it was not always possible if I felt depressed. Since I wanted their attention and affection, I hid my true feelings of sadness, for nobody wants a sad sack around.

At age twenty-four I still gnawed my fingernails. It looked as if I had bloody stumps for fingers, and I rarely had one out of my mouth. This ugly habit lessened only somewhat when I began smoking three packs of cigarettes a day. With these coffin nails in my beak, there was little room for fingers. I smoked a pipe occasionally, in an effort to appear dashing and impressive. The trouble with a pipe was that I inhaled every puff and coughed constantly. Smoking became a real addiction, and I only reduced the number of cigarettes on which I puffed away each day when some of my favorite sports required it. It was hard to smoke while jumping a horse over a steeplechase course or playing tennis or skiing. From childhood, I had been told that smoking stunted one's growth and by the time I reached six feet two inches, I prayed that this was so.

After my first year in Boston, when I realized that most of my friends were getting married, I seriously started to look for a wife. As some of my women friends had told me I would make a great catch, I felt happier about dating. I found it was a cinch to get close to nice girls when they were chasing me and looking me over as a potential partner. There also was less chance of being rejected if they wanted me. This added a new twist to the battle of the sexes, and as a chased rather than a chaste man, I began to blossom around women.

I met Harriet (Patsy) Sturgis, who was to become my wife, at the marriage of one of her first cousins. We were both in the wedding party. She always said she had met me years before at a party on the banks of the Farmington River when she had come back to visit Miss Porter's school.

From every point of view, she was the perfect woman for me. She was attractive, but not so much so that others would chase after her, she had just been jilted by the love of her life so it was a perfect setup for me to step into with no competition, she had splendid family lines (including Cabots, Lowells, Putnams, Jacksons, Cunninghams, Morses and practically every other family that had made Boston great), and she had gone to Miss Porter's, the only school my mother could even speak about.

Her parents lived very grandly in a large house with hot and cold running servants, lovely gardens, priceless antiques, greenhouses and all the other accouterments that go with the territory. I certainly did not marry her for her money—though my father said I did—but I was thrilled she had it.

Even though my family had set up no trust fund for me, I never questioned whether Patsy had more than a modest allowance from her family, along with the salary she earned as a registered nurse. I was to find out, once we were married, that the Sturgises had a great fortune and many trust funds supporting them but, by the time I learned this, I had fallen madly in love with her and was married to her. Thus her wealth was only frosting on the cake for me.

I spent most of our engagement in one of her family's guest rooms, not only to be near her, but, as a man with somewhat of a controlling nature, I wanted her always around me. Longing to marry Patsy and be her life partner, I never wanted her out of my sight. I needed to know that nobody was telling her bad things about me and that she did only things I wanted her to do.

Since she loved me with all her heart, our engagement period was sheer heaven. We got to really know each other very well, even intimately, but she was a virgin on our marriage day. Though I continually pushed her to give up this state when we necked, we never took that final step till the evening of our wedding day, May 4, 1957, in the Ritz Hotel in Boston. It was the very same place where I had asked her to marry me six months earlier.

I adored Patsy's mother and father. Her mother, Harriet Morse Sturgis, had debuted in Boston the same year my mother did, and they had been friends during their school days at Miss Windsor's School. Then Harriet went off to Foxcroft and my mother to Farmington, so their relationship lapsed. When she was three, Harriet had been severely burned from her waist to her nose after her party dress had caught fire as she jumped over a candle playing "Jack be nimble, Jack be quick." With operation after operation, thirty-seven in all, and skin graft after skin graft, she became an absolutely stunning woman but decidedly scarred. She was so incredible that I and others who knew and loved her hardly noticed that she had this disfigurement. She, however, always felt that people were staring at her and it made her uncomfortable. When she was in Venice with her husband after the Second World War, some children in a group started to point at her and laugh. The Sturgis's immediately changed their plane tickets and flew home.

It was not long after meeting Patsy and starting to call upon her at her family's house that I began to love her mother far more than I did my own. She seemed a gift from heaven, a figure I easily could put on a pedestal. She ran a wonderfully efficient house in a magnificent manner, she was involved with countless charities, she had presided over the fabled Vincent Club, she made a wonderful life for her husband, she dressed beautifully, and she was always thoughtful of others. I enjoyed every moment I spent with her.

Patsy's father, George Putnam Sturgis, was a prominent Boston doctor and one of the fairest and kindest men I have ever met. He went out of his way always to do the right thing and to help everyone. He was the pillar of his family and cherished his wife and four children. The only fault I ever found with him was that he made incredible issues out of dividing, amongst his children, such items as money, presents or furniture. He did this so exactly and so evenly that it became a fetish. For example, Patsy was given a mink coat by her grandmother on her eighteenth birthday, so Dr. Sturgis felt that all his other daughters had to have one on their eighteenth birthdays, whether they wanted one or not. One sister, who was never out of blue jeans or off a horse, had a full-length mink coat thus bestowed upon her. I think she used it as a dog bed or horse blanket. She was madly in love with her animals.

Patsy's father also split lovely sets of leather bound books and export porcelain dinner services so that no one would get one speck more than the other. His older brother had, by the English and American aristocracy rules of primogeniture, inherited all the family gold watches, silver and other family mementos. Thus, the doctor was going to make certain that nothing like this happened again in his family. He had coveted a certain gold timepiece, but the brother, who inherited it and knew this, never had the courtesy to offer it to him or present him with another like it. It rankled him always.

George Sturgis finally got far more than his share of valuable objects when his wife, Harriet, an only child, inherited all her father's and mother's possessions. Harriet's father, Robert Cunningham Morse, had made a considerable fortune when he was the founding and senior partner of Paine, Webber, Jackson and Curtis. The company and he had been instrumental in financing the original underwriting of the Gillette Company, among many others. Robert Morse left behind many gold watches, as well as numerous silver pieces made by Paul Revere, a treasure trove of 18th century furniture and forty barrels of fine export porcelain. Patsy's maternal grandparents were major collectors and her grandmother was a great friend of my Clark grandfather, the supplier of my liquor closet at Trinity. They had played bridge together for years at a dollar a point, a huge sum to gamble in those days. My grandfather never felt a bit of remorse at losing my grandmother's money, and Mrs. Morse could well afford it if she lost.

Our wedding, surprisingly, was great fun for me. I had no butterflies or doubts. Consuming champagne and being the center of attention helped, as well. I arrived early at the church, decked out in a top hat, to greet guests as they arrived. Invitees were a bit shocked to see the groom rushing around shaking hands and kissing people. They envisioned me nervously waiting in the vestry with the best man, but the best man was not feeling very well and the ushers were late so I did the job for a while outside the church.

I had an army of ushers compared to Patsy's small coterie of bridesmaids. I obviously was the flamboyant one of this pair and she the conservative. We had nearly two hundred and fifty guests come to our reception at the Sturgis's house. Later in the afternoon, we were driven away from this mob scene in a large 1931 Cadillac (made in the year I was born) to start our life as a couple. Little did we realize it, or even think about it, but we had everything in the world going for us at that particular time. We had social position, money, a house we'd purchased on Boston's North Shore, many, many friends and her incomparable family. We were as happy as clams at high tide and all my insecurity had gone away. At least for the moment it slept.

Like newlyweds in every walk of life, we had aspirations and dreams dictated by our class. We lived in a socially acceptable area, we belonged to the right clubs, we had a house suitable for entertaining, we joined the boards of acceptable charitable organizations, we had help in the house doing domestic work, we gardened, we played certain sports, we worked at leadership jobs. We traveled extensively and we started a family quite soon in order to pass on our inheritance and provide grandchildren. These were the things our background demanded of us. Our blessed life ran smoothly on the surface, though trouble was running deep within it. I still suffered from many problems that money and position could not solve. I worked hard to understand my hang-ups and discussed some of them, though far from enough, with Patsy. Still, in this era of my new marriage and new manhood, the things within me that were unhealed and made me unhappy were mostly plastered over. I let little show.

I was so proud of myself on my wedding night that, at last, I had a wife. I had always convinced myself deep down that I was unlovable and would never take this step. Yet, here I was, a married man making love to my very own wife who was loving me in return. We did not sleep much. I felt as if I had invented sex and was convinced that I performed brilliantly. My dear new wife certainly had no clue what she was getting into, for, as I have said, my fears—of inadequacy, rejection, dysfunctionality and more—were buried deep inside me. I was a much more complicated person than she had ever bargained for or even imagined. I masked as much of the hell as I possibly could behind drink and bravado.

Returning from our month-long honeymoon at the Coral Beach Club in Bermuda, we settled into our newly purchased and renovated house in Beverly Farms on Boston's North Shore. I now worked in a real estate office nearby and I could come home every day for lunch. Early in our marriage this was fun, but eventually Patsy found she needed more space and I stopped. (The Duchess of Windsor once said a couple should "marry for better or worse but never for lunch.") Pretty quickly, after settling in, I realized that, for a better paycheck and Patsy's and my sanity, I needed to get a more demanding job. As luck would have it, I was called by the Shore Country Day School, where I had been volunteering my services with the sports department, and asked to teach all the basic subjects in the sixth grade. They had a problem with the present teacher, who was letting the kids run wild. They wanted my disciplinary skills, which had been evident in my sports work with the school, to help calm the class down and get it back on the proper learning curve.

I leapt at the chance and happily went to work there. After three years teaching the sixth grade, I became an English teacher for the entire seventh grade—sixty students in three sections—and the head of the English department, in charge of developing the curriculum for all the grades of this 400-pupil country day school. The seventh graders had raging hormones, making them somewhat wild. They were a handful, but at the same time, absolutely delightful.

I stayed at Shore Country Day for seven years, when I suddenly found that the taxes on the house that we had built on West Beach were more than my salary. I could still afford to teach, in fact, because Patsy had a great deal of money, but my pride would not let me. After all these years, during which time I also commuted to Harvard to study for a master's degree, my pay was a mere $6,000 a year. Private schools gave faculty the chance to teach at the highest level while being paid at the lowest. As my mother and father still controlled the purse strings of the Smith and Clark monies, I could count on them only for an occasional present but no steady income, ever.

Eleven months after Patsy and I were married, the most incredible and glorious event in our lives transpired. My wife gave birth to an exquisite baby girl, Harriet Morse Smith. I was a father and could not believe it. While growing up, I never dreamed I'd ever be able to create a child, for I thought I would never be man enough. Yet, at the instant of her birth, I understood that I was truly a male and felt so filled with love and pride at the safe delivery of our wonderful child. I was in a dream world and so excited and energized that I must have made sixty calls to proclaim her arrival. Patsy, upon learning it was a girl and fearing someone might nickname the baby "Hatsy," beat everyone to the gun and flatly announced that the baby would be called "Bambi." Since I had been given the choice of the Christian name, "Harriet," Patsy got the choice of the nickname.

For days and days my feet hardly touched the ground, and I kept marveling as I peered into the hospital's nursery window. The fact that I actually now had my very own family was almost too heady. After we had all left the Children's Hospital and gone home, I became a hands-on father and helped feed, change and cuddle Bambi. I swore to myself that she would never have to have a childhood anything like mine and that she would have everything she ever needed, starting with love and support.

After Bambi's arrival, my mother could not help telling me she was glad it was a girl for, as I really should have been one, I now had a daughter to bring up. She also insisted that I immediately enroll Bambi at Farmington. It was the sort of conversation that guaranteed I went home and got stewed.

Within two years we were blessed with our second child, Forrester C. Smith, Jr., Patsy immediately dubbed him "Chippy." My father was delighted with the news and informed me, "It takes a man to make a man." This was probably the first real compliment he had ever given me without the insidious "but" word attached to it. Mother, for her part, said that Chippy should have been a girl because I would be a poor role model. She was convinced that she and my father had been superb ones and she continually pointed out that my brother Philip was the personification of perfect upper-class masculinity. He had gone to Groton and Harvard, joined the AD Club and worked on the New York Stock Exchange. These were her guidelines for complete success. At this point in his life, in fact, Phil had not graduated from Harvard and was "sitting" on a seat on the New York Stock Exchange that my father had owned.

Our two children were the apples of our eyes, and we doted on them. Though wanting to be their primary caregivers, we did not wish to cope with them on a twenty-four-hour basis. As we had a delightful, never-ending social life, we employed two women from Gordon College who came to live with us. They minded the children whenever we went out to play with our friends. This arrangement was one that suited Patsy and me very well. We fed, read, played and prayed with our children but also danced the nights away at all sorts of parties.

Our intention was to make our children's connections with us as parents the antithesis of mine when I was a child. We thought we were accomplishing this, but the truth was we were setting up exactly the childhood for them I had had. It was about compartmentalizing one's life in a way that kept parents absent for a good deal of the time. Certainly with my hidden problems of depression, emotional dysfunctionality and excessive alcohol consumption, the children would suffer eventually, but, for the present, the distractions of our busy schedule and the presence of wonderful nannies helped smooth this over. Money bought us some security and peace on the surface.

The social whirl on the North Shore was ongoing, somewhat decadent and heavily oriented toward huge cocktail parties, stylish dinners on Friday and Saturday nights, dances at the Myopia Hunt Club or the Essex County Club, coming-out parties, and various receptions surrounding sporting events such as fox hunting, Harvard football games or golf tournaments. It never seemed to quiet down. It was much the same life I had known in Far Hills.

After three years in our first house, we built, on a beautiful, four-acre piece of land directly on the ocean, a large house designed to accommodate all sorts of entertaining. We wanted to have big, or even huge, parties, run easily with grace and style. Thus, we designed the house primarily around the orderly flow of guests. The upstairs bedrooms were big and each had a bath. We were more lavish with our own accommodations, for we had a large corner suite with all the closets and dressing space necessary for the demands of our social life. Patsy had a shoe closet, a hat closet, an evening dress closet, a winter dress closet, a summer dress closet and even a jewel safe embedded in the bricks of the fireplace. Obviously I made sure I had my own dressing area in our big bathroom. Dressing rooms are *de rigueur* for the upper class.

The house was rather special, particularly after we put on two additions, so we were asked regularly to put it on fund-raising tours for charities. Many magazines ran features about it. The antiques, both Patsy's and mine, were exceptionally elegant. We gave dances, dinners, luncheons, and teas, hunt breakfasts, fireworks displays and cocktail parties. There was a running beach party always going on in the spring, summer and fall, for we had a marvelous sandy strand to which we issued an open invitation to all our friends. I was forever asking people up from the beach for drinks and then would often have them stay for supper. Not only were our liquor bills staggering but our food bills were outrageous. We were enmeshed in this lifestyle and we loved it. We could well afford the deluxe life.

In the summers we practically ran a hotel. Relatives arrived to visit and dug in for long stretches of time. Their departure at the end of their holidays saw my wife and children collapse in exhaustion and pray for the day when my mother and father, who were in Maine, would stop drinking excessively and long enough to allow these relatives to make pleasant visits to them. In truth, Patsy was not as thrilled as I was about the "hotel" we seemed to be running for my family each summer, our house being preferred over that of my parents. She always ran the place in her own neat and orderly way but the visitors turned it upside down. She was also irritated and upset by the fact that some of these relatives never asked us to their places nor shared with us, during the long winters, the houses they rented in warmer climes. What I loved was that during these visits we drank all day long and I could act out my scapegoat role at my brother's bidding.

Summers, at least as long as I was teaching, were mine to use as playtime and play I did. We joined The Myopia Hunt Club, renowned for its fast-paced style. There I could ride, hunt, swim, golf or play tennis, but each was really just a prelude to heavy drinking.

Though in many ways I was proud of myself as a husband and father, I was still subconsciously unsure of myself amid the Myopia crowd. It was not because my friends there were in any way different from me, for they weren't. We all had the same social background, yet my lack of self-esteem made me feel they were more sophisticated and moved at higher speed than I. Hitting a golf ball with people watching, trying to serve a fast ball while playing tennis, or making a move at the backgammon table, all brought on intense anxiety and fear of criticism, another form of rejection. As I always had, I fortified myself with alcohol. The results, unfortunately, were starting to become a matter of diminishing returns. I was getting the shakes from too much booze—a sure way to invite unwanted scrutiny—and even worse, I tended to get nasty from feeling so terribly—a sure way to be rejected by friends.

When I was drunk, I would quarrel with, insult, or stop speaking to anyone who argued with me even in the slightest. My arrogance was awful. When I sobered up the next day, I'd be terrified about what I might have said and done the night before. The remorse I felt only compounded my insecurity, for it riddled my mind with regrets and stress. I then drank to hide these new fears as well as those old anxieties. People stayed away from me when I drank. One evening at a huge hunt ball in Boston, as Patsy and I were being photographed for the cover of the Boston Globe's rotogravure magazine, a person I never particularly liked passed by and hissed something unpleasant at me. I vividly remember what a foul mood I was in, having fought with Patsy all the way into town over whether or not we should even be going to this party. Minutes after the man's ugly remark, I stormed furiously out of the hotel and drove home, leaving poor Patsy to manage by herself.

The next day I came back to Boston to pick her up at my parents', where she had hastily arranged to stay the night after I left her. I was not going to be forgiven quickly. When the fancy picture appeared about three Sundays later, splashed across the magazine's front page, we looked the essence of elegance in our evening clothes—a scarlet tail coat and a stunning Balenciaga evening dress—and nobody would have guessed the petulant scene the male half of the society couple had staged that evening.

Four years after Chippy's birth, Charles Russell Lowell Smith (Welly) was born to us on June 22, 1964. We had not planned on another baby, for not only were Patsy's reproductive organs giving her problems but also we were satisfied with our family as it was. Two children, one of each sex, both of whom we wanted to give constant attention and affection to, were enough. Patsy's pregnancies were always a real trial, and false labor every two minutes for months before her delivery day was debilitatingly painful. She had ceased using the pill three years before Welly's conception, so it should have been no real surprise to us when the doctor proclaimed her pregnant.

So, given everything, we were overjoyed that Patsy was pregnant because children were themselves bringers of joy. My father's sole remark to me at Welly's birth was that he knew just why we had given him his name. "It was in order to get our hands on the Lowell money." Mother was drinking enough at this point so she was probably not quite sure whether we had a new child or not. When she did finally realize it, she never bothered to learn his name and called him "Lowie" until the day she died.

Our expanding family and our desire to continue partying created an urgent need for us to get a real, full-time nanny. Both Bambi and Chippy went to the Brookwood School and needed to be driven back and forth as well as to be taxied long distances to allow their exhaustive social lives to flourish. They were nearly as heavily scheduled as we were. I was always golfing, playing tennis or sailing, and Patsy and I, when not at parties or sporting events, went to meetings at the children's school, political town meetings and church events on a regular basis. There was no way we could have a little baby at home and still keep up our lives without getting live-in help. Luckily, we soon found a wonderful Welsh woman, Jean, whose arrival, sadly, somehow let me slip slowly into the habit of spending less and less time with my children. I partied even more and so did Patsy. Most times it was I who insisted we go out, but I did not have to work too hard to drag her along. She, at least, was able to say "no" to people, whereas I could not.

As alcohol continued to creep up on me and become a stronger part of my life, I started to forget what I had done or said the evening before. This was worrying, but only fleetingly, for nothing seemed likely to get between me and my six "Beefeater" martinis, or six "Old Forester" bourbons, each evening. I congratulated myself that I could still stop drinking for long stretches of time, such as during Lent, when I tried to prove to others, and myself particularly Patsy, that I did not need it. The fact that one was too many and a hundred not enough drove me to go on the wagon for sometimes up to a year to prove my point. Those times were great when I was sober, but I always started with a vengeance again.

After I stopped teaching, I once again plunged into the world of advertising and public relations. The money I now earned was far better than the $35 a week that I had made nine years before. The firm that hired me was only twenty miles from my house, so I never had a long commute nor did I ever miss the witching hour of six o'clock when my first cocktail of the evening got poured and sipped. I would arrive home at five thirty to find the children fed, Patsy bathed and dressed, and our supper planned. What else was there for me to do but unwind with a drink, or two, or three? Once, after I found that I was having six drinks a night, I told Patsy that I was going to have only one each evening. To hold to this promise I poured myself one martini only, but the trick was I was using a small vase that looked a bit like a normal glass. It fooled Patsy, but, then again, she was having plenty of cocktails.

One July and August, the actor Steve McQueen rented the Wigglesworth place abutting our property. He was on the North Shore to make "The Thomas Crown Affair" and had rented this spectacular house. His wife Neile and their two children, exactly the ages of my two older ones, were delightful, and, from the moment they arrived, our two families had a blast. Not only was I asked to have a speaking part in the movie, but also we were dining, helicoptering and dune-buggying with Steve all over Massachusetts and New Hampshire. We flew to New York on shopping trips with them and also hung out with the Jewisons, as Norman Jewison was directing the picture. We entertained their friends, Faye Dunaway among them, on a regular basis, for the chef they brought from California did not like to cook with Yankee ingredients. The newspapers were forever splashing stories about us on their front pages, with the result being that my ego soared higher every day. When Steve sent me a note that said simply, "I dig you," I went into the stratosphere.

About seven months later, I arranged to have the film open in Boston as a charity benefit. Patsy and I were asked by the studio to be the guests of the McQueen's at all the premiere festivities. I had always wanted to be mobbed and cheered and now my dream came true beyond my wildest expectations. I signed autographs on every pad that was pushed under my nose. People assumed I must be famous if I was with the McQueen's.

We were all on the front pages of all the Boston papers the next day, which caused me to go out and buy at least fifty copies. What I was going to do with them I didn't actually know, but if I could send them to everyone I'd ever known, wouldn't my ego soar!

What I seemed unable to notice was that I was becoming a carbon copy of my mother and father. I was getting more hellish to live with every day. On and off, I was badly depressed, yet not a soul, including myself, recognized this illness in me. For generations, my family had been afflicted with depression, and many of them had lived their whole lives without a clue that they were depressed. They merely thought they were in low spirits and so drank to cheer themselves up. Now, I was joining their ranks, with each drink only making my condition worse. But that was how it had been for them, too. The pattern never changes, but when one is trapped inside it, it's impossible to recognize.

When I was depressed, I felt unwanted and ill at ease with people. I wanted nothing to do with the world around me. When I got high, I wanted to embrace the world and usually became too garrulous. When I began to feel my little world crumbling, I tried to save it by controlling those around me. I began shoring up my world by any method I could think of. Sometimes this consisted of my storming out of the house so that Patsy would then beg me to come back and tell me how much she needed me. I was unreasonable and dictatorial, it was my way or no way, and I paid little if any attention to anyone's wishes or needs. I was like sand under the skins of those around me and at my job. I felt used and abused but, in reality, it was I that was using and abusing everyone. Booze was wreaking havoc with my depressed system.

My job at American Mutual Insurance Company, the place I'd gone to when I stopped teaching, was moderately interesting. But I stopped being satisfied with it after just a few years. Its bureaucracy was a horror to me, as I was too controlling a person to be regulated by this mammoth company. We could not leave at night until a bell went off at exactly 4:35 p.m., a buzzer announced the noon meal at the company cafeteria at 11:45 a.m., the meal ended promptly at 12:45 p.m., when another bell rang. Although I was publishing, writing and editing the company's monthly sales magazine, as well as editing the weekly sales report, daily news sheet and annual report, it simply was not stimulating or imaginative enough work. I found my creative juices were being too confined to the world of insurance. I resigned.

Before very long, I was involved in fundraising and public relations for an offshoot of the Harvard Medical School, the Blood Research Institute. They had asked me to be the assistant business manager and also put me to work on fundraising. This unique institution had invented the blood centrifuge that fractionated blood into its many components. If a patient needed just clotting factors, they got only those out of a whole unit of blood, or if a person needed merely plasma for burns, they could be infused with that one element. I rapidly learned to speak this medical game of fractionating, and I imagined myself a doctor. I was frustrated that I could not do the actual scientific work. It seemed to me that raising money and doing budgets was a trifle dull, but I was delighted that I was my own boss and making a decent salary. The work of the researchers fascinated me and I spent many, many hours with them. Some of them soon became fast friends. Once again, I had proved to myself that I could do a fantastic job with any project I undertook. At the same time I could not give myself credit for the success I was having there for lack of confidence in myself.

I would have been happy to stay at the BRI, but when the Boston Symphony Orchestra and Pops, a magical institution that had the admiration and affection of legions around the world, came after me to manage their development and public relations department, I could not refuse. The job proved to be fascinating, allowing me to interact with people far and wide across the multifaceted world of the arts. It required creativity and was all-consuming. We were always putting on extraordinary benefit events that I helped stage as if I had been born to the job—and, in a sense, I had. I saw more of the globe than I had in the Navy and I dined with presidents, queens, kings, prime ministers, princes, princesses and assorted dukes and duchesses.

Fundraising became the driving force of my life. I had solicited money for churches, local YMCAs, and schools, but now I was in the big leagues. David Rockefeller, Jr., Arthur Fiedler, Fran Fahnestock and

I pulled off some triumphant trips and events while raising millions of dollars. My health suffered from a schedule that kept me busy six days and nights a week, but I loved every second of it. And, in fact, I hadn't left the blood world completely behind me, for, as I worked my contacts and donors, I learned to squeeze blood from a stone!

Through my Symphony connections I was appointed one of the coordinators responsible for setting up the National Endowment for the Arts. I organized all the major cultural institutions in New England to muster together their constituencies into a cohesive lobbying and political force. I spoke throughout the region about the disgraceful lack of support the United States gave to the arts when other countries gave so much more. At the time our country averaged twenty-seven cents per person, compared to four dollars per person in Germany and two dollars and eighty cents in Britain. I asked that letters be sent to Congress asking for support of the arts by allocating at least a dollar per citizen. It obviously worked, for, eventually, the National Endowment for the Arts came into being. I also learned from this special assignment how to be a public speaker, for I addressed thousands of people and was forever being interviewed on television. This was quite an achievement for a person with no self-esteem but as with every job I ever had, I pushed myself to excel. I desperately needed praise.

Each year Patsy and I traveled to some relatively exotic spot with our children for Easter vacation. We went to Nassau, Jamaica, Bermuda, Portugal, Spain and Majorca, among many other places. We would rent a house and hire a driver and really get to know the place. I made a point of finding out ahead of time who were the important people living there and I would then secure from friends the necessary letters of introduction. As the children were usually cared for by women we hired in the various places, our socializing stayed much the same, whether on the North Shore or away. We wove a network of friends throughout the world and I visit them to this day.

When we were at the Mill Reef Club in Antigua, I was asked by a scion of a very famous family to play golf. He was a quadriplegic, but I wanted to get to know him and I assumed he was one person whom I could beat. I readily accepted his invitation and that afternoon arrived on the first tee at the appointed time. He was with his caregiver and caddy, and I with another caddy. My companion won the flip to go first. He was hoisted up out of his wheelchair to tee off. He had the braces on his legs and arms locked in the straight position and then his ball placed on the tee. His aide then pulled his arms back into an upright position and released them. It was a magnificent swing, and the ball went straight as an arrow for at least two hundred and fifty yards. This continued for eighteen holes until I was soundly beaten. Not many people can claim a paralyzed person trounced them at golf.

On Patriot's Day morning of April 19th, 1966, I dragged myself out of bed with my usual hangover and lit the first of my cigarettes, one of the about sixty I would have that day. After breakfast, plans were made to go with the children to a local nursery to buy fruit trees and lilies to plant. Bambi was eight years old and bored to death with the thought of this activity so she managed to make plans of her own. She wanted to visit a friend in Manchester where there was to be some celebration of Paul Revere's ride. We did not have to get Bambi there as the father of her friend would come and pick her up at our house.

At the stroke of ten o'clock, for I had just looked at my watch, the father arrived at our house with his children in the car. Patsy went out to speak to him and I stayed down in the garden with our two-year-old, Welly. I was figuring out what we needed at the nursery. As the driver started the ignition, Patsy called Welly to make sure he was not near the departing car. She did not know he was with me. When I heard her call him, I put him down, as I had just picked him up to hug him. Up from the garden he ran to her and, as fate would have it, his path took him directly in front of the car. It knocked him down and then ran over him. He died instantly from a crushed skull. A ghastly high-pitched wail was the last sound I heard from Welly, followed by a terrified scream from Patsy.

I raced up from the garden and found Patsy sobbing. The driver of the car was yelling hysterically, and I grabbed him and slammed him against his car as hard as I could. I screamed at him to shut up. Suddenly, I stopped. Glancing downward, I saw Welly's blood-spattered body and smashed head. Immediately, waves of blinding pain swept over me and

I vomited. I remember vividly every action and sound that was made in association with the incident and the whole horror became indelibly etched on my brain. I can never erase any of the images I saw or sensations I felt.

We frantically sent the nanny, who had rushed out, in to call the police and to get an ambulance, though I knew full well that Welly was dead and that no medical team would be able to save him. We followed the ambulance that finally came as it carried Welly's broken body to the Beverly Hospital. We did this at the direction of the police, who told us we had to go there in order to give a report and sign a death certificate. Shock engulfed us both, and we moved as if in a dream. Upon returning home, we found that friends and family had materialized out of nowhere. Without them, in the time that followed, we would have been completely lost. They took over everything, from helping with our children, answering phone calls, providing food, arranging flowers and assisting me with funeral arrangements. I started pouring drinks, even though it was not even noon, the socially appointed hour to start cocktailing for the day. This steady flow of alcohol was not to stop for many a day. It was a balm.

A stream of professionals from the community now descended. The minister from our Episcopal church came, as did the insurance agency's representative and an undertaker. Mercifully, Patsy and I were in complete shock, so we moved through all this with preternatural composure. Bambi and Chippy were well cared for by the nanny and friends, yet to this very day I feel guilty that I ignored them. I just couldn't think of anything but Welly's death and its absolute finality. The agony of our child's accident was so excruciating and so devastating that there are few words that can describe it. The mental anguish resulting from the death of one's child is nearly impossible to conceive of by those who have not experienced it. A parent never forgives oneself for the death of a child. One can always find some thing, or reason or action that was not done that could have saved the child's life. It is a ghastly burden to carry forever after and the anguish that the child will be forgotten as if it had never been on the face of the earth, it numbs the brain.

To come even close to understanding the complete desolation a parent feels, a person must understand the intimate and nurturing relationship shared between parent and child. These bonds are so strong and unique that a rupture of them is unthinkable. The interdependence of parents and their children is far different from any other earthly attachments. At the moment of birth, a parent assumes the total commitment and responsibility for the protection of the life of that child. It is a responsibility that can never be shirked. This trust is shattered and the basic order of life blown apart if ever a child should die before the parent. The love one feels for a child is so unconditional and the loss of it so overwhelming that the mind literally cannot rationally cope with it. A child's death, and especially one of this shocking nature, initially causes a shutdown of the system to set in. This is a blessing, for it is our system's way to come to grips with the unfathomable terror and to help somewhat ease the pain of it.

My soul was so savaged, so torn to shreds and my grief was so extreme that my mind could not be mollified. I was in shock for days. Eventually, and it was a long process, I relegated this agony to a place in my mind where mourning continues but is less strong. It is with me to this very day, but the intensity has diminished.

Patsy was devastated beyond belief. She was practically immobile as she sat in one place for hours talking to friends who arrived. Within hours her emotions began to affect her physically with what seemed to be small, but temporary, blackouts and muscle spasms. She cried continually, and she kept saying she could not forgive herself for calling Welly up from the garden. No one would ever have dreamed of blaming her, but she felt culpable and constantly averred that he was her last love child and that she could have no more children. Each time she said this, she wept. I could not answer her questions nor was there any answer.

For a period of time the death made our lives feel surreal. It was as if we were moving about in a vacuum. We feared to love for we had lost someone we had loved so intensely. How could we ever love anyone or anything as much again? Our minds could not focus on anything but Welly and his horrible death. For months, I could hear him running back and forth in the upstairs hall. I would see him poke his head around the corner or I would hear him call from outside. I would see his body in the spot where he was killed each time I drove my car over it. When I woke up each morning, a cold, clammy sweat swept over me when I realized that what I was waking to was not a dream but reality. The mind does let go of the pain but at times it seems to actually intensify it. Dreams and nightmares are all too vivid.

The passing of a child tolls a death knell to about 80% of marriages. It is nearly impossible to console the other spouse when the pain is so intense and so acute for oneself. Patsy and I never stopped blaming ourselves for the accident and we could not help each other's excruciating pain. Our mourning was so intense that we shut each other out. Each of us felt so hopeless and helpless that we were not sure we would survive. Death would have been a blessing for each of us at that time.

When a large part of the shock wore off and my mind became a bit more able to function, I found myself focusing on every minute detail of the accident, whether I wanted to or not. I survived this period only because I kept reminding myself that I could never change what had happened. Welly was dead, and nothing I could do could bring him back. Instead, I must make his short life have some meaning. Dwelling on his death would only destroy my ability to function rationally. Life must go on for Patsy, for me and for our children as, after all, we were still alive. Throughout all this Smith family anguish, I never lost my faith in God nor did I question Him about the death of my son. We were never promised that life would be easy.

I never felt that God was out to get me with this accident, but I did believe that He was a fierce power to deal with. I was deathly afraid of hellfire and damnation. I had for years and years remembered the Sabbath day, particularly during my boarding school years, and, as an adult, I took the children every Sunday to our local Episcopal church. Patsy did not come with us. However, my idea of God was based on fear rather than love, and I continually felt guilty. I was never sure that He really forgave me my trespasses, so I went on carrying a heavy load of sin on my shoulders.

My real walks and talks with God had not started yet but, strangely enough in this time of dire need, my feelings were changing in spite of myself. Patsy, for her part, never had a strong faith to help her through this tragedy. She alternated between feeling guilt and blame, and I was unable to help her. For a long time she felt that she had no right to happiness because she had caused Welly's death. She alone blamed herself. I once read in a book about the George H. W. Bushes that when their daughter, Robin, was dying and after she had died, they had an understanding amongst themselves that when one was down the other would struggle to have his or her spirits up. This way a spouse would know he or she was not to drag the other's spirits further down. Patsy and I were down so often together. We were seldom feeling up as a couple.

Bambi and Chippy were never given a chance to grieve. We foolishly thought they were too young to mourn, and our own grief was such that consoling them was beyond our capabilities. Our children, sadly, were sent back to school the day after the accident for we actually thought it would ease their pain if they were kept busy. They had no time to cry and be with us. Our devastation kept us from realizing that we should be with them, helping them. I pray that they have forgiven us.

We knew they were suffering from little actions and statements of theirs. While walking on the beach one day, Chippy asked Patsy, "Do all little boys die before their mothers?" Bambi, on the night of Welly's death, asked to have her long-put-away security blanket, alias, "her little puppy," in bed with her. That much-loved, stuffed dog had been stowed in the attic for at least three years. Now he was on call, like a doctor or minister or grief counselor. They needed love and we let them down.

My minister advised Patsy and me to get counseling, and so we followed his advice. Unfortunately, it felt too religious to Patsy, and we stopped going after five visits. It was then that this minister suggested that I go to a psychiatrist. Patsy had told him that I had deep problems and she was right. I headed off to the appointment with a touch of fear and trepidation, for it's not easy to bare one's soul and I knew that I would have to or why go or waste the money.

The psychiatrist I was referred to was at the Beverly Hospital. I did not then know it, but many friends and family members had spoken to my minister about my moods, drinking, obsessive behavior and need for help well before the tragedy. Sending me to therapy turned out to be the best advice I ever received, for this marvelous doctor helped me find the way to a new and useful life. It took a very long time, but the end result was worth it. Welly's death was the impetus that gave me an insight into a way of successful living far beyond anything I could have ever dreamed about or expected. Here, I saw, was a way I could try to make a positive change come out of the horror of Welly's tragic death.

It would not be an easy process. I had to visit my subconscious and drag into the light of day all the pains that I had shoved down there over many years. Each session tore me apart mentally but my psychiatrist was brilliant at what he did. Slowly, slowly, tensions were leaving me. One day I accidentally scratched my face and, lo and behold, I had drawn blood from three long scrapes. I had unknowingly gouged my face with my, by now, long fingernails. From childhood I had bitten my nails to the quick and now, without even trying to stop biting them, I had quit. As my inner traumas were vanishing due to working with my doctor, I did not need to "suck my thumb."

The most important advice I got from those early sessions was "not to whine and blame my family for making me the dysfunctional person I was." The doctor laid out a litany for me that made perfect sense. It revolved around accepting myself as I was at that very moment and then finding out why I had certain problems and behaved in certain ways. He emphasized that my parents had done what they thought was right in bringing me up, even if it wasn't, and that they had never purposely tried to do me harm.

They did not know how to love, so how could they love me? How could I have expected them to give me attention when they had never had any themselves? He further explained that they were never going to beg my forgiveness nor could they change what they had said or done to me. Therefore, I was to get on with my life by digging out the hurts and pains that had caused my compulsiveness, addictions and wounded personality. I was to release them. It was going to be painful, he reiterated, but I must try and be willing to work with him.

He further stressed that because of the work I was able to do on my life, changes would ensue drastically and dramatically within my whole family. My relationships outside the family also would improve if I could and would connect with people on a healthy and rational basis. I learned, too, that dysfunctional members of my family would probably be unable to deal with me once I was a functional person. They would envision me as a threat to the precariously constructed security, which they relied upon, the kind that I also had fashioned, in order to survive in our seriously distressed family. Finally, he warned me that my wife might not want me as a changed person. She, after all, had married a spreader of wild oats and not a doer of good deeds.

As session after session of psychotherapy came and went, I began acting as a grounded adult after many long years of behaving like a fool. As the doctor had predicted, now my relationships constantly needed adjustment. My evolving mature personality had reached a point where I had become disgusted with the excesses and dead ends of the life I had lived. Now that I had admitted I had serious problems, I wanted relief. The building blocks that had been so inappropriately built upon were starting to be rearranged to form a solid base, yet I still wanted my evening drinks and this was a tragic mistake.

It was foolish of me to think, but I certainly did at this time, that all my problems were being solved. Yet many remained to be addressed and rectified before all was in order. Many relationships had to be set straight, and, as some could not be made right, setbacks were bound to occur.

I learned important lessons for facing tragedies. Good things do not inevitably come from bad things. So many people say, "out of bad comes good." Sometimes it does, but it is a choice one goes through upon living through such a horror as mine. One makes the choice for going up or down in seconds. At the moment I realized Welly was killed, I was a changed person forever. Nothing would ever be the same for my family or me, and the choice of my direction was instantly flashed through my mind. I chose to go up, and not down. I believe strongly it was the Spark of Divine that guided me. It took tremendous work and pain to bring about this upward change and a great deal of time as well.

After the Navy I moved to Boston and found an apartment overlooking the Public Gardens. Various friends moved in, ensuring a swinging time. This was before the days of men and women living together, but we did our best to uphold male honor with any women we could get to visit us. The parties were constant, and I became quite adept at dancing on the mantle in my kilts or night shirt. With the usual cigarette in my hand, I seem here to be totally out of it. I was, most of the time. My job was horrible and I earned $35 a week. After buying liquor, cigarettes and paying rent, I had little left. I was always in debt.

I believe this is the first picture of Patsy and me together. We had met while both in a wedding and I had asked her to spend a weekend with me on Cape Cod at a friend's house.

My mother was still quite well preserved and looked regal and relatively pretty during the early stages of my marriage. However, she was never far from a drink.

My father looked young until the day he died at 85. Here he is at 60. For a person who ravaged his body with booze and cigarettes, he did amazingly well and had not a gray hair or any baldness. He was a man without a conscience. If you said anything against him, he would stop speaking to you, probably forever. He adored the ladies and baited my mother with the fact that he did. He traveled with them and occasionally my mother would find a corset in her bed left by a damsel. Rage ensued!

Patsy and I were very much in love. Here we are singing a duet at our bridal dinner. We invited few older people such as aunts, uncles, godparents or friends, for Patsy and I were terrified that my family would get stinking drunk.

Our wedding was a large and fun bash. You can see that I had a cast of thousands for ushers, but Patsy had only her sisters and a friend. I was the extravagant one. Patsy was calm and ordered. The laughter emanating from most everyone is due to the fact that my father, who was also taking a picture, had just fallen over backwards. My brothers are not laughing.

Patsy and I were thrilled when our first child, Bambi, arrived. Patsy had been having contractions every four minutes for five months. She gained only seven pounds during her pregnancy. I had never really believed I would be a father and I was delirious at Bambi's arrival. I would get up for her nighttime bottle and feed her and just hug and love her. I wanted her to have everything that I never had. But let's face it; I really did not know what love was or how to give it. It had to be on my terms, and those terms were wrong.

Two years after the arrival of Bambi, our first son, Forrester, Jr., arrived. We called him Chippy, as he had puffed cheeks and looked like a chipmunk. Patsy and I thought the two children made a wonderful family, but what was on the surface hid dark currents. There was entirely too much drinking, partying, fighting, controlling and dysfunctionality. You never would have sensed it, but it was there.

A third child, Welly—a nickname for Lowell, came four years after Chippy. He was a complete surprise. As Patsy had not had the her period for four years, we took no precautions to control birth. He was adorable and the apple of both our eyes. The other children adored him.

This was a picture I took to send to England in order to employ an English nanny. Before long, one came and we could dance the nights away with a permanent babysitter. In the long run, it wasn't such a good idea. Our responsibilities were too diminished.

The picture of Welly was taken one hour before he was killed. The nanny took it in the kitchen and then sent him out to play. We had a portrait done from this snapshot by Madame Shoumatoff. She was the artist doing a portrait of FDR at the instant he died. She was an old friend of Patsy's family. Welly's death was a catastrophe of an unbelievable magnitude to our family, and, as a result, many dynamics changed. Eighty percent of parents divorce when one of their children dies.

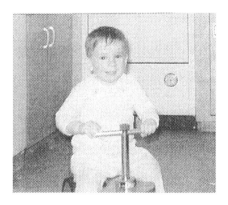

I liked sports as long as they did not interfere with my social life. Golf took too much time away from access to a well-stocked bar, but tennis was OK for it could be done rapidly. My passion was riding, and, in particular, fox hunting. The chase was splendid, exciting and exhilarating. I also always had a sandwich case with a flask attached to my saddle. It never came home empty.

Here Patsy looks adoringly at me, but later in the evening we had a huge fight. A picture of us was taken at the Hunt Ball we went to and later appeared on the cover of *The Boston Globe* magazine—quite a splash, and always a reminder of the terrible fight and her anger at me. I deserved it.

After teaching for a while and watching the taxes on our house exceed
my salary, I left and went to work in the real world. It is quite amazing
that I actually always did really a decent job, whatever I undertook.
One would think that the drink would have interfered but it did not.
I never missed a day due to it, but I must say that I did not always
feel well on the job. Here I am on the first day of my job in the public
relations department of a large insurance company.

I inherited this trusty Purdy shotgun from my grandfather and shot with it continually all over the country. I was not a particularly good shot, but I dressed the part and could discuss guns, which I knew next to nothing about. I loved to eat the duck, pheasant and quail which I had shot. Later on in my life, I was so depressed that I put the double barrel of my beloved Purdy under my chin and pulled the trigger. By the grace of God, it was the wrong trigger. This somehow gave me a "message" to keep on living.

Patsy and I made quite an attractive couple, and we enjoyed life to its
fullest. This is a picture of us with our two older children at Patsy's
cousin's wedding. The cousin married an extremely attractive Jewish
man whose relatives were unhappy that he had married outside his
faith. The cousin's family did not mind one bit, as he had gone to
Harvard, and that was the answer to most of life's problems according
to any Cabot, Lowell, Putnam or Sturgis relatives. When this picture
was taken, I can remember how "high" I felt from the wedding
champagne. Yet, as the picture shows, I look (more or less) sober.

I loved my job with the Boston Symphony. I was on the run here and abroad eighteen hours a day, seven days a week. It involved raising a lot of money and that meant drinking a lot of alcohol. I entertained VIP after VIP. Here are President Nixon's daughter Tricia and son-in-law Edward Cox. RMN was president at the time of this photo and the Secret Service was swarming everywhere. I loved that.

From the looks of the (above) picture, one would assume I was dying my hair or wearing a wig. Neither was true, but I was starting to try to hide my baldness and make my face look less puffy. Frankly, the comb-over made it look dreadful and the double chins, from too much booze, were beginning to appear. Notice that, as I talk to Arthur Fiedler, I desperately clutch a drink and cigarette. I was never without these social aids. This was about the time I got arrested for drunk-driving, a serious problem which I managed to get "fixed." Mr. Fiedler liked his drinks as well, but I don't see one in his hand.

We built this rather stylish house two years after we were married. It was always featured in magazines and on charity tours and we entertained in it constantly. The rug in the living room was worth more than the house, and I never failed to point that out to the troops that piled through the house. This picture, taken for a rotogravure layout, was shot about a month after we had lost our beloved son. We had been asked to do this long before and felt the show must go on. What a mistake. We never sat and contemplated our tragic loss, and, eventually, it caught up with us.

After Welly was killed, we added a conservatory on to the dining room. It gave us tremendous joy and became an obsession. I grubbed in it for hours and hours. You will notice that we were old fashioned enough to keep a silver tea service on the sideboard, but, rest assured, there was no tea time in our house. At the stroke of six on the Simon Willard grandfather clock, the ice came out and the drinks were poured with a very heavy hand.

This was our house that sat on four acres on the ocean. We had our own beach which we shared with massive numbers of friends. We were wildly spoiled and loved it.

Cozy evenings were always spent in this room with booze flowing, a fire going and the television playing. We always ate supper on trays in here, and, unfortunately, never with the children. Communication was lacking, though I, of all people, should have known better.

I could barely contain my excitement the summer when Steve McQueen rented the house next to Patsy's and mine. We became fast friends, and I was asked to take a talking role in *"The Thomas Crown Affair."* I ended up on the cutting room floor, but what a summer I had from hanging out with Faye Dunaway to helicoptering around with director Norman Jewison.

Christmas was a time of mad merriment for all of my family. One trick to keep it merry was not to spend Christmas Day with my mother and father, as they fought constantly and kept leaving the room to "refuel" secretly from hidden bottles. Myself, if I had enough to drink I could manage to sail through the hours of Yuletide stress.

Patsy and I were the toast of the town when *"The Thomas Crown Affair"* opened in Boston. I ran a special benefit premiere for my children's school. We had the McQueen's stay with us and swept through cheering crowds with them on the way to the opening. Here, Patsy, Neile McQueen and Steve sit on the stairs at the theater. I must have been in a corner sobbing that I was cut from the film. Yet I still get residual benefits when it plays on TV.

The Boston Globe — Thursday, June 2o.

Patsy and I always took a vacation in the spring in the Caribbean. On this particular cruise I was consuming three bottles of vermouth a day as I had given up smoking and thought I was going to expire from lack of nicotine. My left hand is cupped around the ever-present glass. The children were with us on this cruise and, unfortunately, they experienced first hand my drinking and temper from lack of cigarettes. They cowered in the bow of the boat we chartered. Patsy was fit to be tied, having reached her limit of endurance when it came to my shenanigans.

NINE

In this day and age psychologists have taken over the jobs formerly held by psychiatrists. Psychiatrists now focus on correcting most mental problems by pushing pills and medications for depression. Psychologists delve into the inner recesses of the mind and bring out problems that can be hurtful and damaging. A fleeting statement uttered by a parent to a child can wreak havoc for years and years, but getting that poison to the surface will heal the damage done. If a child has continually been berated by his or her parents, it can result in a debilitating lack of self-esteem. Such traumas may be helped, even dispelled, by being dealt with in the therapeutic sessions. I know: I have been there. I'm convinced that any cruel remark made to a child is never forgotten, but stored away.

Depression was once almost always treated with talk therapy but today the best remedy is medication. Antidepressant medication has come a long way to help different problems and there are drugs that save thousands of lives every year by preventing suicides.

My parents were outraged when they heard that I was seeing a shrink. Patsy, who had suggested I go in the first place, was not as sure she liked the idea once I started. When I would come home with new ideas, acting less tense, she was convinced that it was not helping our relationship because now I was "different." She was never in favor of change and, quite frankly, my personality was slowly—and I do mean slowly—changing. It was hard for her, grieving as she still was, to understand, really, what was happening with me. We had built our marriage around certain talk, about external events and mutual interests. Now our interests were diverging.

Unfortunately, I was living a Jekyll and Hyde existence. My doctor had told me not to drink, but I continued to do so. It was a habit that was very hard to break. When alcohol dulled my brain, I lapsed into my old behavior. I gained a false sense of security by feeding off people's sympathy. There were many people who since Welly's death had been continually offering love and sympathy. Quite wrongly, I began building my self-esteem on this tragedy because it focused such incredible attention on me. Even my mother, who had swathed herself in black to mourn Welly, and, in turn, my father, showed concern for me. This certainly was a new sensation, and I liked it. However, eventually the sympathy and concern began to lessen for people are not always going to remain sorry for someone. No matter how life stopping a tragedy, the people who are not experiencing it move on. People have their own lives to lead and their own crosses to bear. Time, "like an ever rolling stream," sweeps all this pity away. It becomes tedious for friends and relatives to keep hearing misery, sadness, grief, and personal agony.

All the while I was under psychotherapy I found it necessary to drink. I honestly thought I was just a heavy drinker and it would ease my pain. When my doctor, who was working wonders with my psyche, told me to cut down, I did cut down but you can bet your bottom dollar it was a minuscule amount. My system was craving it. Sadly, alcoholism was increasing my depression. What lifts you up drops you down.

As the pain caused by Welly's death eased, from the healing effects of time, as well as with the help of the doctor, I found I was telling the awful story less and less. It was ceasing to be a crutch for me, and worthwhile ideas for building myself up mentally were the result of my sticking with the therapy. I was starting to provide myself with a firmer foundation for successful living. I could understand loving my family, friends and neighbors, but I had never thought of loving myself, for I really did not. All my life I had been treated by my parents as someone who could not be accepted or loved for who he was. It was difficult to understand love's role in my life. I actually did not believe that God really loved me but only that I loved Him. I still had a long way to go to find His love.

Other than a few Bloody Marys at noon on weekends or on vacations, all my drinking was done in the evening hours. At six o'clock sharp I would make Patsy and myself each a large drink of scotch. Martinis were no longer possible as they produced the most horrific hangovers. I did not sip what I poured but rather gulped it down quickly. In this way, a usual evening meant about six hefty drinks consumed by each of us, though

Patsy's were much weaker. I might have wine with dinner, but I did not drink afterwards. Most people were not aware of my problem as I drank in such a manner as to hide it. I had drinks before I went out to a party so I would have a few drinks at my hosts. They thought of me as a light drinker. Little did they know for I was usually soused on arrival.

After Welly's death, I was always trying to control my children in everything they did. I had been this way to a lesser degree before, but now it was part of my obsession with keeping them safe. I wanted to pick their friends, I wanted to be the only one to give them happy times and, worst of all, I wanted them to be both themselves and Welly combined. This was an impossibility also, as so many of the people and animals in my life whom I had truly loved, from my pony, Capers, to my puppy dogs, to my nurse, Mary, to my son, Welly, had been cruelly snatched from me, I was terrified that I might lose Bambi or Chippy so I kept a tight grip on them.

I had to grab on for dear life to anything and everyone around me. I was the adult child of alcoholics, and I was inculcated with the idea that control was my only means of survival. Unknowingly, I was slowly but surely destroying my relationships both with my children and with Patsy. I was giving them no room to breathe and be themselves.

It was immediately evident to my doctor that I had become a control freak. I always started out my sessions by detailing my plans for the days, weeks and months ahead. I was terrified of chaos and felt I had continually set strict boundaries for myself and those around me. After we talked and talked about this problem, I came to realize that I could do nothing but live in the moment that I was living in. The past was over and done and could not be changed, and the future was impossible to plan for. It would deal with itself. I had to let go of constraints and live in the present, a glorious place of peace, if I could just recognize it. It was a joy to begin to comprehend this truth, but to put it into my system and make it work was another matter. It took years to accomplish.

Practically on cue, on the evenings following my weekly visits to my doctor, Patsy and I would squabble. When she did not appreciate or comment on the small changes psychotherapy was making in my life, I would get irritated and feel rejected. I was doing so many things differently and desperately needed her to support me after the painful digging the doctor was doing into my subconscious. Those sessions with the doctor always left me exhausted and a bit tense. I had made some noticeable switches in my habits and, like a child, craved assurance, recognition and praise. In the very beginning of the therapy, our bickering was not too bad, but it was always there as an irritant—and it never lessened.

A noticeable change involved our ability to love each other. As I had always been afraid of rejection by "good" girls, everything we did as husband and wife was in the dark and very secretive. Being with her physically had always been like two ships meeting and passing in the darkest of nights. If she couldn't really see me, as we loved one another, how could I be rejected? Now as my therapy progressed, our married life became more open, full, warm and exciting. This should have made for greater compatibility, but still lurking were those deep-seated problems that even wonderful sex could not make evaporate.

We made gigantic strides in pulling our lives out of the depths, but we made them separately. By each of us healing our wounds alone, we created cracking flaws in our relationship that proved fatal. The whole world was distorted for us. My psychiatrist made me aware of all these things, but trying to relay them secondhand to my wife never worked. I suggested many times that she go to therapy herself, but she and her family were opposed to it, they felt that only I needed help. They thought her mourning was normal and that only time would make the difference, that anything else was practically unnatural.

To ease our feeling of sorrow for ourselves, we started taking lavish trips. We thought nothing about renting one of the grandest suites at the St. Regis for three or four days of New York, shopping, wining, dining, theater-going and museum-hopping. While traveling, we would refurbish her wardrobe as well as mine, and buy the children extravagant playthings. We got them toys that most of their friends never dreamed of having. There were motorbikes, electric cars, television sets, electric typewriters and the most expensive clothes. They had been far from spoiled, yet now Patsy and I gave these gifts, not only as an expression of our love for them, but, without realizing it, a way of trying to compensate them for Welly's death. We all had a tremendous need for nurturing, but, sadly, we settled for material things. People get so happy with giving and getting gifts that they mistake the exchange for love. It is not love and it vanishes quickly.

We went to Acapulco for an extravagant ten days and then up to Mexico City for five days more of high living in a five-room suite when we needed only one room. We ate and drank from dawn to dusk, and we bought hundreds of things for ourselves and the children that we really never needed or used. Chippy, amongst other things, got a made-to-order bullfighter's outfit, which he adored but outgrew in one month.

We were forever going to Europe for my job and we never went second-class. We had wonderful times, but with an unending supply of booze fueling us, Patsy's and my irritation with each other became worse. We said things we never meant while we were stewed, and worse than that, we each took lasting offense at what the other said. We never seemed to forget the slurs and arrows we exchanged. They festered in us.

We lived high on the hog and set up a lifestyle very much as our families had lived in their heyday. Now I needed to recreate that atmosphere. We had a daily maid for cleaning and someone to do the work outside. We had a nurse for the children, and we always had a butler, a cook and a maid for our dinner parties. As we did not have to do the menial tasks necessary to give splashy dinner parties, we felt that the later our friends stayed the better our bash was. Unfortunately, the later the parties lasted, the more we drank. It led to far worse arguments between Patsy and me and all the good work that the doctor had done and was doing to help me ease my inner problems was being obliterated.

It was easy to see that our failure to get therapy or counseling together was hurting us. The psychiatrist and I worked so well together, but I found it difficult to apply his therapy to my life with Patsy when we were butting heads so constantly. Patsy was not feeling change in her life as she came to terms with Welly's death, so she found it nigh on to impossible to accept or understand the change in me. Ours was not an uncommon problem faced by couples in dire emotional straits, but extenuating circumstances were playing a part in continually pulling us farther apart.

When under the influence of alcohol, I seemed to be getting nicer and sweeter with our friends but meaner and nastier with Patsy. In some odd way, our remarks always brought to the forefront of our minds, the agony of our common grief and the painful guilt that wracked us to our very bones. She was convinced that I could never forgive her for calling Welly up to the car and I was convinced that she could never forgive me for not keeping Welly down with me in the garden. Nothing could have been farther from the truth, but our minds played terrible tricks. As if this was not enough for us, the man who ran over Welly died in a high-speed car crash less than a year later. This stunned us, for we had never thought of the pain he must have constantly been going through. His death really hit home. We felt that Welly's death had caused it. How tragic it all was!

Finally our arguments were getting so bad that we arranged to have two psychiatrists and one psychologist see us as a family group. We wanted them try to analyze our interactions. Patsy did most of the arranging for this encounter but she still thought that it was only I who needed the help and that she would only go along to hear the doctors pronounce how bad I was. She always tried to shield herself from any criticism at all.

Sadly for Patsy, the doctors placed much of our family's problems on her withdrawal into herself with no spiritual power she could turn to for help. They said, in effect, that Patsy subconsciously was now living as if she actually had her mother's burn scars. Her mother, due to her severe burns, had always had special needs because of her scar tissue. Patsy, who from her infancy had internalized this behavioral pattern, now applied this model to the terrible hurt in her own life. Welly's death had increased her need for attention a great deal more than ever before. I wasn't giving it.

This session with the three shrinks hurt her terribly. She felt wounded by their criticism and would not try to correct her supposed deficiencies or undertake any of the steps recommended for us to try. We tried to pray together, but she was unable to. We started to dine as a family, but this lasted only a few nights. Instead of a long cocktail hour, we were told to have family discussions, but Patsy thought the children would not understand these exchanges. I never faulted her for her negativity but I realized, even though I had many problems, that we were solving nothing.

One night, in a fit of anger, I stormed out of the house. Patsy had been nagging at me most of the evening for things I had done and things I had not done. I finally exploded. I was furious and told her to stop her perpetual complaining. I got in my car and headed for Boston for the night. I did not even take a toothbrush. To my surprise, when I called the next day, still quite upset, she told me not to come home as she had had enough of me and my behavior. I had little choice, for not only was the house in her name but she said she would get a restraining order if I dared to darken the doorway. I was incredulous for she had called my bluff at one of my own games, and also she had, in an instant, taken my whole world and smashed it to smithereens.

As her words sank in, I was swept with fear for I had lost everything on earth that I held dear. I would lose the children, not live in the house we built, never dig in the garden, stop swimming on our beach, give up entertaining our friends, and playing with our dogs. I hung up the phone and started to shake as anxiety flooded me. I had little money and absolutely nowhere to go. I had saved nary a cent and never inherited a penny, for we lived perfectly wonderfully together off Patsy's large income. I was making an adequate salary but had always spent it on those things I thought that I needed to enhance my image.

I had fashioned the world I inhabited with what seemed like care. Now it was gone. My ego and emotions were totally annihilated. Within seconds I felt a chill sweep over me, and I was consumed with the need of a good belt of whiskey. I figured it would calm me down and help me solve this dilemma. I also, somewhat ridiculously, rationalized that Patsy would soon take me back. It proved to be a wild dream. As time moved on, her family, and even mine, convinced her that I was a rotten egg who drank far too much. They said I should make radical changes in my behavior if I was to get even a crack at visiting my children. My phone calls to her were filled with my begging and pleading, but she was having none of it. She at last seemed to have the upper hand. She had never had it before in our marriage.

Depression engulfed me for days on end, and I felt myself being pulled lower and lower by its harsh grip. I was living in a small hotel on Commonwealth Avenue where I could just barely pay the bills. Most of my depression was brought on by my delusional belief that drinking eased my pain and helped me face my problems. I brushed aside the fact that the alcohol greatly increased depression. After all, didn't I feel better when I drank?

Financial panic continued to rear its ugly head. My salary from the Boston Symphony was all I had to live on and it was simply not enough for the style I was accustomed to. I put on a facade, but inside I was completely demolished. My mother and father hardly spoke to me and sided with Patsy, and my brothers offered no consolation whatsoever. I was the first in my very large Clark and Smith families to separate, so I was totally ostracized from family activities. Rejection had always been one of my worst fears and here it was in all its hideous fury. At this point only my friends stood by me, and the loyalty they showed was a blessing.

Eventually, I took a small carriage house on Chestnut Street and furnished it sparsely. I rented furniture in Boston that resembled the contents of a third-rate Armenian whorehouse. It was all I could afford, and there were few items of good taste available on the local furniture rental market. A great many of our household possessions in Beverly Farms were mine, for my mother and father had sold their big house in Far Hills and passed on many antiques. However, Patsy would not let me take away a stick of it, nor would she even let me have my clothes. I bought a new wardrobe in Filene's Bargain Basement and lived with frightful furniture.

Ultimately, the ax fell when Patsy's lawyer informed me that she definitely wanted a divorce. After I had learned of this wish of hers, I sank deeper into depression. I made no sense with my lawyer or with Patsy on the phone even though I was trying so hard to be rational. I simply could not handle the total emptiness of my life. I was alone, drinking far, far too much and dwelling on all the pains that had afflicted my life from the day I was born. My existence would never be the same but yet I dimly knew there was a way up and out of this malaise. Should I choose to make something good happen in my life or should I escape in sorrow and drink myself to death? Only I could decide that. The doctor I was seeing for therapy had helped me so much with putting my life in order, bit by bit but, at life-changing moments such as this, one's entire world is blown apart. The therapist's work is blotted out and one can find no rationality in their thoughts. Only alcohol eased the pain until the next day.

For immediate help and solace, I turned, literally with a vengeance, to my friends. They became my saving grace. My life had always brought me into contact with huge numbers of people, most of whom tended to be educated, secure, balanced, sophisticated, connected and wise. I had had the opportunity to be associated with fine people from the moment I went to grammar school. It was, perhaps, an obsession always to amass friends, but what a good obsession it turned out to be. Their presence in my life filled the void left where spousal love should have been. I found security in them and in their families. They had saved my sanity many times before and did so now.

Each weekend I called on them for help and friendship. They gave it. Heading the list of those I now looked to for sanity were my boarding school friends, my college friends, my women friends and my Navy friends. It is not surprising to me that I called on them and made them my new family. Love, they say, makes the world go around and the love of these men and women made my world right and meaningful when I thought I was unable to take another step. As Christ said," God is love," then is not love of friends a perfect example of bringing the power of the Almighty into our midst to give us strength? My friends gave me an inner power to survive my separation.

On far too many occasions I would call Patsy during our separation and either my brother or sister-in-law would answer the phone. Hearing them on the other end of the line and thinking they were forming a wall against me sent me into a tailspin. It seemed to prove to me that all my family and all Patsy's family had risen up against me. These situations increased my feelings of rejection and anxiety and consumed me. The damage both to my psyche and to my family relationships that these telephone encounters engendered was deep. Forgiveness of those involved I found possible, understanding, I find impossible.

As the trouble I was having with depression was becoming obvious to my friends, they pushed hard and insisted that I go back to my psychiatrist. Grudgingly, I did so. After a few sessions, I began to feel somewhat better, for he understood my depression but could not make it go away. He like most physicians at that time knew very little about how the brain's chemical imbalance might cause depression. Those were the days of conventional talk therapy instead of the magic bullet of psychopharmacology. Drugs to cure non-bipolar depression had not yet come on the market. Only lithium was being used for manic depression, a mental problem causing cycles of mania and depression.

This particular pathology ran rampant in my family, and, perhaps, I carried the genes for it, though I did not think mania was part of my behavior. Depression can be a genetically inherited disease and my family was rife with it. It is now obvious to me that many of them drank to ease the pain of it.

What happened next was like an intervention by Cupid. One afternoon after an excellent session in Beverly with my psychiatrist, I took myself to the Myopia Hunt Club. I wanted to watch my children swim in some races. As I was still a member there and knew the junior swimming races were being held, I assumed Patsy would be there and so it was a chance to see her. I didn't get many such opportunities for a friendly confrontation. I was relaxed, full of beans and not feeling low. Patsy and I struck up a delightful conversation and, before I knew it, she had invited me back to the house for the night. I accepted with alacrity and after a wonderful evening together, she asked me to move back in. I was thrilled, and for weeks, floated around in a state of happy shock. I wandered through the house touching and feeling everything. I was home, with my children around me. I played with the beloved dogs, and all my possessions seemed to smile at me. How nice it was to finally have extra underpants and socks at my beck and call.

We both spoke, of course, to our lawyers and told them we were calling the divorce off. Mine, Chris Weld, was thrilled that we were, while Patsy's was not at all sure our renewed marriage would work. Patsy had been far lonelier than I had imagined and overwhelmed with being a single parent. As I had been a pretty good father, had always done my share around the house and had been a social spark in Patsy's life, there was no overriding reason not to give me another chance.

It was foolish to think that all our problems had been solved, for only I had worked on them with professional help when we were apart and I still drank far too much. I was also still depressed; while Patsy was convinced she had no problems. The separation had shown us two things: we could live without each other, and the hideous pain of Welly's death would never leave us. It was always a wedge being driven in and splitting apart our marriage, even if we did not realize it.

In no time at all, we were back in the swing of the fast-moving North Shore set that both of us so loved. I was happy, so why should I see my doctor, even though the psychological problems that had always plagued me hadn't been cured?

As Patsy and I struggled to make our marriage whole again, our lack of trust in it continued to work against us. Never could we forgive ourselves for causing Welly's death. We never blamed one another, only ourselves. It was years before I learned that no parent ever forgives him or herself for a child's death, no matter what the cause. Patsy and I had learned that both of us would survive if we split up again. We had once been so close to divorce that it was always the option lurking in the background if we quarreled.

I provided the final kiss of death to our marriage after Patsy and I had gone on a Caribbean cruise. I was in cigarette withdrawal, for I had just given up smoking—what had been a three-pack-a-day habit for me. Cigarettes were such an addiction that I'd been unable to wake up without grabbing for one before even getting out of bed. The last thing I ever did in the evening was stub one out in my bedside ashtray. I was lost and completely agitated without them. Occasionally, I had given them up, but such denial only lasted about three hours of a morning. By then the craving got the upper hand and I would smoke untold others simply to make up for those I had skipped. Because my coughing was constant and my breathing laborious, I finally got up the nerve to stop cold turkey.

On the cruise I was drinking heavily. I needed to ease my nicotine withdrawal pangs, but I was pouring so much down no one could get any sense out of me. I was high as a kite the entire time on, of all wretched things, vermouth. This dreadful wine mixture that was meant to compensate for the cigarettes helped little to assuage the torturous cravings. My mood swings became unbearable and my temper explosive. I was vile to be around, and the children and Patsy were sick and tired of my behavior. So was I, only I never admitted it.

When we got back to Beverly Farms, Patsy insisted I go for help. I said I would not be criticized anymore and that I, this time, wanted a divorce. I knew I could use help, but I issued this ultimatum to help her realize both of us needed it. She denied, as she always did, that she needed help and stated categorically that she would not stop drinking. To this day I regret my actions, but I left her. Her refusal to beg me to stay was to be the most terrifying rejection I was to ever live through or to suffer as I look back on it. Deep within me I knew I needed her badly and she would now be out of my life for good. I was in for a ghastly ride along a rocky road but felt free as a lark.

All too quickly the children were growing up and becoming very accomplished at whatever they did. Tennis was one of those things they did beautifully. Bambi constantly won tournaments, and to this day plays a brilliant game of tennis and paddle tennis as well. It is wonderful she is such a success in anything she does. My dysfunctional behavior should have left more scars.

Chippy adored water and fast motors. I entered this photo in a contest and nearly won a prize for a snapshot of a happy child. Little did I realize how much I was injuring him with my drinking and attempts at control.

Adolescence has set in as is quite obvious from this photo. Bambi constantly warred with her mother over her hair's length—here it reaches far below her belly button. Chippy warred with me over about everything I said or did and looking back on it, I do not blame him. I was impossible as a father. I was too interested in myself.

My father was a far better grandfather than father and he never missed a graduation or birthday party. Yet he still had never learned to build anyone up. Every sentence ended in "but," as it always had. He would tell someone they were terrific "but" they could be a hell of a lot better, or he would comment someone had done a fabulous job "but" it was not done right. In this way, his conversations were always downers and frustrating beyond belief.

When this picture was taken, Patsy and I were cruising with Bambi and Chippy on a seventy-foot catamaran in the Caribbean. I was drinking at least three bottles of vermouth a day—none of the cheap stuff for me—and I had just stopped smoking three packs of cigarettes a day. I was gaining weight and not only passing out quite often, or, as I called it to the children, resting, but was wetting my bed at night. I was an ornery cuss, insulting and rude, and decidedly on my way to rock bottom. We separated the week we returned home from this cruise.

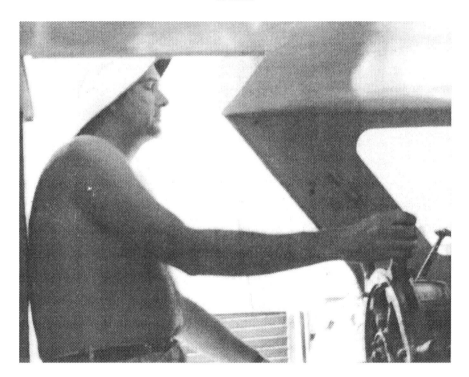

TEN

Loneliness is a terrible thing and especially so if depression is present, for depression feeds on solitude. Loneliness is far more than being alone with oneself, for one can be lonely in a crowd. Loneliness is marked by an emptiness of the spirit deep within a person. Man was made to have love in his life. It takes at least two to love, and we must also love ourselves just as we love our neighbors. Love is the giving of one's self. Constant solitude for the depressed person is tantamount to giving that person a death sentence. As one ruminates on all one's sadness, one tends to spiral downward. As one drops lower and lower, the thought of ending the agony becomes all too real and suicide readily becomes an option. Death can easily seem a solution to a depressive person.

Faith can be severely disrupted by depression. When depressed, the feeling of abandonment is pervasive and prayers seem pointless. Even the possibility of ever being loved is far from one's thoughts, since depression is the nadir of hopelessness. Nothing in this world matters and nothing will ever be right again. To lose faith is agonizing, for the loss of such a positive force spells sure defeat. When I marched out on Patsy, my life became utterly precarious, yet, lacking self-awareness, I could not see what a dire predicament I was in. I knew something was not right, for I often felt deadened and miserable and continued to act in my irrational and dysfunctional ways. I was still convinced that I controlled my life. My psychiatrist and I had talked about all of this, but much of our time together was spent working too hard on my feelings about the death of my son. When I felt that that problem was solved—which it really never was—I had stopped our weekly sessions.

I had for so long lived in controlled situations where I did not need to completely stand on my own feet. From my parents' and grandparents' houses to boarding school to the Navy and on to the privileged routines of my marriage, I had been a creature of the environments around me. But here I was suddenly on my own with no controls. I wasn't exactly standing on my own two feet. I needed my wife and my children.

The Myopia Hunt Club was the perfect place for me to live my single life after leaving Beverly Farms for the second time. There I could entertain at the drop of a hat, I could be waited on and I could golf, swim, play tennis, ride, and drink at will. I always seemed to be searching, subconsciously, for the love I felt I'd never had, and these activities surrounded me with people who, I felt, loved me. This was so much better than the first separation.

My children were nearby as well as some supportive cousins, along with old and dear friends. As my salary at the Boston Symphony was now quite decent, money was no longer a problem. Patsy, I assumed, would take care of the kids' expenses for food, clothing and education so I was saving nary a cent. I still loved her with all my heart but knew we could no longer live together. My dysfunctional behavior and alcoholic mood swings, coupled with her mental detachment from our marriage and the tragedy of Welly's death, had doomed our relationship as husband and wife.

I took my wine cellar to the Club. I had a great deal of Chateau Haut Brion and Chateau Lafite in the cache, most of which Patsy's father had given me as Christmas presents. My drinks closet at Myopia reminded me of my bootleg liquor closet back at Trinity. When my mood was buoyant and I was being enchanted by wine, women and song, I felt I no longer needed help from anyone.

Alcohol made me feel happy and carefree and took away the pain of my being without Patsy. Why should I even consider getting rid of this liquid crutch?

Our separation seemed to be a most civilized one at first. We would see each other at dinners or we would run into each other at weddings, funerals and christenings. We always spoke and kissed as if nothing had happened, but then the sword fell. We started divorce proceedings and began to fight over the basic things that matter to all couples: children, money and possessions. She certainly had a great deal more money than I did, so I was adamant that she should pay for the education of the children. Patsy, however, disagreed with my view, and, to my horror, asked that I pay a large portion of my salary for the children's upkeep. The bickering had started, and we would soon be swallowed up by our squabbles until I finally gave in to her demands and paid what she wanted. It hurt my pocketbook terribly.

Approximately a year after our separation, I secured our divorce in the Dominican Republic. Having a judge running his mouth off to me in Spanish did little to convince me that we were divorced, but a piece of paper assured me that we were. All I had done in court was say "Si" about six times when my attorney jabbed my ribs.

Patsy immediately became involved with someone and they soon married. Unfortunately, the marriage came close to destroying Patsy as it caused her to lose friends, her sense of reality and her good humor. Bambi, by the grace of God, was away most of that time at Miss Porter's School in Farmington, and when things got really bad, Chippy came to live with me.

My life was then much occupied with highly pleasurable social obligations, but Patsy's and her husband's were not. Aware that things were going poorly for them, I made up my mind, with the agreement of her family, whom I occasionally visited for tea, to stick close by in case Patsy's relationship blew up into a major catastrophe and wound up hurting the children. Everyone close to Patsy knew she was not going to be able to stay in this marriage and that she would need friends to be there for her when it collapsed. I was convinced it would fall apart soon and I must stay to help.

In the long run, I was partially right, but, unfortunately for both Patsy and the children, it lasted far longer than anyone would have believed. Patsy said to me, more than once, that she could not face another divorce. I finally gave up trying to help, for it seemed an impossible task. Yet I experienced guilt about this abdication for, deep down inside, I had never stopped feeling that she was my wife. I never referred to her as my ex-wife. Continually crossing my mind was that pronouncement made at our wedding, "Those whom God has joined together, let no man put asunder." Whenever I wrote Patsy, I concluded with "Grow old along with me, the best is yet to be."

During our nearly twenty years of marriage, I was never unfaithful to Patsy nor she to me. We had that wonderful and unbreakable bond of trust throughout all our time together. After our divorce, the blinders were off. I was off and running. Soon I was going out with a tremendous number of attractive women. There were three whom I was actually desperate to marry, but each one rejected me. There also were three who wanted to marry me, but I turned them all down. After this, I found that having girlfriends not in permanent relationships, was far less taxing on my feelings and much easier to deal with. I was still fragile as far as rejection was concerned and I was a clumsy lover when there was too much liquor under my belt. I also found that it was a great deal cheaper to live singly. Not only did I not have to buy jewels and clothes for them but also I did not have to purchase two tickets when I wanted to travel nor did I have to buy two of anything. Such choices reflected my noncommittal and "stay away from being hurt" personality as well as the reality of my pocketbook.

Rushing after women to marry me swept over me when I was feeling up. But such euphoria made me drink more than usual, talk too much and expect too much. The result was I often scared women to death, as we got deeper into the relationships. When I felt down and was moping around, women wanted to mother me, help me, own me and marry me. I was so scared of the intensity of their interest that I soon was overcome by the weight of it. Sadness and occasional impotence afflicted me, and I would send these hovering ladies packing for I could not deal with my inability to love.

After a few hedonistic years in the country at Myopia, I set myself up in a nice apartment in Boston. It looked out on the Charles River. I fixed it up beautifully, for I had finally gotten some of my furniture away from Patsy and had bought a great deal more. This extravagance put me on shaky ground financially, as all of my income came from the Symphony and I could be let go at any moment if alcohol interfered with my work. If that happened, I knew maintaining my lifestyle would be nigh on to impossible. The loss of the job was not at all unlikely, since my social life was putting a strain on my ability to pay strict attention to my duties, while hangovers frequently played funny games with my ability to get to my work on time. The saving grace was that I never missed a day's work.

When my obsessive and compulsive behavior, brought on both by deepening depression and by the strain of dysfunctional thinking, reared its ugly head, as it quite often did, I would go on irrational buying binges. As I felt such a lack of love in my life, when I was feeling low, I always had possessions and bought things I didn't need. I felt a "high" with each and every thing I acquired. Yet all too soon I needed more things to bring the high back again. I was never satisfied, except for the instant when all the furniture, china, sheets, towels, antiques, appliances, flowers and special presents to myself arrived at my doorstep. Only true love can fill the type of void I had. Money or the things it buys never can replace love.

I had little trouble making friends in Boston, as many of my country friends began moving in as fast as they, too, got divorced. We comprised a large circle of people to socialize with, and our partying seemed never to stop. We often went on trips to Maine, South Carolina, Florida, Bermuda or Europe. It was a fabulous life I was leading but, at the same time, somewhat beyond my means. I was always worrying about how I was going to hold up my end of the bargain. My affluence was assumed by everyone and I saw no reason to spoil the illusion.

My mother had moved to Maine to live permanently. She and my father had fought like cats and dogs when they were together, and so she literally fled the scene. They had spoken nary a civil word to each other for at least the last twenty-five years of their fifty-plus years of marriage. In the 1960's they had gotten a small Boston apartment after they left New York and Far Hills. They wanted to be within commuting distance of Tenants Harbor, yet keep the stimulation of city living. Now my father came up to Maine every weekend to spar with her, but at least she had her peace—and her alcohol—when he returned to Boston during the week. She had friends in Maine and, more important to her, a woman who worked for her to pick up a daily supply of liquor. She did not drive much after she moved there as by now a permanent haze had settled over her mind and she was too unsteady on her pins, not to mention too out of touch with reality, to drive a car.

One weekend a close lady friend of mine, Joanie MacDougall, and I went for a stay in the little house I had just finished building in Tenants Harbor. On our first evening there, we went to have cocktails with my mother. She had been "refueling" herself, as my father always called her drinking habit, throughout the day and was having a troublesome time holding her cigarettes. Joanie kept helping her pick them up when they missed the ashtray. My father had put a sheet of aluminum under her table to take care of these "droppings." After a relatively incoherent visit, we left for a dinner party. When it was over, we went home and turned in around twelve.

At three in the morning I got a frantic call from a near neighbor of my mother's to say there was a fire and that I should come immediately. I thought it was probably just some leaves under a window where she might have thrown a cigarette. Nevertheless, I went to check. To my horror, her place was engulfed in flames and I could see her in the room through the window. She was struggling to get up off the sofa, but the smoke and fire suddenly got to her and she fell forward onto the floor. The heat was far too intense to open a window. She died before my eyes. Her drinking and emotional failures had caused me immense problems and pain but I wept as I watched her leave this earth. She was my mother and I had loved her. I had always prayed that someday she would get sober, and now that was not to be. I should have been praying for myself as well.

The manner in which my mother died haunted my dreams for years, and, sometimes, in them I would see myself standing next to her during her last moments. I would awake screaming and sobbing. What a twist of fate that it was I who witnessed her death when her other sons, whom she loved far more than I, were elsewhere. Our relationship had been strained for many years because I was the one forever taking her to drying-out retreats where it was hoped she could solve her alcohol problems. Now I had watched her die in a fire, which her alcoholism and smoking had caused.

As none of my immediate family was in Maine at the time of her death, I organized the undertaker, the funeral arrangements and the autopsy that had to be performed. A death from an accidental fire is always considered suspicious to the authorities until they can determine that death was from the fire and not another cause. My mother had told every member of our family that she never wanted to be cremated, but now there had been an act of God that ignored her wishes. She had not been burned to ashes, but, still, one noted the irony. It is also ironic, given her quite open hostility towards my father that she took with her so many of the things my father cherished most on earth. Their house had been filled with his immensely valuable antiques, as well as his personal artifacts and possessions. All evaporated in the conflagration. He mourned their loss but never mentioned my mother's death again from the moment that I called him in Boston and told him about the fire. He came to live with me for a few weeks after the fire and nary a word was said about my mother but a great deal about the things he had lost.

In 1918, my grandmother, Cornelia Thayer Andrew Clark, had died and left a very large family trust fund. Some of the income from it was to go to Mother after the death of my grandfather, and at her death, the trust was to be divided among her issue. As my grandfather had died, my mother had been living off of this trust, as well as off of money she had inherited outright from her mother when she died. I got my share of the 1918 trust, tax-free, when my mother died. But she had disinherited me in her personal will. I got none of her non-trust money.

Being cut out of her will was a frightful slap in my face, especially as she and I had been getting along a little better before her death. She had informed me earlier that summer that she had put me back in her will, although I had never known I had been out of it. However, she never got around to rectifying my exclusion but only dreamed she had. This turned out to be her final rejection of me and it was unbelievably painful.

When I began to benefit from my grandmother's trust, I moved rapidly into the second phase of my precarious middle age. It changed my life, and now I had more than enough money to spend any way I wished. I had a job income, a consulting income and a trust income, all of which nicely I thought eased my psychological pains and salved over my inner turmoil by subsidizing many delightful diversions. This proved, however, to be exactly what I should not have been doing. It was my road to hell, but I did not heed any warning signs and drove straight down it at full speed. Being completely dysfunctional made this easy for me.

I moved to an elegant house in Louisburg Square in Boston and set about making a glamorous life. I desperately wanted to live it up and prove to the world—especially Patsy and my children—that I had not been torn apart by the divorce. I also thought it might help me banish those episodes which never seemed to stop sweeping over me every time my family relationships worsened. It was heart-rending for me to feel so alone in the world, with my family arrayed against me. I heard nothing but criticism from friends who spent time with my relatives, and I cringed at the negative opinions they passed on to me. Foolishly, I thought that my newfound money would help cure these pains.

My house in the Square, like so many of my previous dwellings, became a magnet for a vast array of friends. I would throw a party at the drop of a hat and my seated dinners for twenty-four became legendary. Conductors, musicians, soloists and singers who were in town for engagements with the Boston Symphony were entertained at my place, as were many of the celebrities opening in plays in Boston.

Nat King Cole's wife, Maria, whose marvelous Ritz Carlton apartment was decorated in a most unusual style with her bathtub placed in the middle of her bedroom, might appear one night or Arthur Fiedler the next night. Both were friends, for we had traveled together throughout Europe. Maria and I would go out on the town occasionally or dine at my place.

One night, she and I swept into a huge and fashionable Red Cross gala on Boston's waterfront. As Maria was unusually beautiful and so superbly dressed, people immediately turned her way as we entered the colossal, flower-filled tent. There we were—I, a Boston Brahmin and she, an exquisite, upper class, black woman. We were the cynosure of all eyes. Friend after friend of mine came over to our table to talk to me and to be introduced to Maria. My phone rang incessantly the next day as I heard from people I had not been in contact with for years. Even Patsy called. I was living it up and loving it.

After a brouhaha with a staff member's wife, who actually was a friend of mine, I got into my first drink-related trouble at work. As I happened to be thoroughly inebriated when I misbehaved towards this woman, I never knew exactly what it was that I had done. Whatever it was, it offended her deeply. When word of the incident reached the ears of the Symphony business manager, he leapt at the chance to get me out of his way. Since I had a larger profile in the eyes of the trustees and nearly everyone else at the BSO, he wanted me gone. I left with my tail between my legs, mortified that alcohol had been the culprit in destroying my job and reputation. Or was the culprit myself?

Within four months, I rectified that loss of income by devising a television show about design and also by buying a nearly defunct design firm. I named it Robinson & Smith, Inc. Robinson had started the firm. I set it up to handle the business I was acquiring from people who saw my television program, or who had come into my apartment and admired my sense of style.

I also started my own travel company, Sporting Ventures Ltd. I could now roam the world at discount prices, and travel I certainly did. It is a conundrum why I did so well in my businesses when I was doing so poorly in coping with my life, but, in fact, I would hardly be the only one in this situation. At one point, I personally was doing over Boston's huge new arts complex (now the Wang Center), the travel venture was booming and I was successfully fundraising as a consultant for two major nonprofit agencies. There seemed to be no stopping me. Yet I had failed so many times in my life, and people close to me had always been so critical, that there was no way I could take anything for granted. Depression kept shoving me down and when one lives alone and works for oneself, one can hide from people as need be. For days on end when I was depressed, I would hibernate and see absolutely nobody except my cleaning woman. When I was on an "upper," I was adept at making the world think all my businesses were successful and that everything I did turned to gold.

I certainly had reason to feel on top of the world. Not only did I have exposure on one of the major television networks, but also I was producing a series for cable called "In Good Taste." The network gig was a segment of a morning talk show on which I was a regular guest demonstrating how people could turn their apartments into showplaces or stage fabulous dinner parties, Christmas shindigs, Easter celebrations and Thanksgiving feasts. I used my own apartment as the set, and with the generous expense allowance I was given, my place became a gem. Business was going well, and I kept on producing these guest spots, which, in turn, brought my design firm more clients. The programs were so successful that a major cable television production company asked me to develop a series that would take an audience through celebrities' houses that I considered to be decorated in good taste. Finding such special residences was easy, for I went to world-famous decorators whom I knew. Sister Parish, who had done over the White House for the Kennedy's, and Mark Hampton, who had overseen a refurbishment of Blair House, the guesthouse of the White House, both participated with me. Before I knew it, I was wandering through houses owned by the likes of Bill Blass and Ted Turner. I was flying high most of the time, but whenever depression reared its ugly head during production—which, I confess, was too often—I simply called in sick with a cold. (Colds made one's on-air voice sound "off" and sometimes even unintelligible, so this was a useful trick.)

My children were by now in secondary school and college, with the expenses of education horrific. As her husband was always on another line and butting in, few phone conversations with Patsy did not end in some form of confrontation. Becoming frustrated with these calls and seeing little of the children at this time, I realized I must get help and talk to a doctor in order to keep my sanity. My depression periods were getting longer and longer. My faith in God, my belief in my future and my belief in myself were all starting to evaporate. Even my sleep was disturbed, but by exerting a great deal of effort, I kept myself going and kept my working life afloat. I compounded this latest spiral downward by breaking up with my long-standing girlfriend and by trying to increase my inheritance through playing the stock market. These were all anxiety provokers, and any attempt at leading a rational and functional life was impossible with these situations hanging over my head. As my problems once again were getting the best of me—or perhaps I should say, the worst of me—I was increasingly helpless. I finally went to a psychiatrist in Boston. The commute to my Beverly doctor's office was too hard to undertake.

When I had been seeing my doctor after Welly's death, there were few pills that could be prescribed to relieve anxiety or depression. Now, eight years later, my new doctor was willing to try some of the new drugs on the market. A few of them were not even available to the public yet. But, in fact, he wound up diagnosing me as manic depressive and prescribing lithium. It helped me not at all. I stayed on it for six months and went further downhill.

It didn't help that the stockbroker handling my account took advantage of both my naiveté about investing and my burning desire to double my money. His advice nearly put me in debtors' prison, for he continually pushed me to sell every stock I owned at pitiful prices. Then he coerced me into the futures market solely to make huge commissions for himself. I had no idea what was going on and wound up losing everything I put into his firm. It was no small sum—about a million dollars in today's money. Naturally this made the plunge into depression even more precipitous.

I began to take more and more chances with my money to make up for my staggering losses, but it was to little avail. Not surprisingly, my life now changed dramatically. My parties, affairs, sporting activities and travel all ground to a halt. The activities that had once made me happy, unfortunately, I could no longer afford them. I wrestled with my depression by taking huge amounts of sleeping pills my doctor was willing to prescribe whenever I asked for them. With alcohol on top of medication, I slept the sleep of the dead but without these aids I did not sleep a wink and thrashed all night in a swirl of fear and worry.

The Boston doctor finally switched my medication, as it was obvious no progress was being made. He tried MAOI medication and I felt somewhat better for a week or two. However, he forgot to tell me that there were certain foods that I must not now eat. One day, after I consumed a large, blue cheese-dressed salad, my blood pressure shot through the sky and I collapsed on the sidewalk. I was disoriented and sick to my stomach, and I had such a splitting headache that I wanted to die rather than suffer any more of the agony I felt. I struggled to a taxi and went home to lie miserably in bed for two days with a racing heart, a pounding skull and heavy sweats drenching me. I thought I was dying but simply did not realize there was a long list of forbidden foods. When the doctor learned of the terrible interaction, he apologized for failing to inform me, but that was the end of my dealings with him. My depression flooded back once I was on no medication.

A month after this nearly fatal episode, I found, through a friend, another psychiatrist who was more interested in psychoanalyzing me than drugging me. But he also sent me to a well-known doctor who specialized in testing new-on-the-market depression medications. Hearing that these trials were producing promising results, I was eager to participate.

It was too bad for me that he turned out to be little better than my first pill-pusher. I was given a large supply of a new anti-anxiety drug, Xanax, which, I was told, I could take whenever I felt anxious. As he said three or four was the dose to take, I took this many about four times a day and, consequently, moved about in a dense fog. Within a month I was in bed, unable to function, sleeping heavily and having nightmares day and night. My television and design jobs nearly evaporated and I could not face life. I was a basket case and felt I had nowhere to turn.

One particularly drugged morning, with every ounce of strength I had, I knelt and swore to God that I would give up this addictive Xanax. Once I had made this pact with Him, I was too scared to break it for fear of His retribution. I climbed back into bed and for the next five days experienced a living hell of delirium tremors, sweats and shaking. It was an agony so intense that I am terrified, even today, to take a pill that noticeably lifts my mood or sedates me.

After this crisis point, life resumed something of a strange financial balance. I remained fretful about the income from my inheritance but fees from my design work had resumed even though they'd diminished since I had let my accounts lapse. Still, I felt healthier than I had in a long time as I was staying in touch with my new psychiatrist, who was a sounder clinician, dealing with me much as my Beverly doctor had done. Avoiding medication, he emphasized psychotherapy. I took a positive, but cautious, hold on my life without the aid of any drugs. It took some real effort but I reduced my intake of liquor to four drinks a day, though, if anyone noticed, they were stiff ones at that.

With reduced drinking I felt better and began to extend myself into the community. I became a very active member of Boston's magnificent jewel, Trinity Church. I was a "believer" but, as I have said, I was scared to death of God as I imagined Him. I felt the power of His love in me, but I cowered in dread at what might happen if I angered Him. Still, I never felt completely abandoned by Him for I knew that He did hear my prayers even in my darkest moments.

The Rector at Trinity Church, Spencer Rice, touched and inspired me Sunday after Sunday with his powerful sermons. They were usually wrapped around the tenet that one must love God, one's neighbor and, most particularly, oneself, if one is to find that unique inner peace necessary to survive in this chaotic world. His homilies infused my soul with the seeds of newly found self-worth. The trouble was that, like so many alcoholics, the better I felt about myself, the more I liked to celebrate and rejoice in that feeling. I rarely in the recent past had felt very lifted up so I relished this new feeling and had a few more drinks thinking they would make me even happier. I can in no way explain these stupid actions for I was by now smart enough to know that drink would pull me down and increase my depression. Unfortunately, my addiction ignored me.

Yet again—and I recognize the repetition here—the ravages of drinking overwhelmed my system. I shook from over-imbibing when passing the plate at church and I felt queasy at the communion rail. I began skipping many church services, activities, lectures and social gatherings. I stayed home to drink and only slipped into Trinity during the week to pray in private. I still was not ready to be sober, and I thought Alcoholics Anonymous was only for old people who were confirmed alcoholics. I was convinced I could give it up anytime I wanted to. And, of course, I was wrong.

One early evening in Maine in the fall of 1985, I was talking to my father as he stood beside the riding lawnmower he used much like a golf cart to move his emphysema-riddled body around his place. As a joke I said, "Smile, Pa, I don't want to remember you scowling and sad. I might never see you again." with that, he smiled, sat down on his already-running mower and died instantly. The mower moved away from me and wove its way erratically down the lawn to the pond with his body slightly slumped off the mower. I wondered, as I watched him, why he was leaning so far forward for, of course, I was unaware that he had died. I trundled off to meet Phyllis Collins for dinner in Camden, not realizing he had fallen off the mower and was lying dead in a glade of tall grass. It was not until I returned from Camden that I found a note on my front door informing me of my father's death. The body had been taken to Thomaston to an undertaker.

From the moment of my father's death, a miasma of greed again enveloped the family. My father's will was poorly planned and written. My younger brother and I were designated as executors, while my older brother was almost disinherited. My father had told me he was going to do this because he felt Philip had received too much from my mother. I had asked my father often not to exclude him, so he did will him some property. My younger brother, my father's lady friend and I were to divide the estate in thirds. (The lady friend's money was to be held in trust for her for her lifetime and then go to my younger brother and me.)

We three were also to divide the Maine and Boston furniture and my sibling was to get my father's house in Maine. At first glance, it seemed as if the division should have been simple, but its poorly constructed legal language produced problems that have not been satisfactorily solved to this day. As untangling it seemed virtually a hopeless task, I signed away, without actually realizing it, all my rights to a family dock, giving them to Philip's children instead. Moreover, I signed other papers, under pressure, in order to secure my brother's written permission to have some special monies that my father had set aside for me. I should have expected such dysfunctional behavior but I was too trusting. The fallout from my father's death and the settling of his estate sent sharp hurts through me that triggered more devastating results. This final family rejection, which I was too depressed to deal with, blindsided me. The impact was enough to drain me of my last shred of self-esteem. I had carried my dysfunctional role-playing into adulthood and now the web, which bound us siblings together, was shredded beyond repair. I was absolutely lost.

As if this was not enough of a pummeling, disaster hit again on January 8, 1986. At two o'clock in the morning the house in Boston in which I lived caught fire because of faulty wiring. The house was burned badly inside but was saved from collapse by the quick work of the Boston Fire Department. I was asleep when it started and just narrowly escaped with my life out a back window, dropping down two stories on knotted bed sheets. It was below zero and I was clad only in my pajama pants. My elegant apartment, which had been featured in magazine articles, used for filming movies and TV shows and was filled with priceless antiques, was very nearly a total loss.

All the furniture I had recently gotten from my father's apartment, plus other items from my family's big house in Far Hills, were ruined or destroyed. Some of the furniture was insured but most of it was not. I had inherited, just two months previously, major pieces from my father so they were still on his insurance policy. I wanted to collect on it but my co executor assured the lawyer handling my father's estate that I had no loss, only smoke damage. This brother never came to see the complete destruction and he nearly ruined my chances of collecting on my loss. Happily, the insurance company did come through and I was able to buy replacements. This second attempt by a sibling to ignore my rights was enraging. Would my family's constant irrational behavior never end? I was incapable of dealing with these affronts in a rational manner.

A fire completely destroys one's identity. All the furniture that had been in my family was gone, the photographs of my family were burned, the beautiful paintings and portraits that I had collected were gone, my papers and books were incinerated, and my personal mementos, clothes, china and silver had been ruined. Once again, I had to start my life over from scratch, much as I did when I left Patsy. I went to live for a few days following the fire with my dear friends the Meads, but within a week or so I was "nakedly" on my own. For some reason or another, I had been on the wagon at the time of the fire, but not for long, the letters arriving from my father's lawyer concerning insurance and fraternal betrayal saw to that.

I soon rented a big apartment on Mt. Vernon Street in Boston to use for both my business and living quarters. It was rather swell, but I thought I deserved it. With the insurance money, my inheritance from my father and a windfall inheritance from my childless Uncle George Clark, I fixed it up nicely. I was still making money on design projects that I had been asked to do for divorced friends moving into Boston. However, I was as far away from contentment as was humanly possible. The family abuses, the constant losses, the fire, the drinking and the void that should have been my self-esteem had finally brought me to a place beyond my breaking point.

One day I struggled to break through the paralysis I felt, trying to grasp just a tinge of joy. I called a friend and made a date for that night at my place. After she arrived we began drinking rather heavily, as both of us imagined it would help bring some cheer into our lives. She was quite depressed as well, for she had been fired from her job just a week prior. Without any warning, and for no reason I could see, she suddenly turned on me in a fury. I was aghast yet drunk enough to turn on her. We screamed and yelled at each other until we were both exhausted. We said vile things about each other and she stormed out. I continued to drink, as tears streamed down my face. My mind raced through all the rejections that had befallen me. I was a total failure and there was no way I would ever be anything else. My depression had completely overwhelmed me. I went to the room where I kept my guns.

My mother was rarely sober in her last few years. She hid bottles throughout the houses she lived in, yet went from time to time to drying out facilities and would drink nothing for a month or two. No retreats ever worked. She did, however, remain well dressed, exquisitely polite and generous, but rather nonsensical in her conversation.

By the time this picture was taken, Mother had lost all her looks to drink. She was puffy faced, and her legs were constantly bleeding and bruised. She developed an alcoholic potbelly, and her hair looked like sea weed in texture and color. She, who once had beauty, friends, a full life and three sons that she "loved," was now totally controlled by alcohol. As such, she was a kind of derelict who could afford to be off the street, and this meant few knew she was in such horrible shape.

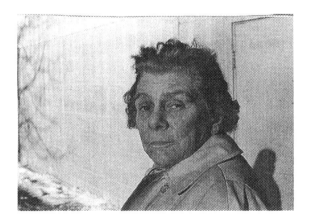

One summer evening, a friend of mine and I were visiting with my mother who, as usual, kept sipping drinks and dropping cigarettes. When it was time to leave, my friend said we should not go as she feared my mother might burn herself. I said not to worry. At three in the morning, I was called and told that Mother's house was on fire. I rushed over and a whole wing was being totally consumed by flames. I just for an instant could see Mother, but I am sure the smoke had gotten her. She was on the sofa, possibly even already dead. My father rushed from Boston to find the aftermath of this inferno. Alcohol always kills one way or another.

My mother left me rather well fixed, enabling me to move to an exquisite townhouse on Louisburg Square in Boston. This is the dining room in which I entertained from eight to a hundred people on a regular basis. I was drinking heavily and had the money to support the habit, and the parties, too.

This is the view of the same room above after an electrical wire shorted at two o'clock in the morning in the dead of winter. I was sober at the time as I had gone on the wagon. A fire alarm saved my life and I dropped from the bedroom window two floors to the garden holding sheets. It was below zero and I was only in a pair of pajama pants.

My living room in the townhouse was filmed for television and magazines many times. I had a TV series called "Good Taste," featuring tips on how to entertain. I became a bit of a celebrity and bought a design firm to handle the work that resulted from the television exposure.

In this picture one can see through the dining room into the living room. Both were destroyed by the fire. As some of the furniture I had only just inherited, it was still insured by one of my late father's policies. When I asked them for the insurance, they hesitated about paying me because the other executor insisted that I'd suffered nothing but smoke damage. Take a look at what the "smoke" did.

I built his little house right at the edge of Maine's rockbound coast. I escaped from Boston to it on a regular basis and it was here that I came to get sober and change my entire life.

Winter here is a bit hard, with the winds constantly blowing. If you went straight out to sea from this house, you would come to Spain. There was no protection from the elements, but I loved it.

This beloved Jack Russell Terrier, Charlie, arrived in my life just before I left Boston. Without him, I doubt I would have survived the first Maine winter. He was my constant companion, a soul to talk to and to hug.

After eight years on the crashing, open ocean, I moved to this house, a little inland. At last, I had central heating, protection from the wind and big wood fireplaces.

One of my greatest delights is gardening. I built this terrace outside my big summer living room and use it as an extra room.

I took this picture of my father the day before he died. The moment before he died I said to him, "Smile, Pa, I might never see you again."

With that, he sat down on this lawn mower, which he used for transportation due to the ravages of drinking and smoking, and died. I did not realize it right away for the mower set off down the hill with him on it. I noticed that the path was quite erratic but thought little of it and left. Three hours later I found that he had fallen off the machine just by the pond at the bottom of the lawn.

I actually became a friend of his in his last few years. I had been to my psychiatrist enough to get on my own feet and realize what he was doing. The death of my mother seemed to calm him down, for they had never stopped fighting. I could hardly remember a civil word between them over their last twenty-five years. They celebrated fifty-five years of marriage with a nasty exchange, but would never divorce because that wasn't done in "proper" families. They are buried half a mile apart in Maine.

ELEVEN

When dawn came and the alcohol and the numbness had only partially worn off, I rolled over as light began filtering into the bedroom. Instantly I realized how close I had come to terminating my life. As my tortured mind started to come to grips with my stupidity, I felt a surging power inexplicably swelling through my body. I rolled over the side of my bed, onto my knees, and prayed.

I had never abandoned my faith in God, just blotted it out at times, and now, at the lowest moment of my life, I knew immediately that I needed a power far greater than myself. Call it what you like but I felt a spirit was pulsating within my head and telling me that this power had saved me from a terrifying end. I knew this force would continue to help me. Instinctively, I felt this was a first stage of my new life. A divine spark was within me and guiding me in a way I had never before experienced. As I was to find out soon, this was but the first of many "sudden awakenings" which brought me to deeper and deeper understanding of the meaning of my life.

As I knelt by the bed in which I had tried to kill myself, I understood that God was within me and I recognized that I had to get my life in order or I would perish. I knew now that I wanted to live, but certainly not as I was presently living. I somehow grasped that it would be a perilous and difficult climb to get out of my pit of despair alone. Yet I knew intuitively that with the help of a higher power I could start to do it. I was alive and I was going to try, with all the force I could muster, to survive. I remained on my knees as my mind raced through possible first steps. What would help would be a mental list of the problems that had to be surmounted and resolved, but I was too weak for that. Even if I could enumerate them, I had never been able to cope with the most severe of them for they were buried too deep inside me and masked by years of dysfunctional behavior and alcohol. It wasn't until I later started peeling back the layers of my psyche that I was able to realize I had far more serious issues to confront than even the death of my son, my fire and my rejections. I had carried my scapegoat and mascot roles into aduldhood and I was completely dysfunctional. My lifestyle forced me to act in totally irrational ways. Alcohol had intensified this ridiculous behavior.

I needed to begin to think clearly and rationally enough to see my whole life, and help myself. It was a daunting task and took tremendous effort for, as we have seen, I was an obsessive, controlling and compulsive person. It was going to be far harder than I ever imagined, but with the sure knowledge of a greater power guiding me, I was soon to set about prayerfully seeking ways to overcome my terrible behavioral afflictions.

It was just days after this epiphany that I realized I should get away from Boston. I could not stay in surroundings that triggered drinking or that were associated with my ongoing depression. I should be off by myself where I could think clearly and seek help. I made a decision to build life anew in Maine.

Rather dramatically and without much planning, I started to move to my own little summerhouse in Tenants Harbor. It was not winterized, but I was convinced that I could both arrange that and adapt to rural living. As I had been both a sophisticated city boy and a country gentleman all my life, this move to Maine was a major change. It was done with little forethought, and it was hardly as simple as I thought it would be. The switch over caused me lots of anxiety. One of the standard alcoholic maneuvers is called the "geographical escape." An alcoholic is convinced that a move is as good as a cure. He blames his problems on his surroundings and friends rather than on himself. This was partially true for me, but I also felt I could better come to terms with myself with no urban distractions and drinking friends on every street corner.

As the lease on my apartment on Mt. Vernon Street, where I had moved after the fire at Louisburg Square, was expiring within a week, I called the owner and said I would not renew it. Within hours I was packing furiously and sloppily. I got hold of as many boxes as I could and stuffed them to the gunnels with all my worldly goods. Then I called a cheap moving man and was off to Maine, one of the last frontiers.

Within two weeks, I found myself settling in Tenants Harbor. I was frightened when I got there but also filled with relief. Such an abrupt change had to be unsettling, so I allowed myself two drinks of white wine in the evening to help allay my fears. Those drinks did the work and calmed me down. I should not have been drinking at all. I was, as usual, fooling myself. I considered wine a light and weak form of alcohol, so why worry.

I soon contracted with carpenter friends to do the work that was needed to let me get through a winter, and I started to shuffle through the problems and situations that arose from my relocation. There were many. The first was the arrival of my things from Boston, with much that I brought broken and torn, as a result of packing so hastily. The second problem was the legions of carpenter ants eating up the sills of my house. They were everywhere and had destroyed the whole foundation. It was a horrendous job to fix but the men I'd hired leapt in and got everything underway.

On the first day they came to work, I lazily sat and watched the work on my house begin. Suddenly, I longed for a stiff drink. Although I reminded myself I was trying to have no noon drinks ever, it did not work. I poured a glass of wine. I gulped it down. A single drink is never seems to be enough, and the aching for more swept through my system, I poured another and was literally driven to keep filling my glass all day long. By nightfall I was thoroughly drunk.

After my near-suicide, I had sworn that I would try and do it differently now. But the alcohol controlled me, and I broke that promise to myself. I was devastated but hopeful that I would not drink the next day.

The next day the same horrifying thing happened. I said to myself that I would have just one at noon, but by nightfall I must have had ten or more. The following day I could not find my car, as I was unable to remember where I had parked it the night before. A friend who lived up the road came to see me for my car was at her place. She suggested, very gently, that I needed help for my alcoholic problem. This was the first time anyone ever had called me an alcoholic. I wished that it had happened years and years before. Immediately sensing that what she had confronted me with was the truth and having just realized that it would be totally impossible for me to stop on my own, I took myself that very night to the Tenants Harbor Alcoholics Anonymous meeting, which is called "Safe Harbor Meeting." As fate would have it, she confronted me on a Tuesday night and this is the one night in the week that the AA meeting is in the village.

Alcoholic Anonymous, dedicated to assisting people to overcome the debilitating and eventually fatal disease of alcoholism, touches the very souls of those who accept its precepts and its Twelve Step Program. It affirms and dignifies lives, for it helps men and women to achieve far more than sobriety. It literally saves them, and brings to their spirit peace and grace. A meaningful relationship with a Higher Power is another result, for AA stresses that a force stronger than oneself is needed. By recognizing this truth, a person can take the necessary leap out of self-centeredness and into a life of healing and giving. As well as emphasizing abstinence from drinking, AA's program focuses on the positive forces that are necessary in our lives. Those include truthfulness, calmness, forgiveness, love and thankfulness, to name but a few.

I felt a tremendous surge of anxiety when I entered the meeting. And I was embarrassed to be there until I realized that all the others were there for the same reason. I thought that rumors would wing their way around the community that I was alcoholic until I remembered the anonymity signified in the name of the organization. The people I saw in the room represented all ages, sexes, many backgrounds and all stages of recovery. I felt at home immediately as people came forward and asked me to sit with them. The organization knows full well that to recover, one needs both a Higher Power and friends.

As I took a seat, I looked around and saw old friends and acquaintances that I had never guessed might have a problem. I did not feel alone. The meeting officially started when the moderator directed us to introduce ourselves. Soon it became my turn and I said for the first time to others, as well as to myself, "I am Forrester and I am an alcoholic." I was stunned to hear myself. A feeling of complete shame hit me. I felt total humiliation at being one of those people I had always considered stupid fools for drinking too much. I had never admitted it to myself: never-never-never!

That was over twenty five years ago and I have been sober since that moment.

The feelings of health and clearness of mind that returned slowly but surely was incredible. It takes a great deal of time to rid the system of alcohol. Once I achieved a modicum of sobriety, after about two months in AA and four meetings a week, I became rational enough to be aware that some of my other major problems must be faced head on. My depression was a big one to be wrestled with. Liquor had continually been exacerbating this condition and now I could try to deal with it. Sobriety was the best medication to cure other problems as well. Most had been caused by abuse of alcohol.

I searched and found a fine psychiatrist in the area to help me try to come to grips with my depression. My new doctor helped me dig deeper into my subconscious than I had ever done before and he began to help me resolve many long-festering issues of rejection that I had not uncovered before. I needed to bring them into my consciousness to be released. My role-playing behavior had to be faced head-on and changed radically. The severely dysfunctional behavior of mine had never been approached directly. When one is dysfunctional our behavior seems normal to us. It's the way we know how to act. When we have the sudden awakening to functional behavior, we are new people.

The combination of AA and psychiatry can work wonders in curing dysfunctionality. Just the very discussion of the situation makes one feel more functional. By accepting truths both large and small about myself and my family, by continuing to work with my psychiatrist and by reading innumerable articles on adult children of alcoholics, I started to heal. I feel strongly that people can never shake off dysfunctional behavior until they wholeheartedly admit to themselves and others that their way of living is not normal. Their reactions to general, everyday happenings are almost never rational for they have carried role-playing into their adult life. They can run the gamut of reactions to a perfectly simple matter or action. As a scapegoat, I spent my days basically, as a jester, for I could not be rational and especially when drunk.

One evening, after about three months of AA meetings, I suddenly felt the urge for a drink quite badly. I kept liquor in the house for guests and could easily have poured myself one. However, I was by now far too disciplined to do that. I was upset, though, by my craving and needed to figure out the trigger for the desire. After some intense introspection over several hours the answer came, like the flash of a camera bulb. I realized that the second I took a swallow and began feeling the buzz from the alcohol, I would like myself better and the painful thoughts would become numb. I suddenly had self-esteem. This particular night,

I had been feeling very low and that had ignited that familiar yearning for a drink. From that awakening moment I lost my desire for alcohol for my sobriety became my self-esteem. Without one doubt I knew I could now build a new lifestyle based on sobriety. Now, at last, I felt genuine courage. It was such a spectacular awakening and it has lasted to this day. I have no desire whatsoever for alcohol. The smell is even abhorrent.

Five years after joining Alcoholics Anonymous, I took a stiff drink totally by accident. It taught me a never-to-be-forgotten lesson. It happened one very hot August day while I was sitting on a glorious porch looking out over Tenants Harbor. A person passed me a glass and told me it was the soda water I had asked for. Thirstily, I gulped the whole thing down as quickly as I could, for the day was hotter than the hinges of Hades. As I caught my breath after swallowing, the whole drink in one big gulp, I let out a yelp, "My God, you gave me a gin and tonic!" The taste of the bitter tonic told me this. Instantly the intense addictive power of the alcohol spread to every nerve in my whole body. My whole being cried out for another. I was aware that I must move quickly to quell the yearning.

I rushed to the kitchen and drank a huge glass of cream, then ate three or four slices of bread. These, I thought, would sop up the liquor in my system. They did a bit, but all day long my whole system was wracked with the intense longing for alcohol. It was a true torment. This accident proved to me, once and for all, that I should never take another drink of alcohol. It would take control of me and the inevitable result would be an agonizing death for me. I never wanted to lose my newly gained "sobriety" self esteem.

When I stopped drowning the higher power within my mind with alcohol, I discovered that loving myself as a sober person could bring me peace and happiness and even contentment. I learned that my single life gave me a superb way to have independence and develop a meaningful, spiritual existence. The depression, which had always been one of my biggest problems, was now getting under control. This was occurring in lock step with my gaining sobriety, but seeing a good doctor and being treated with the right medication, a very new anti depression medication had recently been developed that did the trick for me. Too many people think anti depressant medication is addictive. It is far from it for it gives me no "high." It acts to get brain waves going as they were meant to. Depression is a disease.

I knew I could and must do more to live a full life in rural Maine. I realized I had to give myself a real purpose and direction. I could not just sit all day and repeat to myself that I was alcoholic while going every night to an Alcoholics Anonymous meeting where I would repeat, once again, that I was alcoholic. That might be facing the facts but not getting on with things in a meaningful way. The long nights, the isolation and the somewhat strenuous lifestyle of my first winter in Maine were in no way unpleasant experiences. In fact, they were splendid in every way and opened me up to a more functional existence. I also made room for a regular meditation time as I embraced sobriety, improved behavior and happiness.

With my faith growing stronger each day, for I now liked myself, it made my search for a healing power a great deal easier. I found it impossible to believe that God, in the form of love, was not dwelling inside me. This was my "Divine Spark" and I came to the belief that this is the positive force of love, which is inside all of us. It is the soul of our lives and gives life its purpose. Didn't Jesus say, "God is love"?

With these personal truths as a base for my healing, I haltingly let my egotistical self go. This helped let God bring me into His saving force of love. I said to myself that I could not cope alone and, therefore, I must surrender to a power that will set me free and let me love life and all that is within it. By doing just this, I was to find peace, a peace that only God, and not the world, can give. One never has to be judgmental, condemning, angry or spiteful if one allows love to fill to overflowing. There is no room for negativity. Love gives complete peace.

As I moved forward, I still searched to find some explanation for the shattering tragedy of Welly's death. I realized that it would never be found. Why should I dwell on it? I now knew I must mourn as a remembrance of Welly, but at the same time choosing to make my life more positive by helping others who have suffered similar agonies. I began to run a "grief group" for parents who have also lost their children as I can relate to their sorrow.

As I became more involved in my church, I came to truly believe that the Holy Spirit connects me, in the form of love, to every soul on earth. God's will is done when we let love direct us in word and deed.

I now understand also that God does not purposely inflict pain on us, nor is He responsible for misfortunes that continually plague mankind. Nobody promised us life would be without tragedies. They are part of just living.

These trials and tribulations are always with us as we try to get through each chaotic day. As we spin through space every second of our lives, change is the very essence of it. We have absolutely no control over anything in life. We think we do, but we do not. Even certainty that we, or anyone around, us will be alive in the next second is impossible. We try desperately to regulate everything and everyone around us to fit our needs and wants. This effort will fail every time, for nothing can be counted on except love.

If we can learn to live in the moment—neither looking back at our failures nor forward at our aspirations—and if we can direct our lives by that force of love, we will have a peace within us. I firmly believe Christ came as the messenger of God to teach us to change our lives and live them filled with His love. What more can we ask than to have His peace within us?

So often I wake up in the morning and try to over organize my life. I spend my day committed to this controlling my life. When, at the end of each frenetic day, I assume that I have been successful, I retire happily thinking order has been created. I might even have a feeling of some satisfaction, but the next morning says it was an illusion. I, therefore, must start over trying to gain control over everything again. It's futile. Only that completely positive force of love within me is the single constant and unchanging element. It is there, guiding me when I let go of being self-centered and when I permit love to take over. Then the unique and true peace floods in and the false gods of power, money, events or control evaporate.

I truly believe that all people have an absolute right to follow different paths to find peace and love. Any religion or belief system, which puts a person in harmony with a greater power and offers a message based on the Golden Rule is a route to salvation. Christ said that the Kingdom of God was within us, so who are we to question who "us" may be? Christ taught Christians "the way, the life and the truth," but I do not think that means that Mohammed or Buddha or other prophets were wrong.

I have found that my faith must be constantly practiced and held strong within me, for as an imperfect human being, I constantly fail at my goal of living a perfect life. Conscious of the fact that I should love everyone as myself, I find it most difficult at times not to get upset with myself if someone lashes out at me or rejects me, and I lash back. I need the positive power of love to be replenished in me every day. I can manage to get through only a week before I know deep down that I must refresh my spirit. I choose to go to church on Sundays for this healing power. It is not a sin to me if I do not go to church, but I try to never miss a Sunday service for I am too weak to carry on without God's help. I need the sorting out, the forgiveness and the strength that comes from my time in church.

As I was working on curing my problems, I began carrying my faith out into the community I live. I had always known that rural Maine towns were hard pressed for volunteers to help their service agencies succeed. To conquer my feelings of isolation and to work towards my mission of helping others, I set myself a goal of getting to know at least two new people every single day. AA meetings, church and even the village coffee shop, along with my involvement in local politics, provided a good springboard. What a joy this was for me to set about, and how easy it turned out to be accomplished.

Twenty years later, I know about a thousand people and have been a president, vice-president, chairman, senior warden or trustee of nearly twenty charitable, political, church, environmental and governmental institutions in the state of Maine. I am also a registered Hospice Volunteer. With the help of many others, I have raised millions of dollars, both regionally and nationally, for these groups. The positive direction I have given to my life has also helped keep me from dwelling too long on any of my former sadness and mistakes. It has made my life a truly functional one looking ahead.

One of the most fascinating parts of my new life was my involvement in the political world. When I became Maine's State Finance Chair for the Republican Party, after having held at least fifteen other political positions in my town, the county and statewide, I was tickled pink. I traveled throughout Maine and beyond, meeting and entertaining politicians ranging from Presidents of the United States to Vice Presidents, Senators, Presidential candidates, Governors and just plain VIP's. It was thrilling to meet and dine with both the George Bushes, to breakfast in my house with candidates for President of the U.S., to escort Governors of various states through Maine or to be a confidant of Maine's Senators and Congressional Representatives. I relished all of this activity. My election as a delegate to the Republican National Convention in 1988 fulfilled my wildest dream, for I played a role in nominating George H.W. Bush for President. I had come a long way from being a depressed person afraid to go outdoors and face people without a drink.

I also soon found that I was able to greatly improve my outlook on life by addressing my physical needs along with my psychological ones. I began eating a well balanced diet and exercising every day. I started to experience non-substance-related feelings of euphoria and happiness. How wonderful this was, to feel so good, and so good about myself, without resort to chemicals or stimulants!

Once I was in touch with my healthy self, I knew I must start to mend many of my fences. Most important, it was necessary to repair the one that Patsy and I had built but knocked down. As luck would have it, she had finally kicked her second husband out and divorced him. This helped open the way for us to communicate. He had gone grudgingly, however, and, unfortunately, he had managed to take some of her money with him. I accompanied Patsy the day she went to court to settle accounts and legally shut down their life together. It was not easy for her, and she asked me for my thoughts later that evening, needing my support and understanding in the aftermath of such a humiliating situation. Our new relationship, after such a trauma for her, had its ups and downs, but we muddled through with more of the former than the latter. Stupidly and selfishly, I still wanted her to congratulate me for my sobriety, but she never even mentioned it. As a result, I had to fight against feeling that old, familiar pain of rejection.

Together, we gave our daughter Bambi and her fiancé, Guy Riegel, a wonderful wedding. We experienced a few very minor hitches along the way, as we planned everything together and got through those moments when she was critical of me and the times when I snapped at her for this and that. We had a love that transcended such childishness and was the foundation of our friendship. Well after the wedding we held onto this bond. I would take her plants for her garden and she visited me in Maine on more than one occasion. It was a ghastly shock when, after speaking to her one evening, I was called the next morning and told that she had suddenly died of a heart attack at age sixty.

Her funeral was particularly unbearable for me as so much had been left unsaid between us and now all these issues could never be resolved. Yet I am so glad we mended our fences as far as we had, for the pain of things left undone when death separates two people who love seems intolerable. We had produced a lot of sorrow between us, unintentionally, over the years, but a great deal of it did get resolved.

I sat with her family at the funeral, for I had gotten back to being friends with her father. As fate would have it, it was I who ended up conducting the interment service for her at her gravesite. This was held three weeks after the funeral, as her cremation was not done until after that event. The minister, whom I had called two days before the burial, forgot to show up. At the request of my children and her father I read the Episcopal committal service for her through a flood of tears. By the grace of God, I had brought along my own prayer book from Maine. It was a sad and too early an ending of a life for such a wonderful person, wife, mother and grandmother.

For anyone's well being, one must come to grips with family relationships. This has been true for me, as well, but terribly hard for me to accomplish. I've tried hard, for many of my relationships were, and some still are, in a state of disarray. Adult children of alcoholics are not always functional. One needs to approach these interrelationships with more care so no more hurt will occur.

In some cases, it was easier to leave the situation alone, rising above it and actually blanking out the hurt from my mind. Some members of the family could not and would not accept any apology, nor would they apologize. Dysfunctional behavior never allows it. There is, as I have said, no way to change anyone's behavior except our own. I was my family's scapegoat and mascot for too long a time and, when I shed these roles, I was a totally different person. Now I am simply odd man out and a threat to those who have carried roles and the family's odd behavior into their advancing years.

Even my own children do not understand why my family does not fall into each other's arms. They have no idea about the roles we have played all our lives to, supposedly, hold our family together. Today family members still circle my camp with some dread and fear. I can only think some view me as a threat to their very existence because I have damaged the family's dysfunctional way of coping as a tight unit. I may be wrong, of course, but this is how it seems to me. My children, their spouses and my grandchildren I adore. I love my siblings but do not like them. We are too different and separated by the way I now choose to live.

The most important lesson that I learned—in changing my dysfunctional and alcoholic life to a rational and sober one focused on God's love—was how to seek help for problems beyond my control. I had to come to grips with the fact that I needed help for most of my troubles. We cannot do it alone, or without a rock to build on. Faith, love, medicine and psychiatry helped save me. My life was a disaster until I "got the hell (alcoholism and dysfunctionality) out" of my system and found real love within my life. I also had to change my subconscious behavior so that each time I felt I was being rejected I could see that in reality it was healthy criticism. I formerly could never take any opposition without dysfunctional behavior ensuing. Now my life progresses quite happily. It thus seems logical to me to try to provide some guidelines for others who are similarly challenged in their lives. I trust that by opening my own heart, I have enabled others to open theirs. I pray, if you have any hell in your life, that you can get it out and find peace. God bless!

Winter in Maine is glorious, rewarding and beautiful beyond belief. It's crisp, cold and clear along the coast. The sea is a wonderful thermostat except in the Spring when it keeps it too raw and chilly. Then it's time to head elsewhere.

The garden blooms from May though October and thrives on the summer fog. I grow monster flowers and use manure as if it was going out of style. It pays off to the delight of my family—the functional ones.

I became very involved with politics, church, art and soup kitchens when I started my road to recovery. I found that I could tie them all together in a positive, caring, loving and helpful sense. In each area helping others is the *raison d'etre* for their existence. Here President George Bush and I look over a new book about the Farnsworth Art Museum's collection of Wyeth paintings. I was a vice-president of that museum.

Beautiful women will always be a part of my life. This dear friend, who is rapped in a boa, is but one of the true reasons for living and loving life at its fullest.

A new Jack Russell terrier came into my life. I called her Eloise and she never ceased to amuse me. She talked and chased balls that she thought were rats.

Bill Cohen and Bob Dole sent me this picture signed by each of them. Bob Dole added, "Smile." I was always running around with politicians when I was the Finance Chairman for the Maine State Republican Party.

Life was a whirl of parties for me. Here I am dancing with some fabulous dame behind and on the right of Prince Charles, who was dancing with Nancy Reagan, the wife of the President of the United States. I kept pretty "zappy" company.

Life without "drink" became exhilarating. I gave myself six more hours a day to actually live life to its fullest. I did not wake up with a hangover and I did not spend hours a day in an intoxicated state. It was sheer heaven and I have never looked back with an ounce of regret. The best gift I ever gave myself was my sobriety. I became part of the whole community and could contribute love to the world.

ADDENDUM

There are no captions on the following pictures as the world can be a crazy place and identification could lead to many problems. I added them to this book for they are an integral part of my life and beloved by me. With these heavenly creatures in my life, it is impossible to look at the world without a joyful heart and a belief in Christ's words, "God is love."

The End